JAMES RUSSELL LOWELL'S WRITINGS.

POETICAL WORKS. Cabinet Edition. 2 vols. 16mo. $4.00.

POETICAL WORKS. Blue and Gold. 2 vols. 32mo. $3.00.

POEMS. Complete. *Diamond Edition.* 1 vol. $1.50.

THE VISION OF SIR LAUNFAL. 1 vol. 16mo. 75 cts.

THE VISION OF SIR LAUNFAL. Illustrated. 1 vol. Small 4to. Cloth, gilt. $3.00.

UNDER THE WILLOWS, AND OTHER POEMS. 1 vol. 16mo. Bevelled boards, gilt top. $2.00.

FIRESIDE TRAVELS. 1 vol. 16mo. $1.50.

A FABLE FOR CRITICS. 1 vol. 16mo. 75 cts.

THE BIGLOW PAPERS. 1 vol. 16mo. $1.50.

THE BIGLOW PAPERS. Second Series. $1.50.

AMONG MY BOOKS. 1 vol. 16mo. $2.00.

FIELDS, OSGOOD, & CO., Publishers.

AMONG MY BOOKS.

BY

JAMES RUSSELL LOWELL, A. M.,
PROFESSOR OF BELLES-LETTRES IN HARVARD COLLEGE.

BOSTON:
FIELDS, OSGOOD, & CO.
1870.

University Press: Welch, Bigelow, & Co.,
Cambridge.

To F. D. L.

Love comes and goes with music in his feet,
  And tunes young pulses to his roundelays;
Love brings thee this: will it persuade thee, Sweet,
  That he turns proser when he comes and stays?

CONTENTS.

DRYDEN.*

BENVENUTO CELLINI tells us that when, in his boyhood, he saw a salamander come out of the fire, his grandfather forthwith gave him a sound beating, that he might the better remember so unique a prodigy. Though perhaps in this case the rod had another application than the autobiographer chooses to disclose, and was intended to fix in the pupil's mind a lesson of veracity rather than of science, the testimony to its mnemonic virtue remains. Nay, so universally was it once believed that the senses, and through them the faculties of observation and retention, were quickened by an irritation of the cuticle, that in France it was customary to whip the children annually at the boundaries of the parish, lest the true place of them might ever be lost through neglect of so inexpensive a mordant for the memory. From this practice the older school of critics would seem to

* The Dramatick Works of JOHN DRYDEN, ESQ. In six volumes. London: Printed for Jacob Tonson, in the Strand. MDCCXXXV. 18mo.

The Critical and Miscellaneous Prose-Works of JOHN DRYDEN, now first collected. With Notes and Illustrations. An Account of the Life and Writings of the Author, grounded on Original and Authentick Documents; and a Collection of his Letters, the greatest Part of which has never before been published. By EDMUND MALONE, ESQ. London: T. Cadell and W. Davies, in the Strand. 4 vols. 8vo.

The Poetical Works of JOHN DRYDEN. (Edited by MITFORD.) London: W. Pickering. 1832. 5 vols. 18mo.

have taken a hint for keeping fixed the limits of good taste, and what was somewhat vaguely called *classical* English. To mark these limits in poetry, they set up as Hermæ the images they had made to them of Dryden, of Pope, and later of Goldsmith. Here they solemnly castigated every new aspirant in verse, who in turn performed the same function for the next generation, thus helping to keep always sacred and immovable the *ne plus ultra* alike of inspiration and of the vocabulary. Though no two natures were ever much more unlike than those of Dryden and Pope, and again of Pope and Goldsmith, and no two styles, except in such externals as could be easily caught and copied, yet it was the fashion, down even to the last generation, to advise young writers to form themselves, as it was called, on these excellent models. Wordsworth himself began in this school; and though there were glimpses, here and there, of a direct study of nature, yet most of the epithets in his earlier pieces were of the traditional kind so fatal to poetry during great part of the last century; and he indulged in that alphabetic personification which enlivens all such words as Hunger, Solitude, Freedom, by the easy magic of an initial capital.

> "Where the green apple shrivels on the spray,
> And pines the unripened pear in summer's kindliest ray,
> Even here Content has fixed her smiling reign
> With Independence, child of high Disdain.
> Exulting 'mid the winter of the skies,
> Shy as the jealous chamois, Freedom flies,
> And often grasps her sword, and often eyes."

Here we have every characteristic of the artificial method, even to the triplet, which Swift hated so heartily as "a vicious way of rhyming wherewith Mr. Dryden abounded, imitated by all the bad versifiers of Charles the Second's reign." Wordsworth became, indeed, very early the leader of reform; but, like Wesley, he endeavored a reform within the Establishment. Purifying the substance, he retained the outward forms with a feeling rather than conviction that, in poetry, substance and form are but manifestations of the same inward life, the one fused into the other in the vivid heat of their common expression. Wordsworth could never wholly shake off the influence of the century into which he was born. He began by proposing a reform of the ritual, but it went no further than an attempt to get rid of the words of Latin original where the meaning was as well or better given in derivatives of the Saxon. He would have stricken out the "assemble" and left the "meet together." Like Wesley, he might be compelled by necessity to a breach of the canon; but, like him, he was never a willing schismatic, and his singing robes were the full and flowing canonicals of the church by law established. Inspiration makes short work with the usage of the best authors and ready-made elegances of diction; but where Wordsworth is not possessed by his demon, as Molière said of Corneille, he equals Thomson in verbiage, out-Miltons Milton in artifice of style, and Latinizes his diction beyond Dryden. The fact was, that he took up his early opinions on instinct, and insensibly modified them as he studied the masters of what may be called the Middle Period of English verse.* As a young man, he disparaged Virgil ("We talked a great deal of nonsense in those days," he said when taken to task for it later in life); at fifty-nine he translated three books of the Æneid, in emulation of Dryden, though falling far short of him in everything but closeness, as he seems, after a few years, to have been convinced. Keats was the first resolute and wilful heretic, the true founder of the modern school, which admits no cis-Eliza-

* His "Character of a Happy Warrior" (1806), one of his noblest poems, has a dash of Dryden in it,—still more his "Epistle to Sir George Beaumont (1811)."

bethan authority save Milton, whose own English was formed upon those earlier models. Keats denounced the authors of that style which came in toward the close of the seventeenth century, and reigned absolute through the whole of the eighteenth, as

> "A schism,
> Nurtured by foppery and barbarism,
> . . . . who went about
> Holding a poor decrepit standard out,
> Marked with most flimsy mottoes, and in large
> The name of one Boileau!"

But Keats had never then * studied the writers of whom he speaks so contemptuously, though he might have profited by so doing. Boileau would at least have taught him that *flimsy* would have been an apter epithet for the *standard* than for the mottoes upon it. Dryden was the author of that schism against which Keats so vehemently asserts the claim of the orthodox teaching it had displaced. He was far more just to Boileau, of whom Keats had probably never read a word. "If I would only cross the seas," he says, "I might find in France a living Horace and a Juvenal in the person of the admirable Boileau, whose numbers are excellent, whose expressions are noble, whose thoughts are just, whose language is pure, whose satire is pointed, and whose sense is just. What he borrows from the ancients he repays with usury of his own, in coin as good and almost as universally valuable." †

Dryden has now been in his grave nearly a hundred and seventy years; in the second class of English poets perhaps no one stands, on the whole, so high as he; during his lifetime, in spite of jealousy, detraction, unpopular politics, and a suspicious change of faith, his pre-eminence was conceded; he was the earliest com-

* He studied Dryden's versification before writing his "Lamia."

† On the Origin and Progress of Satire. See Johnson's counter opinion in his life of Dryden.

plete type of the purely literary man, in the modern sense; there is a singular unanimity in allowing him a certain claim to *greatness* which would be denied to men as famous and more read, — to Pope or Swift, for example; he is supposed, in some way or other, to have reformed English poetry. It is now about half a century since the only uniform edition of his works was edited by Scott. No library is complete without him, no name is more familiar than his, and yet it may be suspected that few writers are more thoroughly buried in that great cemetery of the "British Poets." If contemporary reputation be often deceitful, posthumous fame may be generally trusted, for it is a verdict made up of the suffrages of the select men in succeeding generations. This verdict has been as good as unanimous in favor of Dryden. It is, perhaps, worth while to take a fresh observation of him, to consider him neither as warning nor example, but to endeavor to make out what it is that has given so lofty and firm a position to one of the most unequal, inconsistent, and faulty writers that ever lived. He is a curious example of what we often remark of the living, but rarely of the dead, — that they get credit for what they might be quite as much as for what they are, — and posterity has applied to him one of his own rules of criticism, judging him by the best rather than the average of his achievement, a thing posterity is seldom wont to do. On the losing side in politics, it is true of his polemical writings as of Burke's, — whom in many respects he resembles, and especially in that supreme quality of a reasoner, that his mind gathers not only heat, but clearness and expansion, by its own motion, — that they have won his battle for him in the judgment of after times.

To us, looking back at him, he gradually becomes a singularly interesting and even picturesque figure. He is, in more senses than one, in language, in turn of thought, in style of mind, in the direction of his activity, the first of the moderns. He is the first literary man who was also a man of the world, as we understand the term. He succeeded Ben Jonson as the acknowledged dictator of wit and criticism, as Dr. Johnson, after nearly the same interval, succeeded him. All ages are, in some sense, ages of transition; but there are times when the transition is more marked, more rapid; and it is, perhaps, an ill fortune for a man of letters to arrive at maturity during such a period, still more to represent in himself the change that is going on, and to be an efficient cause in bringing it about. Unless, like Goethe, he is of a singularly uncontemporaneous nature, capable of being *tutta in se romita*, and of running parallel with his time rather than being sucked into its current, he will be thwarted in that harmonious development of native force which has so much to do with its steady and successful application. Dryden suffered, no doubt, in this way. Though in creed he seems to have drifted backward in an eddy of the general current; yet of the intellectual movement of the time, so far certainly as literature shared in it, he could say, with Æneas, not only that he saw, but that himself was a great part of it. That movement was, on the whole, a downward one, from faith to scepticism, from enthusiasm to cynicism, from the imagination to the understanding. It was in a direction altogether away from those springs of imagination and faith at which they of the last age had slaked the thirst or renewed the vigor of their souls. Dryden himself recognized that indefinable and gregarious influence which we call nowadays the Spirit of the Age, when he said that "every Age has a kind of universal Genius." * He had also a just notion of that in which

* Essay on Dramatick Poesy.

he lived; for he remarks, incidentally, that "all knowing ages are naturally sceptic and not at all bigoted, which, if I am not much deceived, is the proper character of our own." * It may be conceived that he was even painfully half-aware of having fallen upon a time incapable, not merely of a great poet, but perhaps of any poet at all; for nothing is so sensitive to the chill of a sceptical atmosphere as that enthusiasm which, if it be not genius, is at least the beautiful illusion that saves it from the baffling quibbles of self-consciousness. Thrice unhappy he who, born to see things as they might be, is schooled by circumstances to see them as people say they are, — to read God in a prose translation. Such was Dryden's lot, and such, for a good part of his days, it was by his own choice. He who was of a stature to snatch the torch of life that flashes from lifted hand to hand along the generations, over the heads of inferior men, chose rather to be a link-boy to the stews.

As a writer for the stage, he deliberately adopted and repeatedly reaffirmed the maxim that

"He who lives to please, must please to live."

Without earnest convictions, no great or sound literature is conceivable. But if Dryden mostly wanted that inspiration which comes of belief in and devotion to something nobler and more abiding than the present moment and its petulant need, he had, at least, the next best thing to that, — a thorough faith in himself. He was, moreover, a man of singularly open soul, and of a temper self-confident enough to be candid even with himself. His mind was growing to the last, his judgment widening and deepening, his artistic sense refining itself more and more. He confessed his errors, and was not ashamed to retrace his steps in search of that bet-

* Life of Lucian.

ter knowledge which the omniscience of superficial study had disparaged. Surely an intellect that is still pliable at seventy is a phenomenon as interesting as it is rare. But at whatever period of his life we look at Dryden, and whatever, for the moment, may have been his poetic creed, there was something in the nature of the man that would not be wholly subdued to what it worked in. There are continual glimpses of something in him greater than he, hints of possibilities finer than anything he has done. You feel that the whole of him was better than any random specimens, though of his best, seem to prove. *Incessu patet*, he has by times the large stride of the elder race, though it sinks too often into the slouch of a man who has seen better days. His grand air may, in part, spring from a habit of easy superiority to his competitors; but must also, in part, be ascribed to an innate dignity of character. That this pre-eminence should have been so generally admitted, during his life, can only be explained by a bottom of good sense, kindliness, and sound judgment, whose solid worth could afford that many a flurry of vanity, petulance, and even error should flit across the surface and be forgotten. Whatever else Dryden may have been, the last and abiding impression of him is, that he was thoroughly manly; and while it may be disputed whether he was a great poet, it may be said of him, as Wordsworth said of Burke, that "he was by far the greatest man of his age, not only abounding in knowledge himself, but feeding, in various directions, his most able contemporaries." *

Dryden was born in 1631. He was accordingly six years old when Jonson died, was nearly a quarter of a century younger than Milton, and may have personally

* "The great man must have that intellect which puts in motion the intellect of others." — LANDOR, *Im. Con.*, Diogenes and Plato.

known Bishop Hall, the first English satirist, who was living till 1656. On the other side, he was older than Swift by thirty-six, than Addison by forty-one, and than Pope by fifty-seven years. Dennis says that "Dryden, for the last ten years of his life, was much acquainted with Addison, and drank with him more than he ever used to do, probably so far as to hasten his end," being commonly "an extreme sober man." Pope tells us that, in his twelfth year, he "saw Dryden," perhaps at Will's, perhaps in the street, as Scott did Burns. Dryden himself visited Milton now and then, and was intimate with Davenant, who could tell him of Fletcher and Jonson from personal recollection. Thus he stands between the age before and that which followed him, giving a hand to each. His father was a country clergyman, of Puritan leanings, a younger son of an ancient county family. The Puritanism is thought to have come in with the poet's great-grandfather, who made in his will the somewhat singular statement that he was "assured by the Holy Ghost that he was elect of God." It would appear from this that Dryden's self-confidence was an inheritance. The solid quality of his mind showed itself early. He himself tells us that he had read Polybius "in English, with the pleasure of a boy, before he was ten years of age, and yet even then *had some dark notions of the prudence with which he conducted his design*." * The concluding words are very characteristic, even if Dryden, as men commonly do, interpreted his boyish turn of mind by later self-knowledge. We thus get a glimpse of him browsing — for, like Johnson, Burke, and the full as distinguished from the learned men, he was always a random reader † — in his father's library, and painfully culling

* Character of Polybius (1692).

† "For my own part, who must confess it to my shame that I never read anything but for pleasure." Life of Plutarch (1683).

here and there a spray of his own proper nutriment from among the stubs and thorns of Puritan divinity. After such schooling as could be had in the country, he was sent up to Westminster School, then under the headship of the celebrated Dr. Busby. Here he made his first essays in verse, translating, among other school exercises of the same kind, the third satire of Persius. In 1650 he was entered at Trinity College, Cambridge, and remained there for seven years. The only record of his college life is a discipline imposed, in 1652, for "disobedience to the Vice-Master, and contumacy in taking his punishment, inflicted by him." Whether this punishment was corporeal, as Johnson insinuates in the similar case of Milton, we are ignorant. He certainly retained no very fond recollection of his Alma Mater, for in his "Prologue to the University of Oxford" he says: —

> "Oxford to him a dearer name shall be
> Than his own mother university;
> Thebes did his green, unknowing youth engage,
> He chooses Athens in his riper age."

By the death of his father, in 1654, he came into possession of a small estate of sixty pounds a year, from which, however, a third must be deducted, for his mother's dower, till 1676. After leaving Cambridge, he became secretary to his near relative, Sir Gilbert Pickering, at that time Cromwell's chamberlain, and a member of his Upper House. In 1670 he succeeded Davenant as Poet Laureate,* and Howell as Historiographer, with a yearly salary of two hundred pounds. This place he lost at the Revolution, and had the mortification to see his old enemy and butt, Shadwell, promoted to it, as the best poet the Whig party could muster. If William was

* Gray says petulantly enough that "Dryden was as disgraceful to the office, from his character, as the poorest scribbler could have been from his verses." — GRAY to MASON, 19th December, 1757.

obliged to read the verses of his official minstrel, Dryden was more than avenged. From 1688 to his death, twelve years later, he earned his bread manfully by his pen, without any mean complaining, and with no allusion to his fallen fortunes that is not dignified and touching. These latter years, during which he was his own man again, were probably the happiest of his life. In 1664 or 1665 he married Lady Elizabeth Howard, daughter of the Earl of Berkshire. About a hundred pounds a year were thus added to his income. The marriage is said not to have been a happy one, and perhaps it was not, for his wife was apparently a weak-minded woman; but the inference from the internal evidence of Dryden's plays, as of Shakespeare's, is very untrustworthy, ridicule of marriage having always been a common stock in trade of the comic writers.

The earliest of his verses that have come down to us were written upon the death of Lord Hastings, and are as bad as they can be, — a kind of parody on the worst of Donne. They have every fault of his manner, without a hint of the subtile and often profound thought that more than redeems it. As the Doctor himself would have said, here is Donne outdone. The young nobleman died of the small-pox, and Dryden exclaims pathetically, —

> "Was there no milder way than the small-pox,
> The very filthiness of Pandora's box?"

He compares the pustules to "rosebuds stuck i' the lily skin about," and says that

> "Each little pimple had a tear in it
> To wail the fault its rising did commit."

But he has not done his worst yet, by a great deal. What follows is even finer: —

> "No comet need foretell his change drew on,
> Whose corpse might seem a constellation.

> O, had he died of old, how great a strife
> Had been who from his death should draw their life!
> Who should, by one rich draught, become whate'er
> Seneca, Cato, Numa, Cæsar, were,
> Learned, virtuous, pious, great, and have by this
> An universal metempsychosis!
> Must all these aged sires in one funeral
> Expire? all die in one so young, so small?"

It is said that one of Allston's early pictures was brought to him, after he had long forgotten it, and his opinion asked as to the wisdom of the young artist's persevering in the career he had chosen. Allston advised his quitting it forthwith as hopeless. Could the same experiment have been tried with these verses upon Dryden, can any one doubt that his counsel would have been the same? It should be remembered, however, that he was barely turned eighteen when they were written, and the tendency of his style is noticeable in so early an abandonment of the participial *ed* in *learned* and *aged*. In the next year he appears again in some commendatory verses prefixed to the sacred epigrams of his friend, John Hoddesdon. In these he speaks of the author as a

> "Young eaglet, who, thy nest thus soon forsook,
> So lofty and divine a course hast took
> As all admire, before the down begin
> To peep, as yet, upon thy smoother chin."

Here is almost every fault which Dryden's later nicety would have condemned. But perhaps there is no schooling so good for an author as his own youthful indiscretions. After this effort Dryden seems to have lain fallow for ten years, and then he at length reappears in thirty-seven "heroic stanzas" on the death of Cromwell. The versification is smoother, but the conceits are there again, though in a milder form. The verse is modelled after "Gondibert." A single image from nature (he was almost always happy in these) gives some hint of the maturer Dryden : —

> " And wars, like mists that rise against the sun,
> Made him but greater seem, not greater grow."

Two other verses,

> " And the isle, when her protecting genius went,
> Upon his obsequies loud sighs conferred,"

are interesting, because they show that he had been studying the early poems of Milton. He has contrived to bury under a rubbish of verbiage one of the most purely imaginative passages ever written by the great Puritan poet.

> " From haunted spring and dale,
> Edged with poplar pale,
> The parting genius is with sighing sent."

This is the more curious because, twenty-four years afterwards, he says, in defending rhyme : " Whatever causes he [Milton] alleges for the abolishment of rhyme, his own particular reason is plainly this, that rhyme was not his talent ; he had neither the ease of doing it nor the graces of it : which is manifest in his *Juvenilia*, ... where his rhyme is always constrained and forced, and comes hardly from him, at an age when the soul is most pliant, and the passion of love makes almost every man a rhymer, though not a poet."* It was this, no doubt, that heartened Dr. Johnson to say of " Lycidas " that " the diction was harsh, the rhymes uncertain, and the numbers unpleasing." It is Dryden's excuse that his characteristic excellence is to argue persuasively and powerfully, whether in verse or prose, and that he was amply endowed with the most needful quality of an advocate, — to be always strongly and wholly of his present way of thinking, whatever it might be. Next

* Essay on the Origin and Progress of Satire.

we have, in 1660, "Astræa Redux" on the "happy restoration" of Charles II. In this also we can forebode little of the full-grown Dryden but his defects. We see his tendency to exaggeration, and to confound physical with metaphysical, as where he says of the ships that brought home the royal brothers, that

"The joyful London meets
The princely York, himself alone a freight,
The Swiftsure groans beneath great Gloster's weight

and speaks of the

"Repeated prayer
Which stormed the skies and ravished Charles from thence."

There is also a certain everydayness, not to say vulgarity, of phrase, which Dryden never wholly refined away, and which continually tempts us to sum up at once against him as the greatest poet that ever was or could be made wholly out of prose.

"Heaven would no bargain for its blessings drive"

is an example. On the other hand, there are a few verses almost worthy of his best days, as these: —

"Some lazy ages lost in sleep and ease,
No action leave to busy chronicles;
Such whose *supine felicity* but makes
In story chasms, in epochas mistakes,
O'er whom Time gently shakes his wings of down,
Till with his silent sickle they are mown."

These are all the more noteworthy, that Dryden, unless in argument, is seldom equal for six lines together. In the poem to Lord Clarendon (1662) there are four verses that have something of the "energy divine" for which Pope praised his master.

"Let envy, then, those crimes within you see
From which the happy never must be free;
Envy that does with misery reside,
The joy and the revenge of ruined pride."

In his "Aurengzebe" (1675) there is a passage, of which, as it is a good example of Dryden, I shall quote the whole, though my purpose aims mainly at the latter verses: —

> "When I consider life, 't is all a cheat;
> Yet, fooled with Hope, men favor the deceit,
> Trust on, and think to-morrow will repay;
> To-morrow 's falser than the former day,
> Lies worse, and, while it says we shall be blest
> With some new joys, cuts off what we possest.
> Strange cozenage! none would live past years again,
> Yet all hope pleasure in what yet remain,
> And from the dregs of life think to receive
> What the first sprightly running could not give.
> I 'm tired of waiting for this chymic gold
> Which fools us young and beggars us when old."

The "first sprightly running" of Dryden's vintage was, it must be confessed, a little muddy, if not beery; but if his own soil did not produce grapes of the choicest flavor, he knew where they were to be had; and his product, like sound wine, grew better the longer it stood upon the lees. He tells us, evidently thinking of himself, that in a poet, "from fifty to threescore, the balance generally holds even in our colder climates, for he loses not much in fancy, and judgment, which is the effect of observation, still increases. His succeeding years afford him little more than the stubble of his own harvest, yet, if his constitution be healthful, his mind may still retain a decent vigor, and the gleanings of that of Ephraim, in comparison with others, will surpass the vintage of Abiezer."* Since Chaucer, none of our poets has had a constitution more healthful, and it was his old age that yielded the best of him. In him the understanding was, perhaps, in overplus for his entire good fortune as a poet, and that is a faculty among the earli-

* Dedication of the Georgics.

est to mature. We have seen him, at only ten years, divining the power of reason in Polybius.* The same turn of mind led him later to imitate the French school of tragedy, and to admire in Ben Jonson the most correct of English poets. It was his imagination that needed quickening, and it is very curious to trace through his different prefaces the gradual opening of his eyes to the causes of the solitary pre-eminence of Shakespeare. At first he is sensible of an attraction towards him which he cannot explain, and for which he apologizes, as if it were wrong. But he feels himself drawn more and more strongly, till at last he ceases to resist altogether, and is forced to acknowledge that there is something in this one man that is not and never was anywhere else, something not to be reasoned about, ineffable, divine; if contrary to the rules, so much the worse for *them*. It may be conjectured that Dryden's Puritan associations may have stood in the way of his more properly poetic culture, and that his early knowledge of Shakespeare was slight. He tells us that Davenant, whom he could not have known before he himself was twenty-seven, first taught him to admire the great poet. But even after his imagination had become conscious of its prerogative, and his expression had been ennobled by frequenting this higher society, we find him continually dropping back into that *sermo pedestris* which seems, on the whole, to have been his more natural element. We always feel his epoch in him, that he was the lock which let our language down from its point of highest poetry to its level of easiest and most gently flowing prose. His enthusiasm needs the contagion of other minds to arouse it; but his strong sense, his command of the happy word, his wit,

* Dryden's penetration is always remarkable. His general judgment of Polybius coincides remarkably with that of Mommsen. (Röm. Gesch. II. 448, *seq.*)

which is distinguished by a certain breadth and, as it were, power of generalization, as Pope's by keenness of edge and point, were his, whether he would or no. Accordingly, his poetry is often best and his verse more flowing where (as in parts of his version of the twenty-ninth ode of the third book of Horace) he is amplifying the suggestions of another mind.* Viewed from one side, he justifies Milton's remark of him, that "he was a good rhymist, but no poet." To look at all sides, and to distrust the verdict of a single mood, is, no doubt, the duty of a critic. But how if a certain side be so often presented as to thrust forward in the memory and disturb it in the effort to recall that total impression (for the office of a critic is not, though often so misunderstood, to say *guilty* or *not guilty* of some particular fact) which is the only safe ground of judgment? It is the weight of the whole man, not of one or the other limb of him, that we want. *Expende Hannibalem.* Very good, but not in a scale capacious only of a single quality at a time, for it is their union, and not their addition, that assures the value of each separately. It was not this or that which gave him his weight in council, his swiftness of decision in battle that outran the forethought of other men, — it was Hannibal. But this prosaic element in Dryden will force itself upon me. As I read him, I cannot help thinking of an ostrich, to be classed with flying things, and capable, what with leap and flap together, of leaving the earth for a longer or shorter space, but loving the open plain, where wing and foot help each other to something that is both flight and run at once. What with his haste and a certain dash, which,

* "I have taken some pains to make it my masterpiece in English." Preface to Second Miscellany. Fox said that it "was better than the original." J. C. Scaliger said of Erasmus: "Ex alieno ingenio poeta, ex suo versificator."

according to our mood, we may call florid or splendid, he seems to stand among poets where Rubens does among painters, — greater, perhaps, as a colorist than an artist, yet great here also, if we compare him with any but the first.

We have arrived at Dryden's thirty-second year, and thus far have found little in him to warrant an augury that he was ever to be one of the *great* names in English literature, the most perfect type, that is, of his class, and that class a high one, though not the highest. If Joseph de Maistre's axiom, *Qui n'a pas vaincu à trente ans, ne vaincra jamais,* were true, there would be little hope of him, for he has won no battle yet. But there is something solid and doughty in the man, that can rise from defeat, the stuff of which victories are made in due time, when we are able to choose our position better, and the sun is at our back. Hitherto his performances have been mainly of the *obbligato* sort, at which few men of original force are good, least of all Dryden, who had always something of stiffness in his strength. Waller had praised the living Cromwell in perhaps the manliest verses he ever wrote, — not *very* manly, to be sure, but really elegant, and, on the whole, better than those in which Dryden squeezed out melodious tears. Waller, who had also made himself conspicuous as a volunteer Antony to the country squire turned Cæsar,

("With ermine clad and purple, let him hold
A royal sceptre made of Spanish gold,")

was more servile than Dryden in hailing the return of *ex officio* Majesty. He bewails to Charles, in snuffling heroics,

"Our sorrow and our crime
To have accepted life so long a time,
Without you here."

A weak man, put to the test by rough and angry times,

as Waller was, may be pitied, but meanness is nothing but contemptible under any circumstances. If it be true that "every conqueror creates a Muse," Cromwell was unfortunate. Even Milton's sonnet, though dignified, is reserved if not distrustful. Marvell's "Horatian Ode," the most truly classic in our language, is worthy of its theme. The same poet's Elegy, in parts noble, and everywhere humanly tender, is worth more than all Carlyle's biography as a witness to the gentler qualities of the hero, and of the deep affection that stalwart nature could inspire in hearts of truly masculine temper. As it is little known, a few verses of it may be quoted to show the difference between grief that thinks of its object and grief that thinks of its rhymes : —

"Valor, religion, friendship, prudence died
At once with him, and all that 's good beside,
And we, death's refuse, nature's dregs, confined
To loathsome life, alas! are left behind.
Where we (so once we used) shall now no more,
To fetch day, press about his chamber-door,
No more shall hear that powerful language charm,
Whose force oft spared the labor of his arm,
No more shall follow where he spent the days
In war or counsel, or in prayer and praise.

. . . . .

I saw him dead; a leaden slumber lies,
And mortal sleep, over those wakeful eyes;
Those gentle rays under the lids were fled,
Which through his looks that piercing sweetness shed;
That port, which so majestic was and strong,
Loose and deprived of vigor stretched along,
All withered, all discolored, pale, and wan,
How much another thing! no more That Man!
O human glory! vain! O death! O wings!
O worthless world! O transitory things!
Yet dwelt that greatness in his shape decayed
That still, though dead, greater than Death he laid,
And, in his altered face, you something feign
That threatens Death he yet will live again."

Such verses might not satisfy Lindley Murray, but

they are of that higher mood which satisfies the heart. These couplets, too, have an energy worthy of Milton's friend : —

> "When up the armëd mountains of Dunbar
> He marched, and through deep Severn, ending war."
>
> "Thee, many ages hence, in martial verse
> Shall the English soldier, ere he charge, rehearse."

On the whole, one is glad that Dryden's panegyric on the Protector was so poor. It was purely official verse-making. Had there been any feeling in it, there had been baseness in his address to Charles. As it is, we may fairly assume that he was so far sincere in both cases as to be thankful for a chance to exercise himself in rhyme, without much caring whether upon a funeral or a restoration. He might naturally enough expect that poetry would have a better chance under Charles than under Cromwell, or any successor with Commonwealth principles. Cromwell had more serious matters to think about than verses, while Charles might at least care as much about them as it was in his base good-nature to care about anything but loose women and spaniels. Dryden's sound sense, afterwards so conspicuous, shows itself even in these pieces, when we can get at it through the tangled thicket of tropical phrase. But the authentic and unmistakable Dryden first manifests himself in some verses addressed to his friend Dr. Charlton in 1663. We have first his common sense, which has almost the point of wit, yet with a tang of prose : —

> "The longest tyranny that ever swayed
> Was that wherein our ancestors betrayed
> Their freeborn reason to the Stagyrite,
> And made his torch their universal light.
> *So truth, while only one supplied the state,*
> *Grew scarce and dear and yet sophisticate.*
> *Still it was bought, like emp'ric wares or charms,*
> *Hard words sealed up with Aristotle's arms.*"

Then we have his graceful sweetness of fancy, where he speaks of the inhabitants of the New World: —

> "Guiltless men who danced away their time,
> Fresh as their groves and happy as their clime."

And, finally, there is a hint of imagination where "mighty visions of the Danish race" watch round Charles sheltered in Stonehenge after the battle of Worcester. These passages might have been written by the Dryden whom we learn to know fifteen years later. They have the advantage that he wrote them to please himself. His contemporary, Dr. Heylin, said of French cooks, that "their trade was not to feed the belly, but the palate." Dryden was a great while in learning this secret, as available in good writing as in cookery. He strove after it, but his thoroughly English nature, to the last, would too easily content itself with serving up the honest beef of his thought, without regard to daintiness of flavor in the dressing of it.* Of the best English poetry, it might be said that it is understanding aërated by imagination. In Dryden the solid part too often refused to mix kindly with the leaven, either remaining lumpish or rising to a hasty puffiness. Grace and lightness were with him much more a laborious achievement than a natural gift, and it is all the more remarkable that he should so often have attained to what seems such an easy perfection in both. Always a hasty

* In one of the last letters he ever wrote, thanking his cousin Mrs. Steward for a gift of marrow-puddings, he says: "A chine of honest bacon would please my appetite more than all the marrow-puddings; for I like them better plain, having a very vulgar stomach." So of Cowley he says: "There was plenty enough, but ill sorted, whole pyramids of sweetmeats for boys and women, but little of solid meat for men." The physical is a truer antitype of the spiritual man than we are willing to admit, and the brain is often forced to acknowledge the inconvenient country-cousinship of the stomach.

writer,* he was long in forming his style, and to the last was apt to snatch the readiest word rather than wait for the fittest. He was not wholly and unconsciously poet, but a thinker who sometimes lost himself on enchanted ground and was transfigured by its touch. This preponderance in him of the reasoning over the intuitive faculties, the one always there, the other flashing in when you least expect it, accounts for that inequality and even incongruousness in his writing which makes one revise his judgment at every tenth page. In his prose you come upon passages that persuade you he is a poet, in spite of his verses so often turning state's evidence against him as to convince you he is none. He is a prose-writer, with a kind of Æolian attachment. For example, take this bit of prose from the dedication of his version of Virgil's Pastorals, 1694: "He found the strength of his genius betimes, and was even in his youth preluding to his Georgicks and his Æneis. He could not forbear to try his wings, though his pinions were not hardened to maintain a long, laborious flight; yet sometimes they bore him to a pitch as lofty as ever he was able to reach afterwards. But when he was admonished by his subject to descend, he came down gently circling in the air and singing to the ground, like a lark melodious in her mounting and continuing her song till she alights, still preparing for a higher flight at her next sally, and tuning her voice to better music." This is charming, and yet even this wants the ethereal tincture that pervades the style of Jeremy Taylor, making

* In his preface to "All for Love," he says, evidently alluding to himself: "If he have a friend whose hastiness in writing is his greatest fault, Horace would have taught him to have minced the matter, and to have called it readiness of thought and a flowing fancy." And in the Preface to the Fables he says of Homer: "This vehemence of his, I confess, is more suitable to my temper." He makes other allusions to it.

it, as Burke said of Sheridan's eloquence, "neither prose nor poetry, but something better than either." Let us compare Taylor's treatment of the same image: "For so have I seen a lark rising from his bed of grass and soaring upwards, singing as he rises, and hopes to get to heaven and climb above the clouds; but the poor bird was beaten back by the loud sighings of an eastern wind, and his motion made irregular and inconstant, descending more at every breath of the tempest than it could recover by the libration and frequent weighing of his wings, till the little creature was forced to sit down and pant, and stay till the storm was over, and then it made a prosperous flight, and did rise and sing as if it had learned music and motion of an angel as he passed sometimes through the air about his ministries here below." Taylor's fault is that his sentences too often smell of the library, but what an open air is here! How unpremeditated it all seems! How carelessly he knots each new thought, as it comes, to the one before it with an *and*, like a girl making lace! And what a slidingly musical use he makes of the sibilants with which our language is unjustly taxed by those who can only make them hiss, not sing! There are twelve of them in the first twenty words, fifteen of which are monsyllables. We notice the structure of Dryden's periods, but this grows up as we read. It gushes, like the song of the bird itself, —

"In profuse strains of unpremeditated art."

Let us now take a specimen of Dryden's bad prose from one of his poems. I open the "Annus Mirabilis" at random, and hit upon this: —

"Our little fleet was now engaged so far,
That, like the swordfish in the whale, they fought:
The combat only seemed a civil war,
Till through their bowels we our passage wrought."

Is this Dryden, or Sternhold, or Shadwell, those Toms who made him say that "dulness was fatal to the name of Tom"? The natural history of Goldsmith in the verse of Pye! His thoughts did not "voluntary move harmonious numbers." He had his choice between prose and verse, and seems to be poetical on second thought. I do not speak without book. He was more than half conscious of it himself. In the same letter to Mrs. Steward, just cited, he says, "I am still drudging on, always a poet and never a good one"; and this from no mock-modesty, for he is always handsomely frank in telling us whatever of his own doing pleased him. This was written in the last year of his life, and at about the same time he says elsewhere: "What judgment I had increases rather than diminishes, and thoughts, such as they are, come crowding in so fast upon me that my only difficulty is to choose or to reject, to run them into verse or to give them the other harmony of prose; I have so long studied and practised both, that they are grown into a habit and become familiar to me."* I think that a man who was primarily a poet would hardly have felt this equanimity of choice.

I find a confirmation of this feeling about Dryden in his early literary loves. His taste was not an instinct, but the slow result of reflection and of the manfulness with which he always acknowledged to himself his own mistakes. In this latter respect few men deal so magnanimously with themselves as he, and accordingly few have been so happily inconsistent. *Ancora imparo* might have served him for a motto as well as Michael Angelo. His prefaces are a complete log of his life, and the habit of writing them was a useful one to him, for it forced him to think with a pen in his hand, which, according to Goethe, "if it do no other good, keeps the mind from

* Preface to the Fables.

staggering about." In these prefaces we see his taste gradually rising from Du Bartas to Spenser, from Cowley to Milton, from Corneille to Shakespeare. "I remember when I was a boy," he says in his dedication of the "Spanish Friar," 1681, "I thought inimitable Spenser a mean poet in comparison of Sylvester's *Du Bartas*, and was rapt into an ecstasy when I read these lines: —

'Now when the winter's keener breath began
To crystallize the Baltic oceän,
To glaze the lakes, to bridle up the floods,
And periwig with snow * the baldpate woods.'

I am much deceived if this be not abominable fustian." Swift, in his "Tale of a Tub," has a ludicrous passage in this style: "Look on this globe of earth, you will find it to be a very complete and fashionable dress. What is that which some call *land*, but a fine coat faced with green? or the *sea*, but a waistcoat of water-tabby? Proceed to the particular works of creation, you will find how curious journeyman Nature has been to trim up the vegetable *beaux*; observe how *sparkish a periwig adorns the head of a beech*, and what a fine doublet of white satin is worn by the birch." The fault is not in any inaptness of the images, nor in the mere vulgarity of the things themselves, but in that of the associations they awaken. The "prithee, undo this button" of Lear, coming where it does and expressing what it does, is one of those touches of the pathetically sublime, of which only Shakespeare ever knew the secret. Herrick, too, has a charming poem on "Julia's petticoat," the charm

* *Wool* is Sylvester's word. Dryden reminds us of Burke in this also, that he always quotes from memory and seldom exactly. His memory was better for things than for words. This helps to explain the length of time it took him to master that vocabulary at last so various, full, and seemingly extemporaneous. He is a large quoter, though, with his usual inconsistency, he says, "I am no admirer of quotations." (Essay on Heroic Plays.)

being that he lifts the familiar and the low to the region of sentiment. In the passage from Sylvester, it is precisely the reverse, and the wig takes as much from the sentiment as it adds to a Lord Chancellor. So Pope's proverbial verse,

> "True wit is Nature to advantage drest,"

unpleasantly suggests Nature under the hands of a lady's-maid.* We have no word in English that will exactly define this want of propriety in diction. *Vulgar* is too strong, and *commonplace* too weak. Perhaps *bourgeois* comes as near as any. It is to be noticed that Dryden does not unequivocally condemn the passage he quotes, but qualifies it with an "if I am not much mistaken." Indeed, though his judgment in substantials, like that of Johnson, is always worth having, his taste, the negative half of genius, never altogether refined itself from a colloquial familiarity, which is one of the charms of his prose, and gives that air of easy strength in which his satire is unmatched. In his "Royal Martyr" (1669), the tyrant Maximin says to the gods:—

> "Keep you your rain and sunshine in the skies,
> And I'll keep back my flame and sacrifice;
> *Your trade of Heaven shall soon be at a stand,*
> *And all your goods lie dead upon your hand,*"—

a passage which has as many faults as only Dryden was capable of committing, even to a false idiom forced by the last rhyme. The same tyrant in dying exclaims:—

> "And after thee I'll go,
> Revenging still, and following e'en to th' other world my blow,
> And, *shoving back this earth on which I sit,*
> *I'll mount and scatter all the gods I hit.*"

* In the *Epimetheus* of a poet usually as elegant as Gray himself, one's finer sense is a little jarred by the

> "Spectral gleam their snow-white *dresses.*"

In the "Conquest of Grenada" (1670), we have: —

> "This little loss in our vast body shews
> So small, that half *have never heard the news;*
> *Fame's out of breath e'er she can fly so far*
> *To tell 'em all that you have e'er made war.*" *

And in the same play,

> "That busy thing,
> *The soul, is packing up*, and just on wing
> Like parting swallows when they seek the spring,"

where the last sweet verse curiously illustrates that inequality (poetry on a prose background) which so often puzzles us in Dryden. Infinitely worse is the speech of Almanzor to his mother's ghost: —

> "I'll rush into the covert of the night
> And pull thee backward by the shroud to light,
> Or else I'll squeeze thee like a bladder there,
> And make thee groan thyself away to air."

What wonder that Dryden should have been substituted for Davenant as the butt of the "Rehearsal," and that the parody should have had such a run? And yet it was Dryden who, in speaking of Persius, hit upon the happy phrase of "boisterous metaphors"; † it was Dryden who said of Cowley, whom he elsewhere calls "the darling of my youth," ‡ that he was "sunk in reputation because he could never forgive any conceit which came in his

* This probably suggested to Young the grandiose image in his "Last Day" (B. ii.): —

> "Those overwhelming armies . . . .
> Whose rear lay wrapt in night, while breaking dawn
> Roused the broad front and called the battle on."

This, to be sure, is no plagiarism; but it should be carried to Dryden's credit that we catch the poets of the next half-century oftener with their hands in his pockets than in those of any one else.

† Essay on Satire.

‡ Ibid.

way, but swept, like a drag-net, great and small."* But the passages I have thus far cited as specimens of our poet's coarseness (for poet he surely was *intus*, though not always *in cute*) were written before he was forty, and he had an odd notion, suitable to his healthy complexion, that poets on the whole improve after that date. Man at forty, he says, "seems to be fully in his summer tropic, ... and I believe that it will hold in all great poets that, though they wrote before with a certain heat of genius which inspired them, yet that heat was not perfectly digested." † But artificial heat is never to be digested at all, as is plain in Dryden's case. He was a man who warmed slowly, and, in his hurry to supply the market, forced his mind. The result was the same after forty as before. In "Œdipus" (1679) we find,

"Not one bolt
Shall err from Thebes, but more be called for, more,
New-moulded thunder of a larger size!"

This play was written in conjunction with Lee, of whom

* Preface to Fables. Men are always inclined to revenge themselves on their old idols in the first enthusiasm of conversion to a purer faith. Cowley had all the faults that Dryden loads him with, and yet his popularity was to some extent deserved. He at least had a theory that poetry should soar, not creep, and longed for some expedient, in the failure of natural wings, by which he could lift himself away from the conventional and commonplace. By beating out the substance of Pindar very thin, he contrived a kind of balloon which, tumid with gas, did certainly mount a little, *into* the clouds, if not above them, though sure to come suddenly down with a bump. His odes, indeed, are an alternation of upward jerks and concussions, and smack more of Chapelain than of the Theban, but his prose is very agreeable,— Montaigne and water, perhaps, but with some flavor of the Gascon wine left. The strophe of his ode to Dr. Scarborough, in which he compares his surgical friend, operating for the stone, to Moses striking the rock, more than justifies all the ill that Dryden could lay at his door. It was into precisely such mud-holes that Cowley's Will-o'-the-Wisp had misguided him. Men may never wholly shake off a vice but they are always conscious of it, and hate the tempter.

† Dedication of Georgics.

Dryden relates * that, when some one said to him, "It is easy enough to write like a madman," he replied, "No, it is hard to write like a madman, but easy enough to write like a fool," — perhaps the most compendious lecture on poetry ever delivered. The splendid bit of eloquence, which has so much the sheet-iron clang of impeachment thunder (I hope that Dryden is not in the Library of Congress!) is perhaps Lee's. The following passage almost certainly is his: —

> "Sure 't is the end of all things! Fate has torn
> The lock of Time off, and his head is now
> The ghastly ball of round Eternity!"

But the next, in which the soul is likened to the pocket of an indignant housemaid charged with theft, is wholly in Dryden's manner: —

> "No; I dare challenge heaven to turn me outward,
> And shake my soul quite empty in your sight."

In the same style, he makes his Don Sebastian (1690) say that he is as much astonished as "drowsy mortals" at the last trump,

> "When, called in haste, *they fumble for their limbs*,"

and propose to take upon himself the whole of a crime shared with another by asking Heaven *to charge the bill* on him. And in "King Arthur," written ten years after the Preface from which I have quoted his confession about Dubartas, we have a passage precisely of the kind he condemned: —

> "Ah for the many souls as but this morn
> Were clothed with flesh and warmed with vital blood,
> But naked now, or *shirted* but with air."

Dryden too often violated his own admirable rule, that "an author is not to write all he can, but only all he ought."† In his worst images, however, there is often a vividness that half excuses them. But it is a grotesque

* In a letter to Dennis, 1693.

† Preface to Fables.

vividness, as from the flare of a bonfire. They do not flash into sudden lustre, as in the great poets, where the imaginations of poet and reader leap toward each other and meet half-way.

English prose is indebted to Dryden for having freed it from the cloister of pedantry. He, more than any other single writer, contributed, as well by precept as example, to give it suppleness of movement and the easier air of the modern world. His own style, juicy with proverbial phrases, has that familiar dignity, so hard to attain, perhaps unattainable except by one who, like Dryden, feels that his position is assured. Charles Cotton is as easy, but not so elegant; Walton as familiar, but not so flowing; Swift as idiomatic, but not so elevated; Burke more splendid, but not so equally luminous. That his style was no easy acquisition (though, of course, the aptitude was innate) he himself tells us. In his dedication of "Troilus and Cressida" (1679), where he seems to hint at the erection of an Academy, he says that "the perfect knowledge of a tongue was never attained by any single person. The Court, the College, and the Town must all be joined in it. And as our English is a composition of the dead and living tongues, there is required a perfect knowledge, not only of the Greek and Latin, but of the Old German, French, and Italian, and to help all these, a conversation with those authors of our own who have written with the fewest faults in prose and verse. But how barbarously we yet write and speak your Lordship knows, and I am sufficiently sensible in my own English.* For I am often put to a stand in considering whether what I write be the idiom of the tongue, or false grammar and non-

* More than half a century later, Orrery, in his "Remarks" on Swift, says: "We speak and we write at random; and if a man's common conversation were committed to paper, he would be startled *for*

sense couched beneath that specious name of *Anglicism*, and have no other way to clear my doubts but by translating my English into Latin, and thereby trying what sense the words will bear in a more stable language." *Tantæ molis erat.* Five years later: "The proprieties and delicacies of the English are known to few; it is impossible even for a good wit to understand and practise them without the help of a liberal education, long reading and digesting of those few good authors we have amongst us, the knowledge of men and manners, *the freedom of habitudes and conversation with the best company of both sexes*, and, in short, without wearing off the rust which he contracted while he was laying in a stock of learning." In the passage I have italicized, it will be seen that Dryden lays some stress upon the influence of women in refining language. Swift, also, in his plan for an Academy, says: "Now, though I would by no means give the ladies the trouble of advising us in the reformation of our language, yet I cannot help thinking that, since they have been left out of all meetings except parties at play, or where worse designs are carried on, our conversation has very much degenerated." * Swift affirms that the language had grown corrupt since the Restoration, and that "the Court, which used to be the standard of propriety and correctness of speech, was then, and, I think, has ever since continued, the worst school in England." † He lays the blame partly on the

to find himself guilty in *so few* sentences of so many solecisms and such false English." I do not remember *for to* anywhere in Dryden's prose. *So few* has long been denizened; no wonder, since it is nothing more than *si peu* Anglicized.

* Letter to the Lord High Treasurer.

† Ibid. He complains of "manglings and abbreviations." "What does your Lordship think of the words drudg'd, disturb'd, rebuk'd, fledg'd, and a thousand others?" In a contribution to the "Tatler" (No. 230) he ridicules the use of *'um* for *them*, and a number of slang

general licentiousness, partly upon the French education of many of Charles's courtiers, and partly on the poets. Dryden undoubtedly formed his diction by the usage of the Court. The age was a very free-and-easy, not to say a very coarse one. Its coarseness was not external, like that of Elizabeth's day, but the outward mark of an inward depravity. What Swift's notion of the refinement of women was may be judged by his anecdotes of Stella. I will not say that Dryden's prose did not gain by the conversational elasticity which his frequenting men and women of the world enabled him to give it. It is the best specimen of every-day style that we have. But the habitual dwelling of his mind in a commonplace atmosphere, and among those easy levels of sentiment which befitted Will's Coffee-house and the Bird-cage Walk, was a damage to his poetry. Solitude is as needful to the imagination as society is wholesome for the character. He cannot always distinguish between enthusiasm and extravagance when he sees them. But apart from these influences which I have adduced in exculpation, there was certainly a vein of coarseness in him, a want

phrases, among which is *mob.* "The war," he says, "has introduced abundance of polysyllables, which will never be able to live many more campaigns." *Speculations, operations, preliminaries, ambassadors, pallisadoes, communication, circumvallation, battalions,* are the instances he gives, and all are now familiar. No man, or body of men, can dam the stream of language. Dryden is rather fond of *'em* for *them,* but uses it rarely in his prose. Swift himself prefers *'t is* to *it is,* as does Emerson still. In what Swift says of the poets, he may be fairly suspected of glancing at Dryden, who was his kinsman, and whose prefaces and translation of Virgil he ridicules in the "Tale of a Tub." Dryden is reported to have said of him, "Cousin Swift is no poet." The Dean began his literary career by Pindaric odes to Athenian Societies and the like, — perhaps the greatest mistake as to his own powers of which an author was ever guilty. It was very likely that he would send these to his relative, already distinguished, for his opinion upon them. If this was so, the justice of Dryden's judgment must have added to the smart. Swift never forgot or forgave; Dryden was careless enough to do the one, and large enough to do the other.

of that exquisite sensitiveness which is the conscience of the artist. An old gentleman, writing to the Gentleman's Magazine in 1745, professes to remember "plain John Dryden (before he paid his court with success to the great) in one uniform clothing of Norwich drugget. I have eat tarts at the Mulberry Garden with him and Madam Reeve, when our author advanced to a sword and Chadreux wig." * I always fancy Dryden in the drugget, with wig, lace ruffles, and sword superimposed. It is the type of this curiously incongruous man.

The first poem by which Dryden won a general acknowledgment of his power was the "Annus Mirabilis," written in his thirty-seventh year. Pepys, himself not altogether a bad judge, doubtless expresses the common opinion when he says: "I am very well pleased this night with reading a poem I brought home with me last night from Westminster Hall, of Dryden's, upon the present war; a very good poem." † And a very good poem, in some sort, it continues to be, in spite of its

* Both Malone and Scott accept this gentleman's evidence without question, but I confess suspicion of a memory that runs back more than eighty-one years, and recollects a man before he had any claim to remembrance. Dryden was never poor, and there is at Oxford a portrait of him painted in 1664, which represents him in a superb periwig and laced band. This was "before he had paid his court with success to the great." But the story is at least *ben trovato*, and morally true enough to serve as an illustration. Who the "old gentleman" was has never been discovered. Of Crowne (who has some interest for us as a sometime student at Harvard) he says: "Many a cup of metheglin have I drank with little starch'd Johnny Crown; we called him so, from the stiff, unalterable primness of his long cravat." Crowne reflects no more credit on his Alma Mater than Downing. Both were sneaks, and of such a kind as, I think, can only be produced by a debauched Puritanism. Crowne, as a rival of Dryden, is contemptuously alluded to by Cibber in his "Apology."

† Diary, III. 390. Almost the only notices of Dryden that make him alive to me I have found in the delicious book of this Polonius-Montaigne, the only man who ever had the courage to keep a sincere journal, even under the shelter of cipher.

amazing blemishes. We must always bear in mind that Dryden lived in an age that supplied him with no ready-made inspiration, and that big phrases and images are apt to be pressed into the service when great ones do not volunteer. With this poem begins the long series of Dryden's prefaces, of which Swift made such excellent, though malicious, fun that I cannot forbear to quote it. "I do utterly disapprove and declare against that pernicious custom of making the *preface* a bill of fare to the book. For I have always looked upon it as a high point of indiscretion in monster-mongers and other retailers of strange sights to hang out a fair picture over the door, drawn after the life, with a most eloquent description underneath; this has saved me many a threepence. . . . . Such is exactly the fate at this time of *prefaces*. . . . . This expedient was admirable at first; our great Dryden has long carried it as far as it would go, and with incredible success. He has often said to me in confidence, 'that the world would never have suspected him to be so great a poet, if he had not assured them so frequently, in his prefaces, that it was impossible they could either doubt or forget it.' Perhaps it may be so; however, I much fear his instructions have edified out of their place, and taught men to grow wiser in certain points where he never intended they should." * The *monster-mongers* is a terrible thrust, when we remember some of the comedies and heroic plays which Dryden ushered in this fashion. In the dedication of the "Annus" to the city of London is one of those pithy sentences of which Dryden is ever afterwards so full, and which he lets fall with a carelessness that seems always to deepen the meaning: "I have heard, indeed, of some virtuous persons who

* Tale of a Tub, Sect. V. Pepys also speaks of buying the "Maiden Queen" of Mr. Dryden's, which he himself, in his preface, seems to brag of, and indeed is a good play. — 18th January, 1668.

have ended unfortunately, but never of any virtuous nation; Providence is engaged too deeply when the cause becomes so general." In his "account" of the poem in a letter to Sir Robert Howard he says: "I have chosen to write my poem in quatrains or stanzas of four in alternate rhyme, because I have ever judged them more noble and of greater dignity, both for the sound and number, than any other verse in use amongst us. . . . . The learned languages have certainly a great advantage of us in not being tied to the slavery of any rhyme. . . . . But in this necessity of our rhymes, I have always found the couplet verse most easy, though not so proper for this occasion; for there the work is sooner at an end, every two lines concluding the labor of the poet." A little further on: "They [the French] write in alexandrines, or verses of six feet, such as amongst us is the old translation of Homer by Chapman: all which, by lengthening their chain,* makes the sphere of their activity the greater." I have quoted these passages because, in a small compass, they include several things characteristic of Dryden. "I have ever judged," and "I have always found," are particularly so. If he took up an opinion in the morning, he would have found so many arguments for it before night that it would seem already old and familiar. So with his reproach of rhyme; a

* He is fond of this image. In the "Maiden Queen" Celadon tells Sabina that, when he is with her rival Florimel, his heart is still her prisoner, "it only draws a longer chain after it." Goldsmith's fancy was taken by it; and everybody admires in the "Traveller" the extraordinary conceit of a heart dragging a lengthening chain. The smoothness of too many rhymed pentameters is that of thin ice over shallow water; so long as we glide along rapidly, all is well; but if we dwell a moment on any one spot, we may find ourselves knee-deep in mud. A later poet, in trying to improve on Goldsmith, shows the ludicrousness of the image: —

"And round my heart's leg ties its galling chain."

To write imaginatively a man should have — imagination!

year or two before he was eagerly defending it; * again a few years, and he will utterly condemn and drop it in his plays, while retaining it in his translations; afterwards his study of Milton leads him to think that blank verse would suit the epic style better, and he proposes to try it with Homer, but at last translates one book as a specimen, and behold, it is in rhyme! But the charm of this great advocate is, that, whatever side he was on, he could always find excellent reasons for it, and state them with great force, and abundance of happy illustration. He is an exception to the proverb, and is none the worse pleader that he is always pleading his own cause. The blunder about Chapman is of a kind into which his hasty temperament often betrayed him. He remembered that Chapman's "Iliad" was in a long measure, concluded without looking that it was alexandrine, and then attributes it generally to his "Homer." Chapman's "Iliad" is done in fourteen-syllable verse, and his "Odyssee" in the very metre that Dryden himself used in his own version.† I remark also what he says of the couplet, that it was easy because the second verse concludes the labor of the poet. And yet it was Dryden who found it hard for that very reason. His vehement abundance refused those narrow banks, first running

* See his epistle dedicatory to the "Rival Ladies" (1664). For the other side, see particularly a passage in his "Discourse on Epic Poetry" (1697).

† In the same way he had two years before assumed that Shakespeare "was the first who, to shun the pains of continued rhyming, invented that kind of writing which we call blank verse!" Dryden was never, I suspect, a very careful student of English literature. He seems never to have known that Surrey translated a part of the "Æneid" (and with great spirit) into blank verse. Indeed, he was not a scholar, in the proper sense of the word, but he had that faculty of rapid assimilation without study, so remarkable in Coleridge and other rich minds, whose office is rather to impregnate than to invent. These brokers of thought perform a great office in literature, second only to that of originators.

over into a triplet, and, even then uncontainable, rising to an alexandrine in the concluding verse. And I have little doubt that it was the roominess, rather than the dignity, of the quatrain which led him to choose it. As apposite to this, I may quote what he elsewhere says of octosyllabic verse: "The thought can turn itself with greater ease in a larger compass. When the rhyme comes too thick upon us, it straightens the expression: we are thinking of the close, when we should be employed in adorning the thought. It makes a poet giddy with turning in a space too narrow for his imagination." *

Dryden himself, as was not always the case with him, was well satisfied with his work. He calls it his best hitherto, and attributes his success to the excellence of his subject, "incomparably the best he had ever had, *excepting only the Royal Family.*" The first part is devoted to the Dutch war; the last to the fire of London. The martial half is infinitely the better of the two. He altogether surpasses his model, Davenant. If his poem lack the gravity of thought attained by a few stanzas of "Gondibert," it is vastly superior in life, in picturesqueness, in the energy of single lines, and, above all, in imagination. Few men have read "Gondibert," and almost every one speaks of it, as commonly of the dead, with a certain subdued respect. And it deserves respect as an honest effort to bring poetry back to its highest office in the ideal treatment of life. Davenant emulated Spenser, and if his poem had been as good as his preface, it could still be read in another spirit than that of investigation. As it is, it always reminds me of Goldsmith's famous verse. It is remote, unfriendly, solitary, and, above

* Essay on Satire. What he has said just before this about Butler is worth noting. Butler had had a chief hand in the "Rehearsal," but Dryden had no grudges where the question was of giving its just praise to merit.

all, slow. Its shining passages, for there are such, remind one of distress-rockets sent up at intervals from a ship just about to founder, and sadden rather than cheer.*

The first part of the "Annus Mirabilis" is by no means clear of the false taste of the time,† though it has some of Dryden's manliest verses and happiest comparisons, always his two distinguishing merits. Here, as almost everywhere else in Dryden, measuring him merely as poet, we recall what he, with pathetic pride, says of himself in the prologue to "Aurengzebe": —

"Let him retire, betwixt two ages cast,
The first of this, the hindmost of the last."

What can be worse than what he says of comets? —

"Whether they unctuous exhalations are
Fired by the sun, or seeming so alone,
Or each some more remote and slippery star
Which loses footing when to mortals shown."

Or than this, of the destruction of the Dutch India-ships? —

"Amidst whole heaps of spices lights a ball,
And now their odors armed against them fly;
Some preciously by shattered porcelain fall,
And some by aromatic splinters die."

Dear Dr. Johnson had his doubts about Shakespeare, but

* The conclusion of the second canto of Book Third is the best continuously fine passage. Dryden's poem has nowhere so much meaning in so small space as Davenant, when he says of the sense of honor that,

"Like Power, it grows to nothing, growing less."

Davenant took the hint of the stanza from Sir John Davies. Wyatt first used it, so far as I know, in English.

† Perhaps there is no better lecture on the prevailing vices of style and thought (if thought this frothy ferment of the mind may be called) than in Cotton Mather's "Magnalia." For Mather, like a true provincial, appropriates only the mannerism, and, as is usual in such cases, betrays all its weakness by the unconscious parody of exaggeration.

here at least was poetry! This is one of the quatrains which he pronounces "worthy of our author."*

But Dryden himself has said that "a man who is resolved to praise an author with any appearance of justice must be sure to take him on the strongest side, and where he is least liable to exceptions." This is true also of one who wishes to measure an author fairly, for the higher wisdom of criticism lies in the capacity to admire.

Leser, wie gefall ich dir?
Leser, wie gefällst du mir?

are both fair questions, the answer to the first being more often involved in that to the second than is sometimes thought. The poet in Dryden was never more fully revealed than in such verses as these:—

"And threatening France, placed like a painted Jove,†
Kept idle thunder in his lifted hand";

"Silent in smoke of cannon they come on";

"And his loud guns speak thick, like angry men";

* The Doctor was a capital judge of the substantial value of the goods he handled, but his judgment always seems that of the thumb and forefinger. For the shades, the disposition of colors, the beauty of the figures, he has as good as no sense whatever. The critical parts of his Life of Dryden seem to me the best of his writing in this kind. There is little to be gleaned after him. He had studied his author, which he seldom did, and his criticism is sympathetic, a thing still rarer with him. As illustrative of his own habits, his remarks on Dryden's reading are curious.

† Perhaps the hint was given by a phrase of Corneille, *monarque en peinture*. Dryden seldom borrows, unless from Shakespeare, without improving, and he borrowed a great deal. Thus in "Don Sebastian" (of suicide):—

"Brutus and Cato might discharge their souls,
And give them furloughs for the other world;
But we, like sentries, are obliged to stand
In starless nights and wait the appointed hour."

The thought is Cicero's, but how it is intensified by the "starless nights"! Dryden, I suspect, got it from his favorite, Montaigne, who says, "Que nous ne pouvons abandonner cette garnison du monde, sans

"The vigorous seaman every port-hole plies,
And adds his heart to every gun he fires";

"And, though to me unknown, they sure fought well,
Whom Rupert led, and who were British born."

This is masculine writing, and yet it must be said that there is scarcely a quatrain in which the rhyme does not trip him into a platitude, and there are too many swaggering with that *expression forte d'un sentiment faible* which Voltaire condemns in Corneille, — a temptation to which Dryden always lay too invitingly open. But there are passages higher in kind than any I have cited, because they show imagination. Such are the verses in which he describes the dreams of the disheartened enemy: —

"In dreams they fearful precipices tread,
Or, shipwrecked, labor to some distant shore,
Or in dark churches walk among the dead";

and those in which he recalls glorious memories, and sees where

"The mighty ghosts of our great Harries rose,
And armëd Edwards looked with anxious eyes."

A few verses, like the pleasantly alliterative one in which he makes the spider, "from the silent ambush of his den," "feel far off the trembling of his thread," show that he was beginning to study the niceties of verse, instead of trusting wholly to what he would have called his natural *fougue*. On the whole, this part of the poem is very good war poetry, as war poetry goes (for there is but one first-rate poem of the kind in English, — short, national, eager as if the writer were personally engaged, with the rapid metre of a drum beating the charge, —

le commandement exprez de celuy qui nous y a mis." (L. ii. chap. 3.) In the same play, by a very Drydenish verse, he gives new force to an old comparison: —

"And I should break through laws divine and human,
And think 'em cobwebs spread for little man,
Which all the bulky herd of Nature breaks."

and that is Drayton's "Battle of Agincourt" *), but it shows more study of Lucan than of Virgil, and for a long time yet we shall find Dryden bewildered by bad models. He is always imitating — no, that is not the word, always emulating — somebody in his more strictly poetical attempts, for in that direction he always needed some external impulse to set his mind in motion. This is more or less true of all authors; nor does it detract from their originality, which depends wholly on their being able so far to forget themselves as to let something of themselves slip into what they write.† Of absolute originality we will not speak till authors are raised by some Deucalion-and-Pyrrha process; and even then our faith would be small, for writers who have no past are pretty sure of having no future. Dryden, at any rate, always had to have his copy set him at the top of the page, and wrote ill or well accordingly. His mind (somewhat solid for a poet) warmed slowly, but, once fairly heated through, he had more of that good-luck of self-oblivion than most men. He certainly gave even a liberal interpretation to Molière's rule of taking his own property wherever he found it, though he sometimes blundered awkwardly about what was properly *his;* but in literature, it should be remembered, a thing always becomes his at last who says it best, and thus makes it his own.‡

* Not his solemn historical droning under that title, but addressed "To the Cambrio-Britons on their harp."

† "Les poëtes euxmêmes s'animent et s'échauffent par la lecture des autres poëtes. Messieurs de Malherbe, Corneille, &c., se disposoient au travail par la lecture des poëtes qui étoient de leur gout." — Vigneul, Marvilliana, I. 64, 65.

‡ For example, Waller had said,

> "Others may use the ocean as their road,
> Only the English *make it their abode;*
> . . . . .
> We *tread on billows with a steady foot,*" —

Mr. Savage Landor once told me that he said to Wordsworth: "Mr. Wordsworth, a man may mix poetry with prose as much as he pleases, and it will only elevate and enliven; but the moment he mixes a particle of prose with his poetry, it precipitates the whole." Wordsworth, he added, never forgave him. The always hasty Dryden, as I think I have already said, was liable, like a careless apothecary's 'prentice, to make the same confusion of ingredients, especially in the more mischievous way. I cannot leave the "Annus Mirabilis" without giving an example of this. Describing the Dutch prizes, rather like an auctioneer than a poet, he says that

> "Some English wool, vexed in a Belgian loom,
> And into cloth of spongy softness made,
> Did into France or colder Denmark doom,
> To ruin with worse ware our staple trade."

One might fancy this written by the secretary of a board of trade in an unguarded moment; but we should remember that the poem is dedicated to the city of London. The depreciation of the rival fabrics is exquisite; and Dryden, the most English of our poets, would not be so thoroughly English if he had not in him some fibre of *la nation boutiquière*. Let us now see how he succeeds in attempting to infuse science (the most obsti-

long before Campbell. Campbell helps himself to both thoughts, enlivens them into

> "Her march is o'er the mountain wave,
> Her home is on the deep,"

and they are his forevermore. His "leviathans afloat" he *lifted* from the "Annus Mirabilis"; but in what court could Dryden sue? Again, Waller in another poem calls the Duke of York's flag

> "His dreadful streamer, like a comet's hair";

and this, I believe, is the first application of the celestial portent to this particular comparison. Yet Milton's "imperial ensign" waves defiant behind his impregnable lines, and even Campbell flaunts his "meteor flag" in Waller's face. Gray's bard might be sent to the lock-up, but even he would find bail.

> "C'est imiter quelqu'un que de planter des choux."

nately prosy material) with poetry. Speaking of "a more exact knowledge of the longitudes," as he explains in a note, he tells us that,

"Then we upon our globe's last verge shall go,
And view the ocean leaning on the sky;
From thence our rolling neighbors we shall know,
And on the lunar world securely pry."

Dr. Johnson confesses that he does not understand this. Why should he, when it is plain that Dryden was wholly in the dark himself? To understand it is none of my business, but I confess that it interests me as an Americanism. We have hitherto been credited as the inventors of the "jumping-off place" at the extreme western verge of the world. But Dryden was beforehand with us. Though he doubtless knew that the earth was a sphere (and perhaps that it was flattened at the poles), it was always a flat surface in his fancy. In his "Amphitryon," he makes Alcmena say: —

"No, I would fly thee to the ridge of earth,
And leap the precipice to 'scape thy sight."

And in his "Spanish Friar," Lorenzo says to Elvira that they "will travel together to the ridge of the world, and then drop together into the next." It is idle for us poor Yankees to hope that we can invent anything. To say sooth, if Dryden had left nothing behind him but the "Annus Mirabilis," he might have served as a type of the kind of poet America would have produced by the biggest-river-and-tallest-mountain recipe, — longitude and latitude in plenty, with marks of culture scattered here and there like the *carets* on a proof-sheet.

It is now time to say something of Dryden as a dramatist. In the thirty-two years between 1662 and 1694 he produced twenty-five plays, and assisted Lee in two. I have hinted that it took Dryden longer than most men to find the true bent of his genius. On a superficial view, he might almost seem to confirm that theory, maintained by Johnson, among others, that genius was nothing more than great intellectual power exercised persistently in some particular direction which chance decided, so that it lay in circumstance merely whether a man should turn out a Shakespeare or a Newton. But when we come to compare what he wrote, regardless of Minerva's averted face, with the spontaneous production of his happier muse, we shall be inclined to think his example one of the strongest cases against the theory in question. He began his dramatic career, as usual, by rowing against the strong current of his nature, and pulled only the more doggedly the more he felt himself swept down the stream. His first attempt was at comedy, and, though his earliest piece of that kind (the "Wild Gallant," 1663) utterly failed, he wrote eight others afterwards. On the 23d February, 1663, Pepys writes in his diary: "To Court, and there saw the 'Wild Gallant' performed by the king's house; but it was ill acted, and the play so poor a thing as I never saw in my life almost, and so little answering the name, that, from the beginning to the end, I could not, nor can at this time, tell certainly which was the Wild Gallant. The king did not seem pleased at all the whole play, nor anybody else." After some alteration, it was revived with more success. On its publication in 1669 Dryden honestly admitted its former failure, though with a kind of salvo for his self-love. "I made the town my judges, and the greater part condemned it. After which I do not think it my concernment to defend it with the ordinary zeal of a poet for his decried poem, though Corneille is more resolute in his preface before 'Pertharite,'* which was condemned more universally

* Corneille's tragedy of "Pertharite" was acted unsuccessfully in 1659. Racine made free use of it in his more fortunate "Andromaque."

than this. . . . . Yet it was received at Court, and was more than once the divertisement of his Majesty, by his own command." Pepys lets us amusingly behind the scenes in the matter of his Majesty's divertisement. Dryden does not seem to see that in the condemnation of something meant to amuse the public there can be no question of degree. To fail at all is to fail utterly.

" *Tous les genres sont permis, hors le genre ennuyeux.*"

In the reading, at least, all Dryden's comic writing for the stage must be ranked with the latter class. He himself would fain make an exception of the "Spanish Friar," but I confess that I rather wonder at than envy those who can be amused by it. His comedies lack everything that a comedy should have, — lightness, quickness of transition, unexpectedness of incident, easy cleverness of dialogue, and humorous contrast of character brought out by identity of situation. The comic parts of the "Maiden Queen" seem to me Dryden's best, but the merit even of these is Shakespeare's, and there is little choice where even the best is only tolerable. The common quality, however, of all Dryden's comedies is their nastiness, the more remarkable because we have ample evidence that he was a man of modest conversation. Pepys, who was by no means squeamish (for he found "Sir Martin Marall" "the most entire piece of mirth . . . . that certainly ever was writ . . . . very good wit therein, not fooling"), writes in his diary of the 19th June, 1668 : " My wife and Deb to the king's playhouse to-day, thinking to spy me there, and saw the new play 'Evening Love,' of Dryden's, which, though the world commends, she likes not." The next day he saw it himself, "and do not like it, it being very smutty, and nothing so good as the 'Maiden Queen' or the 'Indian Emperor' of Dryden's making. *I was troubled at* *it.*" On the 22d he adds: "Calling this day at Herringman's,* he tells me Dryden do himself call it but a fifth-rate play." This was no doubt true, and yet, though Dryden in his preface to the play says, "I confess I have given [yielded] too much to the people in it, and am ashamed for them as well as for myself, that I have pleased them at so cheap a rate," he takes care to add, "not that there is anything here that I would not defend to an ill-natured judge." The plot was from Calderon, and the author, rebutting the charge of plagiarism, tells us that the king ("without whose command they should no longer be troubled with anything of mine") had already answered for him by saying, "that he only desired that they who accused me of theft would always steal him plays like mine." Of the morals of the play he has not a word, nor do I believe that he was conscious of any harm in them till he was attacked by Collier, and then (with some protest against what he considers the undue severity of his censor) he had the manliness to confess that he had done wrong. "It becomes me not to draw my pen in the defence of a bad cause, when I have so often drawn it for a good one." † And in a letter to his correspondent, Mrs. Thomas, written only a few weeks before his death, warning her against the example of Mrs. Behn, he says, with remorseful sincerity: "I confess I am the last man in the world who ought in justice to arraign her, who have been myself too much a libertine in most of my poems, which I should be well contented I had time either to purge or to see them fairly burned." Congreve was less patient, and even Dryden, in the last epilogue he ever wrote, attempts an excuse: —

"Perhaps the Parson stretched a point too far,
When with our Theatres he waged a war;
He tells you that this very moral age
Received the first infection from the Stage,

* Dryden's publisher.

† Preface to the Fables.

> But sure a banished Court, with lewdness fraught,
> The seeds of open vice returning brought.
>
> . . . . . .
>
> Whitehall the naked Venus first revealed,
> Who, standing, as at Cyprus, in her shrine,
> The strumpet was adored with rites divine.
>
> . . . . .
>
> The poets, who must live by courts or starve,
> Were proud so good a Government to serve,
> And, mixing with buffoons and pimps profane,
> Tainted the Stage for some small snip of gain."

Dryden least of all men should have stooped to this palliation, for he had, not without justice, said of himself: "The same parts and application which have made me a poet might have raised me to any honors of the gown." Milton and Marvell neither lived by the Court, nor starved. Charles Lamb most ingeniously defends the Comedy of the Restoration as "the sanctuary and quiet Alsatia of hunted casuistry," where there was no pretence of representing a real world.* But this was certainly not so. Dryden again and again boasts of the superior advantage which his age had over that of the elder dramatists, in painting polite life, and attributes it to a greater freedom of intercourse between the poets and the frequenters of the Court.† We shall be less surprised at the *kind* of refinement upon which Dryden congratulated himself, when we learn (from the dedication of "Marriage à la Mode") that the Earl of Rochester was its exemplar: "The best comic writers of our age will join with me to acknowledge that they have copied the gallantries of courts, the delicacy of expression, and the decencies of behavior from your Lordship." In judging

* I interpret some otherwise ambiguous passages in this charming and acute essay by its title: "On the *artificial* comedy of the last century."

† See especially his defence of the epilogue to the Second Part of the "Conquest of Granada" (1672).

Dryden, it should be borne in mind that for some years he was under contract to deliver three plays a year, a kind of bond to which no man should subject his brain who has a decent respect for the quality of its products. We should remember, too, that in his day *manners* meant what we call *morals*, that custom always makes a larger part of virtue among average men than they are quite aware, and that the reaction from an outward conformity which had no root in inward faith may for a time have given to the frank expression of laxity an air of honesty that made it seem almost refreshing. There is no such hotbed for excess of license as excess of restraint, and the arrogant fanaticism of a single virtue is apt to make men suspicious of tyranny in all the rest. But the riot of emancipation could not last long, for the more tolerant society is of private vice, the more exacting will it be of public decorum, that excellent thing, so often the plausible substitute for things more excellent. By 1678 the public mind had so far recovered its tone that Dryden's comedy of "Limberham" was barely tolerated for three nights. I will let the man who looked at human nature from more sides, and therefore judged it more gently than any other, give the only excuse possible for Dryden: —

> "Men's judgments are
> A parcel of their fortunes, and things outward
> Do draw the inward quality after them
> To suffer all alike."

Dryden's own apology only makes matters worse for him by showing that he committed his offences with his eyes wide open, and that he wrote comedies so wholly in despite of nature as never to deviate into the comic. Failing as clown, he did not scruple to take on himself the office of Chiffinch to the palled appetite of the public. "For I confess my chief endeavours are to delight the age in which I live. If the humour of this be for low comedy, small accidents, and raillery, I will force my genius to obey it, though with more reputation I could write in verse. I know I am not so fitted by nature to write comedy; I want that gayety of humour which is requisite to it. My conversation is slow and dull, my humour saturnine and reserved: In short, I am none of those who endeavour to break jests in company or make repartees. So that those who decry my comedies do me no injury, except it be in point of profit: Reputation in them is the last thing to which I shall pretend."* For my own part, though I have been forced to hold my nose in picking my way through these ordures of Dryden, I am free to say that I think them far less morally mischievous than that *corps-de-ballet* literature in which the most animal of the passions is made more temptingly naked by a veil of French gauze. Nor does Dryden's lewdness leave such a reek in the mind as the filthy cynicism of Swift, who delighted to uncover the nakedness of our common mother.

It is pleasant to follow Dryden into the more congenial region of heroic plays, though here also we find him making a false start. Anxious to please the king,† and so able a reasoner as to convince even himself of the justice of whatever cause he argued, he not only wrote tragedies in the French style, but defended his practice in an essay which is by far the most delightful reproduction of the classic dialogue ever written in English. Eugenius (Lord Buckhurst), Lisideius (Sir Charles Sidley), Crites (Sir R. Howard), and Neander (Dryden) are the four partakers in the debate. The comparative

* Defence of an Essay on Dramatick Poesy.

† "The favor which heroick plays have lately found upon our theatres has been wholly derived to them from the countenance and approbation they have received at Court." (Dedication of "Indian Emperor" to Duchess of Monmouth.)

merits of ancients and moderns, of the Shakespearian and contemporary drama, of rhyme and blank verse, the value of the three (supposed) Aristotelian unities, are the main topics discussed. The tone of the discussion is admirable, midway between bookishness and talk, and the fairness with which each side of the argument is treated shows the breadth of Dryden's mind perhaps better than any other one piece of his writing. There are no men of straw set up to be knocked down again, as there commonly are in debates conducted upon this plan. The "Defence" of the Essay is to be taken as a supplement to Neander's share in it, as well as many scattered passages in subsequent prefaces and dedications. All the interlocutors agree that "the sweetness of English verse was never understood or practised by our fathers," and that "our poesy is much improved by the happiness of some writers yet living, who first taught us to mould our thoughts into easy and significant words, to retrench the superfluities of expression, and to make our rhyme so properly a part of the verse that it should never mislead the sense, but itself be led and governed by it." In another place he shows that by "living writers" he meant Waller and Denham. "Rhyme has all the advantages of prose besides its own. But the excellence and dignity of it were never fully known till Mr. Waller taught it: he first made writing easily an art; first showed us to conclude the sense, most commonly in distiches, which in the verse before him runs on for so many lines together that the reader is out of breath to overtake it." * Dryden afterwards changed his mind, and one of the excellences of his own rhymed verse is, that his sense is too ample to be concluded by the distich. Rhyme had been censured as unnatural in dialogue; but Dryden replies that it is no more so than blank verse, since no man

* Dedication of "Rival Ladies."

talks any kind of verse in real life. But the argument for rhyme is of another kind. "I am satisfied if it cause delight, for delight is the chief if not the only end of poesy [he should have said *means*]; instruction can be admitted but in the second place, for poesy only instructs as it delights. . . . . The converse, therefore, which a poet is to imitate must be heightened with all the arts and ornaments of poesy, and must be such as, strictly considered, could never be supposed spoken by any without premeditation. . . . . Thus prose, though the rightful prince, yet is by common consent deposed as too weak for the government of serious plays, and, he failing, there now start up two competitors; one the nearer in blood, which is blank verse; the other more fit for the ends of government, which is rhyme. Blank verse is, indeed, the nearer prose, but he is blemished with the weakness of his predecessor. Rhyme (for I will deal clearly) has somewhat of the usurper in him; but he is brave and generous, and his dominion pleasing."* To the objection that the difficulties of rhyme will lead to circumlocution, he answers in substance, that a good poet will know how to avoid them.

It is curious how long the superstition that Waller was the refiner of English verse has prevailed since Dryden first gave it vogue. He was a very poor poet and a purely mechanical versifier. He has lived mainly on the credit of a single couplet,

> "The soul's dark cottage, battered and decayed,
> Lets in new light through chinks that Time hath made,"

in which the melody alone belongs to him, and the con-

* Defence of the Essay. Dryden, in the happiness of his illustrative comparisons, is almost unmatched. Like himself, they occupy a middle ground between poetry and prose, — they are a cross between metaphor and simile.

ceit, such as it is, to Samuel Daniel, who said, long before, that the body's

> "Walls, grown thin, permit the mind
> To look out thorough and his frailty find."

Waller has made worse nonsense of it in the transfusion. It might seem that Ben Jonson had a prophetic foreboding of him when he wrote: "Others there are that have no composition at all, but a kind of tuning and rhyming fall, in what they write. It runs and slides and only makes a sound. Women's poets they are called, as you have women's tailors.

> They write a verse as smooth, as soft, as cream
> In which there is no torrent, nor scarce stream.

You may sound these wits and find the depth of them with your middle-finger." * It seems to have been taken for granted by Waller, as afterwards by Dryden, that our elder poets bestowed no thought upon their verse. "Waller was smooth," but unhappily he was also flat, and his importation of the French theory of the couplet as a kind of thought-coop did nothing but mischief.† He never compassed even a smoothness approaching this description of a nightingale's song by a third-rate poet of the earlier school, —

> "Trails her plain ditty in one long-spun note
> Through the sleek passage of her open throat,
> A clear, unwrinkled song," —

* Discoveries.

† What a wretched rhymer he could be we may see in his *alteration* of the "Maid's Tragedy" of Beaumont and Fletcher: —

> "Not long since walking in the field,
> My nurse and I, we there beheld
> A goodly fruit; which, tempting me,
> I would have plucked; but, trembling, she,
> Whoever eat those berries, cried,
> In less than half an hour died!"

What intolerable seesaw! Not much of Byron's "fatal facility" in *these* octosyllabics!

one of whose beauties is its running over into the third verse. Those poets indeed

> "Felt music's pulse in all her arteries";

and Dryden himself found out, when he came to try it, that blank verse was not so easy a thing as he at first conceived it, nay, that it is the most difficult of all verse, and that it must make up in harmony, by variety of pause and modulation, for what it loses in the melody of rhyme. In what makes the chief merit of his later versification, he but rediscovered the secret of his predecessors in giving to rhymed pentameters something of the freedom of blank verse, and not mistaking metre for rhythm.

Voltaire, in his Commentary on Corneille, has sufficiently lamented the awkwardness of movement imposed upon the French dramatists by the gyves of rhyme. But he considers the necessity of overcoming this obstacle, on the whole, an advantage. Difficulty is his tenth and superior muse. How did Dryden, who says nearly the same thing, succeed in his attempt at the French manner? He fell into every one of its vices, without attaining much of what constitutes its excellence. From the nature of the language, all French poetry is purely artificial, and its high polish is all that keeps out decay. The length of their dramatic verse forces the French into much tautology, into bombast in its original meaning, the stuffing out a thought with words till it fills the line. The rigid system of their rhyme, which makes it much harder to manage than in English, has accustomed them to inaccuracies of thought which would shock them in prose. For example, in the "Cinna" of Corneille, as originally written, Emilie says to Augustus, —

> "Ces flammes dans nos cœurs dès longtemps étoient nées,
> Et ce sont des secrets de plus de quatre années."

I say nothing of the second verse, which is purely prosaic surplusage exacted by the rhyme, nor of the jingling together of *ces, dès, étoient, nées, des,* and *secrets,* but I confess that *nées* does not seem to be the epithet that Corneille would have chosen for *flammes,* if he could have had his own way, and that flames would seem of all things the hardest to keep secret. But in revising, Corneille changed the first verse thus, —

> " Ces flammes dans nos cœurs *sans votre ordre* étoient nées."

Can anything be more absurd than flames born to order? Yet Voltaire, on his guard against these rhyming pitfalls for the sense, does not notice this in his minute comments on this play. Of extravagant metaphor, the result of this same making sound the file-leader of sense, a single example from " Heraclius " shall suffice : —

> " La vapeur de mon sang ira grossir la foudre
> Que Dieu tient déjà prête à le reduire en poudre."

One cannot think of a Louis Quatorze Apollo except in a full-bottomed periwig, and the tragic style of their poets is always showing the disastrous influence of that portentous comet. It is the *style perruque* in another than the French meaning of the phrase, and the skill lay in dressing it majestically, so that, as Cibber says, "upon the head of a man of sense, *if it became him,* it could never fail of drawing to him a more partial regard and benevolence than could possibly be hoped for in an ill-made one." It did not become Dryden, and he left it off.*

Like his own Zimri, Dryden was "all for" this or that fancy, till he took up with another. But even while he was writing on French models, his judgment could not be blinded to their defects. "Look upon the

* In more senses than one. His last and best portrait shows him in his own gray hair.

'Cinna' and the 'Pompey,' they are not so properly to be called plays as long discourses of reason of State, and 'Polieucte' in matters of religion is as solemn as the long stops upon our organs; . . . . their actors speak by the hour-glass like our parsons. . . . . I deny not but this may suit well enough with the French, for as we, who are a more sullen people, come to be diverted at our plays, so they, who are of an airy and gay temper, come thither to make themselves more serious." * With what an air of innocent unconsciousness the sarcasm is driven home! Again, while he was still slaving at these bricks without straw, he says: "The present French poets are generally accused that, wheresoever they lay the scene, or in whatever age, the manners of their heroes are wholly French. Racine's Bajazet is bred at Constantinople, but his civilities are conveyed to him by some secret passage from Versailles into the Seraglio." It is curious that Voltaire, speaking of the *Bérénice* of Racine, praises a passage in it for precisely what Dryden condemns: "Il semble qu'on entende *Henriette* d'Angleterre elle-même parlant au marquis de *Vardes*. La politesse de la cour de *Louis XIV.*, l'agrément de la langue Française, la douceur de la versification la plus naturelle, le sentiment le plus tendre, tout se trouve dans ce peu de vers." After Dryden had broken away from the heroic style, he speaks out more plainly. In the Preface to his "All for Love," in reply to some cavils upon "little, and not essential decencies," the decision about which he refers to a master of ceremonies, he goes on to say: "The French poets, I confess, are strict observers of these punctilios; . . . . in this nicety of manners does the excellency of French poetry consist. Their heroes are the most civil people breathing, but their good breeding seldom extends to a word of

* Essay on Dramatick Poesy.

sense. All their wit is in their ceremony; they want the genius which animates our stage, and therefore 't is but necessary, when they cannot please, that they should take care not to offend. . . . . They are so careful not to exasperate a critic that they never leave him any work, ... for no part of a poem is worth our discommending where the whole is insipid, as when we have once tasted palled wine we stay not to examine it glass by glass. But while they affect to shine in trifles, they are often careless in essentials. . . . . For my part, I desire to be tried by the laws of my own country." This is said in heat, but it is plain enough that his mind was wholly changed. In his discourse on epic poetry he is as decided, but more temperate. He says that the French heroic verse "runs with more activity than strength.* Their language is not strung with sinews like our English; it has the nimbleness of a greyhound, but not the bulk and body of a mastiff. Our men and our verses overbear them by their weight, and *pondere, non numero,* is the British motto. The French have set up purity for the standard of their language, and a masculine vigor is that of ours. Like their tongue is the genius of their poets, — light and trifling in comparison of the English." †

Dryden might have profited by an admirable saying

* A French hendecasyllable verse runs exactly like our ballad measure: —

A cobbler there was and he lived in a stall, ...
La raison, pour marcher, n'a souvent qu'une voye.
(Dryden's note.)

The verse is not a hendecasyllable. "Attended watchfully to her recitative (Mlle. Duchesnois), and find that, in nine lines out of ten, 'A cobbler there was,' &c., *is* the tune of the French heroics." — *Moore's Diary*, 24th April, 1821.

† "The language of the age is never the language of poetry, except among the French, whose verse, where the thought or image does not support it, differs in nothing from prose." — GRAY to WEST.

of his own, that "they who would combat general authority with particular opinion must first establish themselves a reputation of understanding better than other men." He understood the defects much better than the beauties of the French theatre. Lessing was even more one-sided in his judgment upon it.* Goethe, with his usual wisdom, studied it carefully without losing his temper, and tried to profit by its structural merits. Dryden, with his eyes wide open, copied its worst faults, especially its declamatory sentiment. He should have known that certain things can never be transplanted, and that among these is a style of poetry whose great excellence was that it was in perfect sympathy with the genius of the people among whom it came into being. But the truth is, that Dryden had no aptitude whatever for the stage, and in writing for it he was attempting to make a trade of his genius, — an arrangement from which the genius always withdraws in disgust. It was easier to make loose thinking and the bad writing which betrays it pass unobserved while the ear was occupied with the sonorous music of the rhyme to which they marched. Except in "All for Love," "the only play," he tells us, "which he wrote to please himself," † there is no trace of real passion in any of his tragedies. This, indeed, is inevitable, for there are no characters, but only personages, in any except that. That is, in many respects, a noble play, and there are few finer scenes,

* Diderot and Rousseau, however, thought their language unfit for poetry, and Voltaire seems to have half agreed with them. No one has expressed this feeling more neatly than Fauriel : "Nul doute que l'on ne puisse dire en prose des choses éminemment poétiques, tout comme il n'est que trop certain que l'on peut en dire de fort prosaïques en vers, et même en excellents vers, en vers élégamment tournés, et en beau langage. C'est un fait dont je n'ai pas besoin d'indiquer d'exemples : aucune littérature n'en fournirait autant que le nôtre." — Hist. de la Poésie Provençale, II. 237.

† Parallel of Poetry and Painting.

whether in the conception or the carrying out, than that between Antony and Ventidius in the first act.*

As usual, Dryden's good sense was not blind to the extravagances of his dramatic style. In "Mac Flecknoe" he makes his own Maximin the type of childish rant,

> "And little Maximins the gods defy";

but, as usual also, he could give a plausible reason for his own mistakes by means of that most fallacious of all fallacies which is true so far as it goes. In his Prologue to the "Royal Martyr" he says:—

> "And he who servilely creeps after sense
> Is safe, but ne'er will reach an excellence.
> . . . . .
> But, when a tyrant for his theme he had,
> He loosed the reins and let his muse run mad,
> And, though he stumbles in a full career,
> Yet rashness is a better fault than fear;
> . . . . .
> They then, who of each trip advantage take,
> Find out those faults which they want wit to make."

And in the Preface to the same play he tells us: "I have not everywhere observed the equality of numbers in my verse, partly by reason of my haste, but more especially because I *would not have my sense a slave to syllables.*" Dryden, when he had not a bad case to argue, would have had small respect for the wit whose skill lay in the making of faults, and has himself, where his self-love was not engaged, admirably defined the boundary which divides boldness from rashness. What Quintilian says of Seneca applies very aptly to Dryden: "Velles eum suo ingenio dixisse, alieno judicio." † He was thinking of himself, I fancy, when he makes Ventidius say of Antony,—

* "Il y a seulement la scène de *Ventidius* et d'*Antoine* qui est digne de Corneille. C'est là le sentiment de milord Bolingbroke et de tous les bons auteurs; c'est ainsi que pensait Addisson." — Voltaire to M. de Fromont, 15th November, 1735.

† Inst. X., i. 129.

"He starts out wide
And bounds into a vice that bears him far
From his first course, and plunges him in ills;
But, when his danger makes him find his fault,
Quick to observe, and full of sharp remorse,
He censures eagerly his own misdeeds,
Judging himself with malice to himself,
And not forgiving what as man he did
Because his other parts are more than man."

But bad though they nearly all are as wholes, his plays contain passages which only the great masters have surpassed, and to the level of which no subsequent writer for the stage has ever risen. The necessity of rhyme often forced him to a platitude, as where he says, —

"My love was blind to your deluding art,
But blind men feel when stabbed so near the heart." *

But even in rhyme he not seldom justifies his claim to the title of "glorious John." In the very play from which I have just quoted are these verses in his best manner: —

"No, like his better Fortune I'll appear,
With open arms, loose veil, and flowing hair,
Just flying forward from her rolling sphere."

His comparisons, as I have said, are almost always happy. This, from the "Indian Emperor," is tenderly pathetic: —

"As callow birds,
Whose mother 's killed in seeking of the prey,
Cry in their nest and think her long away,
And, at each leaf that stirs, each blast of wind,
Gape for the food which they must never find."

And this, of the anger with which the Maiden Queen, striving to hide her jealousy, betrays her love, is vigorous: —

"Her rage was love, and its tempestuous flame,
Like lightning, showed the heaven from whence it came.

* Conquest of Grenada, Second Part.

The following simile from the "Conquest of Grenada" is as well expressed as it is apt in conception: —

> "I scarcely understand my own intent;
> But, silk-worm like, so long within have wrought,
> That I am lost in my own web of thought."

In the "Rival Ladies," Angelina, walking in the dark, describes her sensations naturally and strikingly: —

> "No noise but what my footsteps make, and they
> Sound dreadfully and louder than by day:
> They double too, and every step I take
> Sounds thick, methinks, and more than one could make."

In all the rhymed plays* there are many passages which one is rather inclined to like than sure he would be right in liking them. The following verses from "Aurengzebe" are of this sort: —

> "My love was such it needed no return,
> Rich in itself, like elemental fire,
> Whose pureness does no aliment require."

This is Cowleyish, and *pureness* is surely the wrong word; and yet it is better than mere commonplace. Perhaps what oftenest turns the balance in Dryden's favor, when we are weighing his claims as a poet, is his persistent capability of enthusiasm. To the last he kindles, and sometimes *almost* flashes out that supernatural light which is the supreme test of poetic genius. As he himself so finely and characteristically says in "Aurengzebe," there was no period in his life when it was not true of him that

> "He felt the inspiring heat, the absent god return."

The verses which follow are full of him, and, with the exception of the single word *underwent*, are in his luckiest manner: —

> "One loose, one sally of a hero's soul,
> Does all the military art control.

* In most, he mingles blank verse.

While timorous wit goes round, or fords the shore,
He shoots the gulf, and is already o'er,
And, when the enthusiastic fit is spent,
Looks back amazed at what he underwent." *

Pithy sentences and phrases always drop from Dryden's pen as if unawares, whether in prose or verse. I string together a few at random:—

"The greatest argument for love is love."

"Few know the use of life before 't is past."

"Time gives himself and is not valuëd."

"Death in itself is nothing; but we fear
To be we know not what, we know not where."

"Love either finds equality or makes it;
Like death, he knows no difference in degrees."

"That 's empire, that which I can give away."

"Yours is a soul irregularly great,
Which, wanting temper, yet abounds in heat."

"Forgiveness to the injured does belong,
But they ne'er pardon who have done the wrong."

"Poor women's thoughts are all extempore."

"The cause of love can never be assigned,
'T is in no face, but in the lover's mind." †

"Heaven can forgive a crime to penitence,
For Heaven can judge if penitence be true;
But man, who knows not hearts, should make examples."

"Kings' titles commonly begin by force,
Which time wears off and mellows into right."

"Fear 's a large promiser; who subject live
To that base passion, know not what they give."

"The secret pleasure of the generous act
Is the great mind's great bribe."

"That bad thing, gold, buys all good things."

"Why, love does all that 's noble here below."

* Conquest of Grenada.

† This recalls a striking verse of Alfred de Musset:—

"La muse est toujours belle,
Même pour l'insensé, même pour l'impuissant,
Car sa beauté pour nous, c'est notre amour pour elle."

> "To prove religion true,
> If either wit or sufferings could suffice,
> All faiths afford the constant and the wise."

But Dryden, as he tells us himself,

> "Grew weary of his long-loved mistress, Rhyme;
> Passion 's too fierce to be in fetters bound,
> And Nature flies him like enchanted ground."

The finest things in his plays were written in blank verse, as vernacular to him as the alexandrine to the French. In this he vindicates his claim as a poet. His diction gets wings, and both his verse and his thought become capable of a reach which was denied them when set in the stocks of the couplet. The solid man becomes even airy in this new-found freedom: Anthony says,

> "How I loved,
> Witness ye days and nights, and all ye hours
> That *danced away with down upon your feet.*"

And what image was ever more delicately exquisite, what movement more fadingly accordant with the sense, than in the last two verses of the following passage?

> "I feel death rising higher still and higher,
> Within my bosom; every breath I fetch
> Shuts up my life within a shorter compass,
> *And, like the vanishing sound of bells, grows less*
> *And less each pulse, till it be lost in air.*" *

Nor was he altogether without pathos, though it is rare with him. The following passage seems to me tenderly full of it: —

> "Something like
> That voice, methinks, I should have somewhere heard;
> But floods of woe have hurried it far off
> Beyond my ken of soul." †

And this single verse from "Aurengzebe": —

> "Live still! oh live! live even to be unkind!"

with its passionate eagerness and sobbing repetition, is

* Rival Ladies. † Don Sebastian.

worth a ship-load of the long-drawn treacle of modern self-compassion.

Now and then, to be sure, we come upon something that makes us hesitate again whether, after all, Dryden was not grandiose rather than great, as in the two passages that next follow : —

"He looks secure of death, superior greatness,
Like Jove when he made Fate and said, Thou art
The slave of my creation." *

"I 'm pleased with my own work; Jove was not more
With infant nature, when his spacious hand
Had rounded this huge ball of earth and seas,
To give it the first push and see it roll
Along the vast abyss." †

I should say that Dryden is more apt to dilate our fancy than our thought, as great poets have the gift of doing. But if he have not the potent alchemy that transmutes the lead of our commonplace associations into gold, as Shakespeare knows how to do so easily, yet his sense is always up to the sterling standard ; and though he has not added so much as some have done to the stock of bullion which others afterwards coin and put in circulation, there are few who have minted so many phrases that are still a part of our daily currency. The first line of the following passage has been worn pretty smooth, but the succeeding ones are less familiar : —

"Men are but children of a larger growth,
Our appetites as apt to change as theirs,
And full as craving too and full as vain;
And yet the soul, shut up in her dark room,
Viewing so clear abroad, at home sees nothing;
But, like a mole in earth, busy and blind,
Works all her folly up and casts it outward
In the world's open view." ‡

The image is mixed and even contradictory, but the thought obtains grace for it. I feel as if Shakespeare would have written *seeing* for *viewing*, thus gaining the

* Don Sebastian. † Cleomenes. ‡ All for Love.

strength of repetition in one verse and avoiding the sameness of it in the other. Dryden, I suspect, was not much given to correction, and indeed one of the great charms of his best writing is that everything seems struck off at a heat, as by a superior man in the best mood of his talk. Where he rises, he generally becomes fervent rather than imaginative; his thought does not incorporate itself in metaphor, as in purely poetic minds, but repeats and reinforces itself in simile. Where he *is* imaginative, it is in that lower sense which the poverty of our language, for want of a better word, compels us to call *picturesque*, and even then he shows little of that finer instinct which suggests so much more than it tells, and works the more powerfully as it taxes more the imagination of the reader. In Donne's "Relic" there is an example of what I mean. He fancies some one breaking up his grave and spying

> "A bracelet of bright hair about the bone," —

a verse that still shines there in the darkness of the tomb, after two centuries, like one of those inextinguishable lamps whose secret is lost.* Yet Dryden sometimes showed a sense of this magic of a mysterious hint, as in the "Spanish Friar": —

> "No, I confess, you bade me not in words;
> The dial spoke not, but it made shrewd signs,
> And pointed full upon the stroke of murder."

This is perhaps a solitary example. Nor is he always so possessed by the image in his mind as unconsciously

* Dryden, with his wonted perspicacity, follows Ben Jonson in calling Donne "the greatest wit, though not the best poet, of our nation." (Dedication of Eleonora.) Even as a poet Donne

> "Had in him those brave translunary things
> That our first poets had."

To open vistas for the imagination through the blind wall of the senses, as he could sometimes do, is the supreme function of poetry.

to choose even the picturesquely imaginative word. He has done so, however, in this passage from "Marriage à la Mode": —

"You ne'er must hope again to see your princess,
Except as prisoners view fair walks and streets,
And careless passengers going by their grates."

But after all, he is best upon a level, table-land, it is true, and a very high level, but still somewhere between the loftier peaks of inspiration and the plain of every-day life. In those passages where he moralizes he is always good, setting some obvious truth in a new light by vigorous phrase and happy illustration. Take this (from "Œdipus") as a proof of it: —

"The gods are just,
But how can finite measure infinite?
Reason! alas, it does not know itself!
Yet man, vain man, would with his short-lined plummet
Fathom the vast abyss of heavenly justice.
Whatever is, is in its causes just,
Since all things are by fate. But purblind man
Sees but a part o' th' chain, the nearest links,
His eyes not carrying to that equal beam
That poises all above."

From the same play I pick an illustration of that ripened sweetness of thought and language which marks the natural vein of Dryden. One cannot help applying the passage to the late Mr. Quincy: —

"Of no distemper, of no blast he died,
But fell like autumn fruit that mellowed long,
E'en wondered at because he dropt no sooner;
Fate seemed to wind him up for fourscore years;
Yet freshly ran he on ten winters more,
Till, like a clock worn out with eating Time,
The wheels of weary life at last stood still." *

Here is another of the same kind from "All for Love": —

* My own judgment is my sole warrant for attributing these extracts from Œdipus to Dryden rather than Lee.

> "Gone so soon!
> Is Death no more? He used him carelessly,
> With a familiar kindness; ere he knocked,
> Ran to the door and took him in his arms,
> As who should say, You 're welcome at all hours,
> A friend need give no warning."

With one more extract from the same play, which is in every way his best, for he had, when he wrote it, been feeding on the bee-bread of Shakespeare, I shall conclude. Antony says,

> "For I am now so sunk from what I was,
> Thou find'st me at my lowest water-mark.
> The rivers that ran in and raised my fortunes
> Are all dried up, or take another course:
> What I have left is from my native spring;
> I 've a heart still that swells in scorn of Fate,
> And lifts me to my banks."

This is certainly, from beginning to end, in what used to be called the *grand* style, at once noble and natural. I have not undertaken to analyze any one of the plays, for (except in "All for Love") it would have been only to expose their weakness. Dryden had *no* constructive faculty; and in every one of his longer poems that required a plot, the plot is bad, always more or less inconsistent with itself, and rather hitched-on to the subject than combining with it. It is fair to say, however, before leaving this part of Dryden's literary work, that Horne Tooke thought "Don Sebastian" "the best play extant." * Gray admired the plays of Dryden, "not as dramatic compositions, but as poetry." † "There are as many things finely said in his plays as almost by anybody," said Pope to Spence. Of their rant, their fustian, their bombast, their bad English, of their innumerable sins against Dryden's own better conscience both as poet and critic, I shall excuse myself from

* Recollections of Rogers, p. 165.

† Nicholls's Reminiscences of Gray. Pickering's edition of Gray's Works, Vol. V. p. 35.

giving any instances.* I like what is good in Dryden so much, and it *is* so good, that I think Gray was justified in always losing his temper when he heard "his faults criticised." †

It is as a satirist and pleader in verse that Dryden is best known, and as both he is in some respects unrivalled. His satire is not so sly as Chaucer's, but it is distinguished by the same good-nature. There is no malice in it. I shall not enter into his literary quarrels further than to say that he seems to me, on the whole, to have been forbearing, which is the more striking as he tells us repeatedly that he was naturally vindictive. It was he who called revenge "the darling attribute of heaven." "I complain not of their lampoons and libels, though I have been the public mark for many years. I am vindictive enough to have repelled force by force, if I could imagine that any of them had ever reached me." It was this feeling of easy superiority, I suspect, that made him the mark for so much jealous vituperation. Scott is wrong in attributing his onslaught upon Settle to jealousy because one of the latter's plays had been performed at Court, — an honor never paid to any of Dryden's.‡ I have found nothing like a trace of jealousy in

* Let one suffice for all. In the "Royal Martyr," Porphyrius, awaiting his execution, says to Maximin, who had wished him for a son-in-law: —

"Where'er thou stand'st, I 'll level at that place
My gushing blood, and spout it at thy face;
Thus not by marriage we our blood will join;
Nay, more, my arms shall throw my head at thine."

"It is no shame," says Dryden himself, "to be a poet, though it is to be a bad one."

† Gray, *ubi supra*, p. 38.

‡ Scott had never seen Pepys's Diary when he wrote this, or he would have left it unwritten: "Fell to discourse of the last night's work at Court, where the ladies and Duke of Monmouth acted the 'Indian Emperor,' wherein they told me these things most remarkable that not any woman but the Duchess of Monmouth and Mrs. Corn-

that large and benignant nature. In his vindication of the "Duke of Guise," he says, with honest confidence in himself: "Nay, I durst almost refer myself to some of the angry poets on the other side, whether I have not rather countenanced and assisted their beginnings than hindered them from rising." He seems to have been really as indifferent to the attacks on himself as Pope pretended to be. In the same vindication he says of the "Rehearsal," the only one of them that had any wit in it, and it has a great deal: "Much less am I concérned at the noble name of Bayes; that 's a brat so like his own father that he cannot be mistaken for any other body. They might as reasonably have called Tom Sternhold Virgil, and the resemblance would have held as well." In his Essay on Satire he says: "And yet we know that in Christian charity all offences are to be forgiven as we expect the like pardon for those we daily commit against Almighty God. And this consideration has often made me tremble when I was saying our Lord's Prayer; for the plain condition of the forgiveness which we beg is the pardoning of others the offences which they have done to us; for which reason I have many times avoided the commission of that fault, even when I have been notoriously provoked."* And in another passage he says, with his usual wisdom: "Good sense and good-nature are never separated, though the ignorant world has thought otherwise. Good-nature, by which I mean beneficence and candor, is the product of right reason, which of necessity will give allowance to the failings of others, by considering that there is nothing

wallis did anything but like fools and stocks, but that these two did do most extraordinary well; that not any man did anything well but Captain O'Bryan, who spoke and did well, but above all things did dance most incomparably." — 14th January, 1668.

* See also that noble passage in the "Hind and Panther" (1573-1591), where this is put into verse. Dryden always thought in prose.

perfect in mankind." In the same Essay he gives his own receipt for satire: "How easy it is to call rogue and villain, and that wittily! but how hard to make a man appear a fool, a blockhead, or a knave, without using any of those opprobrious terms! .... This is the mystery of that noble trade. .... Neither is it true that this fineness of raillery is offensive: a witty man is tickled while he is hurt in this manner, and a fool feels it not. .... There is a vast difference between the slovenly butchering of a man and the fineness of a stroke that separates the head from the body, and leaves it standing in its place. A man may be capable, as Jack Ketch's wife said of his servant, of a plain piece of work, of a bare hanging; but to make a malefactor die sweetly was only belonging to her husband. I wish I could apply it to myself, if the reader would be kind enough to think it belongs to me. The character of Zimri in my 'Absalom' is, in my opinion, worth the whole poem. It is not bloody, but it is ridiculous enough, and he for whom it was intended was too witty to resent it as an injury. .... I avoided the mention of great crimes, and applied myself to the representing of blind sides and little extravagances, to which, the wittier a man is, he is genrally the more obnoxious."

Dryden thought his genius led him that way. In his elegy on the satirist Oldham, whom Hallam, without reading him, I suspect, ranks next to Dryden,* he says: —

"For sure our souls were near allied, and thine
Cast in the same poetic mould with mine;
One common note in either lyre did strike,
And knaves and fools we both abhorred alike."

His practice is not always so delicate as his theory; but

* Probably on the authority of this very epitaph, as if epitaphs were to be believed even under oath! A great many authors live because we read nothing but their tombstones. Oldham was, to borrow one of Dryden's phrases, "a bad or, which is worse, an indifferent poet."

if he was sometimes rough, he never took a base advantage. He knocks his antagonist down, and there an end. Pope seems to have nursed his grudge, and then, watching his chance, to have squirted vitriol from behind a corner, rather glad than otherwise if it fell on the women of those he hated or envied. And if Dryden is never dastardly, as Pope often was, so also he never wrote anything so maliciously depreciatory as Pope's unprovoked attack on Addison. Dryden's satire is often coarse, but where it is coarsest, it is commonly in defence of himself against attacks that were themselves brutal. Then, to be sure, he snatches the first ready cudgel, as in Shadwell's case, though even then there is something of the good-humor of conscious strength. Pope's provocation was too often the mere opportunity to say a biting thing, where he could do it safely. If his victim showed fight, he tried to smooth things over, as with Dennis. Dryden could forget that he had ever had a quarrel, but he never slunk away from any, least of all from one provoked by himself.* Pope's satire is too much occupied with the externals of manners, habits, personal defects, and peculiarities. Dryden goes right to the rooted character of the man, to the weaknesses of his nature, as where he says of Burnet: —

> "Prompt to assail, and careless of defence,
> Invulnerable in his impudence,
> He dares the world, and, eager of a name,
> He thrusts about and *justles into fame.*
> So fond of loud report that, not to miss
> Of being known (his last and utmost bliss),
> *He rather would be known for what he is.*"

It would be hard to find in Pope such compression of meaning as in the first, or such penetrative sarcasm as

* "He was of a nature exceedingly humane and compassionate, easily forgiving injuries, and capable of a prompt and sincere reconciliation with them that had offended him." — CONGREVE.

in the second of the passages I have underscored. Dryden's satire is still quoted for its comprehensiveness of application, Pope's rather for the elegance of its finish and the point of its phrase than for any deeper qualities.* I do not remember that Dryden ever makes poverty a reproach.† He was above it, alike by generosity of birth and mind. Pope is always the *parvenu*, always giving himself the airs of a fine gentleman, and, like Horace Walpole and Byron, affecting superiority to professional literature. Dryden, like Lessing, was a hack-writer, and was proud, as an honest man has a right to be, of being able to get his bread by his brains. He lived in Grub Street all his life, and never dreamed that where a man of genius lived was not the best quarter of the town. "Tell his Majesty," said sturdy old Jonson, "that his soul lives in an alley."

Dryden's prefaces are a mine of good writing and judicious criticism. His *obiter dicta* have often the penetration, and always more than the equity, of Voltaire's, for Dryden never loses temper, and never altogether qualifies his judgment by his self-love. "He was a more universal writer than Voltaire," said Horne Tooke, and perhaps it is true that he had a broader view, though his learning was neither so extensive nor so accurate.

* Coleridge says excellently: "You will find this a good gauge or criterion of genius, — whether it progresses and evolves, or only spins upon itself. Take Dryden's Achitophel and Zimri; every line adds to or modifies the character, which is, as it were, a-building up to the very last verse; whereas in Pope's Timon, &c. the first two or three couplets contain all the pith of the character, and the twenty or thirty lines that follow are so much evidence or proof of overt acts of jealousy, or pride, or whatever it may be that is satirized." (Table-Talk, 192.) Some of Dryden's best satirical *hits* are let fall by seeming accident in his prose, as where he says of his Protestant assailants, "Most of them love all whores but her of Babylon." They had first attacked him on the score of his private morals.

† That he taxes Shadwell with it is only a seeming exception, as any careful reader will see.

My space will not afford many extracts, but I cannot forbear one or two. He says of Chaucer, that "he is a perpetual fountain of good sense," * and likes him better than Ovid, — a bold confession in that day. He prefers the pastorals of Theocritus to those of Virgil. "Virgil's shepherds are too well read in the philosophy of Epicurus and of Plato"; "there is a kind of rusticity in all those pompous verses, somewhat of a holiday shepherd strutting in his country buskins"; † "Theocritus is softer than Ovid, he touches the passions more delicately, and performs all this out of his own fund, without diving into the arts and sciences for a supply. Even his Doric dialect has an incomparable sweetness in his clownishness, like a fair shepherdess, in her country russet, talking in a Yorkshire tone." ‡ Comparing Virgil's verse with that of some other poets, he says, that his "numbers are perpetually varied to increase the delight of the reader, so that the same sounds are never repeated twice together. On the contrary, Ovid and Claudian, though they write in styles different from each other, yet have each of them but one sort of music in their verses. All the versification and little variety of Claudian is included within the compass of four or five lines, and then he begins again in the same tenor, perpetually closing his sense at the end of a verse, and that verse commonly which they call golden, or two substantives and two adjectives with a verb betwixt them to keep the peace. Ovid, with all his sweetness, has as little variety of numbers and sound as he; he is always, as it were, upon the hand-gallop, and his verse runs upon carpet-ground." § What a dreary half-century would have been saved to English poetry, could Pope have laid these sentences to heart! Upon translation, no one has written so much

* Preface to Fables.

† Dedication of the Georgics.

‡ Preface to Second Miscellany.

§ Ibid.

and so well as Dryden in his various prefaces. Whatever has been said since is either expansion or variation of what he had said before. His general theory may be stated as an aim at something between the literalness of metaphrase and the looseness of paraphase. "Where I have enlarged," he says, "I desire the false critics would not always think that those thoughts are wholly mine, but either *they are secretly in the poet*, or may be fairly deduced from him." Coleridge, with his usual cleverness of *assimilation*, has condensed him in a letter to Wordsworth: "There is no medium between a prose version and one on the avowed principle of *compensation* in the widest sense, i.e. manner, genius, total effect." *

I have selected these passages, not because they are the best, but because they have a near application to Dryden himself. His own characterization of Chaucer (though too narrow for the greatest but one of English poets) is the best that could be given of himself: "He is a perpetual fountain of good sense." And the other passages show him a close and open-minded student of the art he professed. Has his influence on our literature, but especially on our poetry, been on the whole for good or evil? If he could have been read with the liberal understanding which he brought to the works of others, I should answer at once that it had been beneficial. But his translations and paraphrases, in some ways the best things he did, were done, like his plays, under contract to deliver a certain number of verses for a specified sum. The versification, of which he had learned the art by long practice, is excellent, but his haste has led him to fill out the measure of lines with phrases that add only to dilute, and thus the clearest, the most direct, the most manly versifier of his time became, without meaning it, the source (*fons et origo ma-*

* Memoirs of Wordsworth, Vol. II. p. 74 (American edition).

lorum) of that poetic diction from which our poetry has not even yet recovered. I do not like to say it, but he has sometimes smothered the childlike simplicity of Chaucer under feather-beds of verbiage. What this kind of thing came to in the next century, when everybody ceremoniously took a bushel-basket to bring a wren's egg to market in, is only too sadly familiar. It is clear that his natural taste led Dryden to prefer directness and simplicity of style. If he was too often tempted astray by Artifice, his love of Nature betrays itself in many an almost passionate outbreak of angry remorse. Addison tells us that he took particular delight in the reading of our old English ballads. What he valued above all things was Force, though in his haste he is willing to make a shift with its counterfeit, Effect. As usual, he had a good reason to urge for what he did: "I will not excuse, but justify myself for one pretended crime for which I am liable to be charged by false critics, not only in this translation, but in many of my original poems, — that I Latinize too much. It is true that when I find an English word significant and sounding, I neither borrow from the Latin or any other language; but when I want at home I must seek abroad. If sounding words are not of our growth and manufacture, who shall hinder me to import them from a foreign country? I carry not out the treasure of the nation which is never to return; but what I bring from Italy I spend in England: here it remains, and here it circulates; for if the coin be good, it will pass from one hand to another. I trade both with the living and the dead for the enrichment of our native language. We have enough in England to supply our necessity; but if we will have things of magnificence and splendor, we must get them by commerce. . . . . Therefore, if I find a word in a classic author, I propose it to be naturalized by using it myself, and if the public approve of it the bill passes. But every man cannot distinguish betwixt pedantry and poetry; every man, therefore, is not fit to innovate." * This is admirably said, and with Dryden's accustomed penetration to the root of the matter. The Latin has given us most of our canorous words, only they must not be confounded with merely sonorous ones, still less with phrases that, instead of supplementing the sense, encumber it. It was of Latinizing in this sense that Dryden was guilty. Instead of stabbing, he "with steel invades the life." The consequence was that by and by we have Dr. Johnson's poet, Savage, telling us, —

> "In front, a parlor meets my entering view,
> Opposed a room to sweet refection due";

Dr. Blacklock making a forlorn maiden say of her "dear," who is out late, —

> "Or by some apoplectic fit deprest
> Perhaps, alas! he seeks eternal rest";

and Mr. Bruce, in a Danish war-song, calling on the vikings to "assume their oars." But it must be admitted of Dryden that he seldom makes the second verse of a couplet the mere trainbearer to the first, as Pope was continually doing. In Dryden the rhyme waits upon the thought; in Pope and his school the thought courtesies to the tune for which it is written.

Dryden has also been blamed for his gallicisms.† He tried some, it is true, but they have not been accepted.

* A Discourse of Epick Poetry. "If the *public* approve." "On ne peut pas admettre dans le développement des langues aucune révolution artificielle et sciemment executée; il n'y a pour elles ni conciles, ni assemblées délibérantes; on ne les réforme pas comme une constitution vicieuse." — RENAN, De l'Origine du Langage, p. 95.

† This is an old complaint. Puttenham sighs over such innovation in Elizabeth's time, and Carew in James's. A language grows, and is not made. Almost all the new-fangled words with which Jonson taxes Marston in his "Poetaster" are now current.

I do not think he added a single word to the language, unless, as I suspect, he first used *magnetism* in its present sense of moral attraction. What he did in his best writing was to use the English as if it were a spoken, and not merely an inkhorn language; as if it were his own to do what he pleased with it, as if it need not be ashamed of itself.* In this respect, his service to our prose was greater than any other man has ever rendered. He says he formed his style upon Tillotson's (Bossuet, on the other hand, formed *his* upon Corneille's); but I rather think he got it at Will's, for its great charm is that it has the various freedom of talk.† In verse, he had a pomp which, excellent in itself, became pompousness in his imitators. But he had nothing of Milton's ear for various rhythm and interwoven harmony. He knew how to give new modulation, sweetness, and force to the pentameter; but in what used to be called pindarics, I am heretic enough to think he generally failed. His so much praised "Alexander's Feast" (in parts of it, at least) has no excuse for its slovenly metre and awkward expression, but that it was written for music. He himself tells us, in the epistle dedicatory to "King Arthur," "that the numbers of poetry and vocal music are sometimes so contrary, that in many places I have been obliged to cramp my verses and make them rugged

* Like most idiomatic, as distinguished from correct writers, he knew very little about the language historically or critically. His prose and poetry swarm with locutions that would have made Lindley Murray's hair stand on end. *How* little he knew is plain from his criticising in Ben Jonson the use of *ones* in the plural, of "Though Heaven should speak with all *his* wrath," and *be* "as false English for *are*, though the rhyme hides it." Yet all are good English, and I have found them all in Dryden's own writing! Of his sins against idiom I have a longer list than I have room for. And yet he is one of our highest authorities for *real* English.

† To see what he rescued us from in pedantry on the one hand, and vulgarism on the other, read Feltham and Tom Brown — if you can.

to the reader that they may be harmonious to the hearer." His renowned ode suffered from this constraint, but this is no apology for the vulgarity of conception in too many passages.*

Dryden's conversion to Romanism has been commonly taken for granted as insincere, and has therefore left an abiding stain on his character, though the other mud thrown at him by angry opponents or rivals brushed off so soon as it was dry. But I think his change of faith susceptible of several explanations, none of them in any way discreditable to him. Where Church and State are habitually associated, it is natural that minds even of a high order should unconsciously come to regard religion as only a subtler mode of police.† Dryden, conservative by nature, had discovered before Joseph de Maistre, that Protestantism, so long as it justified its name by continuing to be an active principle, was the abettor of Republicanism. I think this is hinted in more than one passage in his preface to "The Hind and Panther." He may very well have preferred Romanism because of its elder claim to authority in all matters of doctrine, but I think he had a deeper reason in the constitution of his own mind. That he was "naturally inclined to scepticism in philosophy," he tells us of himself in the preface to the "Religio Laici"; but he was a sceptic

* "Cette ode mise en musique par Purcell (si je ne me trompe), passe en Angleterre pour le chef-d'œuvre de la poësie la plus sublime et la plus variée; et je vous avoue que, comme je sais mieux l'anglais que le grec, j'aime cent fois mieux cette ode que tout Pindare." — VOLTAIRE to M. DE CHABANON, 9 mars, 1772.

Dryden would have agreed with Voltaire. When Chief-Justice Marlay, then a young Templar, "congratulated him on having produced the finest and noblest Ode that had ever been written in any language, 'You are right, young gentleman' (replied Dryden), 'a nobler Ode never *was* produced, nor ever *will*.'" — MALONE.

† This was true of Coleridge, Wordsworth, and still more of Southey, who in some respects was not unlike Dryden.

with an imaginative side, and in such characters scepticism and superstition play into each other's hands. This finds a curious illustration in a letter to his sons, written four years before his death : "Towards the latter end of this month, September, Charles will begin to recover his perfect health, according to his Nativity, which, casting it myself, I am sure is true, and all things hitherto have happened accordingly to the very time that I predicted them." Have we forgotten Montaigne's votive offerings at the shrine of Loreto?

Dryden was short of body, inclined to stoutness, and florid of complexion. He is said to have had "a sleepy eye," but was handsome and of a manly carriage. He "was not a very genteel man, he was intimate with none but poetical men.* He was said to be a very good man by all that knew him: he was as plump as Mr. Pitt, of a fresh color and a down look, and not very conversible." So Pope described him to Spence. He still reigns in literary tradition, as when at Will's his elbow-chair had the best place by the fire in winter, or on the balcony in summer, and when a pinch from his snuff-box made a young author blush with pleasure as would now-a-days a favorable notice in the "Saturday Review." What gave and secures for him this singular eminence? To put it in a single word, I think that his qualities and faculties were in that rare combination which makes character. This gave *flavor* to whatever he wrote, — a very rare quality.

Was he, then, a great poet? Hardly, in the narrow-

* Pope's notion of gentility was perhaps expressed in a letter from Lord Cobham to him : "I congratulate you upon the fine weather. 'T is a strange thing that people of condition and men of parts must enjoy it in common with the rest of the world." (Ruffhead's Pope, p. 276, *note.*) His Lordship's naïve distinction between people of condition and men of parts is as good as Pope's between genteel and poetical men. I fancy the poet grinning savagely as he read it.

est definition. But he was a strong thinker who sometimes carried common sense to a height where it catches the light of a diviner air, and warmed reason till it had wellnigh the illuminating property of intuition. Certainly he is not, like Spenser, the poets' poet, but other men have also their rights. Even the Philistine is a man and a brother, and is entirely right so far as he sees. To demand more of him is to be unreasonable. And he sees, among other things, that a man who undertakes to write should first have a meaning perfectly defined to himself, and then should be able to set it forth clearly in the best words. This is precisely Dryden's praise,* and amid the rickety sentiment looming big through misty phrase which marks so much of modern literature, to read him is as bracing as a northwest wind. He blows the mind clear. In ripeness of mind and bluff heartiness of expression, he takes rank with the best. His phrase is always a short-cut to his sense, for his estate was too spacious for him to need that trick of winding the path of his thought about, and planting it out with clumps of epithet, by which the landscape-gardeners of literature give to a paltry half-acre the air of a park. In poetry, to be next-best is, in one sense, to be nothing; and yet to be among the first in any kind of writing, as Dryden certainly was, is to be one of a very small company. He had, beyond most, the gift of the right word. And if he does not, like one or two of the greater masters of song, stir our sympathies by that indefinable aroma so magical in arousing the subtile associations of the soul, he has this in common with the few great writers, that the winged seeds of his thought embed themselves in the memory and germinate there. If I could be guilty of the absurdity of recommending

* "Nothing is truly sublime," he himself said, "that is not just and proper."

to a young man any author on whom to form his style, I should tell him that, next to having something that will not stay unsaid, he could find no safer guide than Dryden.

Cowper, in a letter to Mr. Unwin (5th January, 1782), expresses what I think is the common feeling about Dryden, that, with all his defects, he had that indefinable something we call Genius. "But I admire Dryden most [he had been speaking of Pope], who has succeeded by mere dint of genius, and in spite of a laziness and a carelessness almost peculiar to himself. His faults are numberless, and so are his beauties. His faults are those of a great man, and his beauties are such (at least sometimes) as Pope with all his touching and retouching could never equal." But, after all, perhaps no man has summed him up so well as John Dennis, one of Pope's typical dunces, a dull man outside of his own sphere, as men are apt to be, but who had some sound notions as a critic, and thus became the object of Pope's fear and therefore of his resentment. Dennis speaks of him as his "departed friend, whom I infinitely esteemed when living for the solidity of his thought, for the spring and the warmth and the beautiful turn of it; for the power and variety and fulness of his harmony; for the purity, the perspicuity, the energy of his expression; and, whenever these great qualities are required, for the pomp and solemnity and majesty of his style." *

* Dennis in a letter to Tonson, 1715.

WITCHCRAFT.*

CREDULITY, as a mental and moral phenomenon, manifests itself in widely different ways, according as it chances to be the daughter of fancy or terror. The one lies warm about the heart as Folk-lore, fills moonlit dells

* Salem Witchcraft, with an Account of Salem Village, and a History of Opinions on Witchcraft and Kindred Subjects. By CHARLES W. UPHAM. Boston: Wiggin and Lunt. 1867. 2 vols.

IOANNIS WIERI de praestigiis daemonum, et incantationibus ac veneficiis libri sex, postrema editione sexta aucti et recogniti. Accessit liber apologeticus et pseudomonarchia daemonum. Cum rerum et verborum copioso indice. Cum Caes. Maiest. Regisq; Galliarum gratia et privelegio. Basiliæ ex officina Oporiniani, 1583.

SCOT'S Discovery of Witchcraft: proving the common opinions of Witches contracting with Divels, Spirits, or Familiars; and their power to kill, torment, and consume the bodies of men, women, and children, or other creatures by diseases or otherwise; their flying in the Air, &c.; To be but imaginary Erronious conceptions and novelties; Wherein also the lewde, unchristian practises of Witchmongers, upon aged, melancholy, ignorant and superstitious people in extorting confessions by inhumane terrors and Tortures, is notably detected. Also The knavery and confederacy of Conjurors. The impious blasphemy of Inchanters. The imposture of Soothsayers, and infidelity of Atheists. The delusion of Pythonists, Figure-casters, Astrologers, and vanity of Dreamers. The fruitlesse beggarly art of Alchimistry. The horrible art of Poisoning and all the tricks and conveyances of juggling and liegerdemain are fully deciphered. With many other things opened that have long lain hidden: though very necessary to be known for the undeceiving of Judges, Justices, and Juries, and for the preservation of poor, aged, deformed, ignorant people; frequently taken, arraigned, condemned and executed for Witches, when according to a right understanding, and a good conscience, Physick, Food, and necessaries with dancing fairies, sets out a meal for the Brownie, hears the tinkle of airy bridle-bells as Tamlane rides away with the Queen of Dreams, changes Pluto and

should be administered to him. Whereunto is added a treatise upon the nature and substance of Spirits and Divels &c., all written and published in Anno 1584. By REGINALD SCOT, Esquire. Printed by R. C. and are to be sold by Giles Calvert dwelling at the Black Spread-Eagle, at the West-End of Pauls, 1651.

De la Demonomanie des Sorciers. A MONSEIGNEUR M. CHRESTOFE DE THOU, Chevalier, Seigneur de Cœli, premier President en la Cour de Parlement et Conseiller du Roy en son privé Conseil. Reveu, Corrigé, et augmenté d'une grande partie. Par I. BODIN ANGEVIN. A Paris: Chez Iacques Du Puys, Libraire Iuré, à la Samaritaine. M.D.LXXXVII. Avec privilege du Roy.

Magica, seu mirabilium historiarum de Spectris et Apparitionibus spirituum: Item, de magicis et diabolicis incantationibus. De Miraculis, Oraculis, Vaticiniis, Divinationibus, Prædictionibus, Revelationibus et aliis eiusmodi multis ac varijs præstigijs, ludibrijs et imposturis malorum Dæmonum. Libri II. Ex probatis et fide dignis historiarum scriptoribus diligenter collecti. Islebiæ, cura, Typis et sumptibus Henningi Grossij Bibl. Lipo. 1597. Cum privilegio.

The displaying of supposed Witchcraft wherein is affirmed that there are many sorts of Deceivers and Impostors, and divers persons under a passive delusion of Melancholy and Fancy. But that there is a corporeal league made betwixt the Devil and the Witch, or that he sucks on the Witch's body, has carnal copulation, or that Witches are turned into Cats, Dogs, raise Tempests or the like is utterly denied and disproved. Wherein is also handled, The existence of Angels and Spirits, the truth of Apparitions, the Nature of Astral and Sydereal Spirits, the force of Charms and Philters; with other abstruse matters. By JOHN WEBSTER, Practitioner in Physick. Falsa etenim opiniones Hominum non solum surdos sed et cœcos faciunt, ita ut videre nequeant quæ aliis perspicua apparent. Galen. lib. 8, de Comp. Med. London: Printed by I. M. and are to be sold by the booksellers in London. 1677.

Sadducismus Triumphatus: or Full and Plain Evidence concerning Witches and Apparitions. In two Parts. The First treating of their Possibility; the Second of their Real Existence. By JOSEPH GLANVIL, late Chaplain in Ordinary to His Majesty, and Fellow of the Royal Society. The third edition. The advantages whereof above the former, the Reader may understand out of Dr H. More's Account prefixed therunto. With two Authentick, but wonderful Stories of certain Swedish Witches. Done into English by A. HORNECK DD. London, Printed for S. L. and are to be sold by Anth. Baskerville at the Bible, the corner of Essex-street, without Temple-Bar. M.DCLXXXIX.

Proserpine into Oberon and Titania, and makes friends with unseen powers as Good Folk; the other is a bird of night, whose shadow sends a chill among the roots

Demonologie ou Traitte des Demons et Sorciers: De leur puissance et impuissance: Par FR. PERRAUD. Ensemble L'Antidemon de Mascon, ou Histoire Veritable de ce qu'un Demon a fait et dit, il y a quelques années en la maison dudit Sr Perreaud à Mascon. I. Jacques iv. 7, 8. "Resistez au Diable, et il s'enfuira de vous. Approchez vous de Dieu, et il s'approchera de vous." A Geneve, chez Pierre Aubert. M,DC,LIII.

The Wonders of the Invisible World. Being an account of the tryals of several witches lately executed in New-England. By COTTON MATHER, D. D. To which is added a farther account of the tryals of the New England Witches. By INCREASE MATHER, D. D., President of Harvard College. London: John Russell Smith, Soho Square. 1862. (First printed in Boston, 1692.)

I. N. D. N. J. C. Dissertatio Juridica de Lamiis earumque processu criminali, Von Hexen und dem peinl. Prozeß wider dieselben, Quam, auxiliante Divina Gratia, Consensu et Authoritate Magnifici JCtorum Ordinis in illustribus Athenis Salanis sub præsidio Magnifici, Nobilissimi, Amplissimi, Consultissimi, atque Excellentissimi DN. ERNESTI FRIDER. Schröter hereditarii in Wickerstädt, JCti et Antecessoris hujus Salanæ Famigeratissimi, Consiliarii Saxonici, Curiæ Provincialis, Facultatis Juridicæ, et Scabinatus Assessoris longe Gravissimi, Domini Patroni Præceptoris et Promotoris sui nullo non honoris et observantiæ cultu sanctè devenerandi, colendi, publicæ Eruditorum censuræ subjicit Michael Paris Walburger, Grœbzigâ Anhaltinus, in Acroaterio JCtorum ad diem 1. Maj. A. 1670. Editio Tertia. Jenæ, Typis Pauli Ehrichii. 1707.

Histoire de Diables de Loudun, ou de la Possession des Religieuses Ursulines, et de la condemnation et du suplice d'Urbain Grandier, Curé de la même ville. Cruels effets de la Vengeance du Cardinal de Richelieu. A Amsterdam Aux depens de la Compagnie. M.DCC.LII.

A view of the Invisible World, or General History of Apparitions. Collected from the best Authorities, both Antient and Modern, and attested by Authors of the highest Reputation and Credit. Illustrated with a Variety of Notes and parallel Cases; in which some Account of the Nature and Cause of Departed Spirits visiting their former Stations by returning again into the present World, is treated in a Manner different to the prevailing Opinions of Mankind. And an Attempt is made from Rational Principles to account for the Species of such supernatural Appearances, when they may be suppos'd consistent with the Divine Appointment in the Government of the World. With the sentiments of Monsieur LE CLERC, Mr. LOCKE, Mr. ADDISON, and Others on this important Subject. In which some humorous and di-of the hair: it sucks with the vampire, gorges with the ghoule, is choked by the night-hag, pines away under the witch's charm, and commits uncleanness with the embodied Principle of Evil, giving up the fair realm of innocent belief to a murky throng from the slums and stews of the debauched brain. Both have vanished from among educated men, and such superstition as comes to the surface now-a-days is the harmless Jacobitism of sentiment, pleasing itself with the fiction all the more because there is no exacting reality behind it to impose a duty or demand a sacrifice. And as Jacobitism survived the Stuarts, so this has outlived the dynasty to which it professes an after-dinner allegiance. It nails a horseshoe over the door, but keeps a rattle by its bedside to summon a more substantial watchman; it hangs a crape on the beehives to get a taste of ideal sweetness, but obeys the teaching of the latest bee-book for material and marketable honey. This is the æsthetic variety of the malady, or rather, perhaps, it is only the old complaint robbed of all its pain, and lapped in waking dreams by

verting instances are remark'd, in order to divert that Gloom of Melancholy that naturally arises in the Human Mind, from reading or meditating on such Subjects. Illustrated with suitable Cuts. London: Printed in the year M,DCC,LII. [Mainly from DeFoe's "History of Apparitions."]

Satan's Invisible World discovered; or, a choice Collection of Modern Relations, proving evidently, against the Atheists of this present Age, that there are Devils, Spirits, Witches and Apparitions, from Authentic Records, Attestations of Witnesses, and undoubted Verity. To which is added that marvellous History of Major Weir and his Sister, the Witches of Balgarran, Pittenweem and Calder, &c. By GEORGE SINCLAIR, late Professor of Philosophy in Glasgow. No man should be vain that he can injure the merit of a Book; for the meanest rogue may burn a City or kill a Hero; whereas he could never build the one, or equal the other. Sir George M'Kenzie, Edinburgh: Sold by P. Anderson, Parliament Square. M.DCC.LXXX.

La Magie et l'Astrologie dans l'Antiquité et au Moyen Age, ou Étude sur les superstitions païennes qui se sont perpétuées jusqu'à nos jours. Par L. F. ALFRED MAURY. Troisième Edition revue et corrigée. Paris: Didier. 1864.

the narcotism of an age of science. To the world at large it is not undelightful to see the poetical instincts of friends and neighbors finding some other vent than that of verse. But there has been a superstition of very different fibre, of more intense and practical validity, the deformed child of faith, peopling the midnight of the mind with fearful shapes and phrenetic suggestions, a monstrous brood of its own begetting, and making even good men ferocious in imagined self-defence.

Imagination, has always been, and still is, in a narrower sense, the great mythologizer; but both its mode of manifestation and the force with which it reacts on the mind are one thing in its crude form of childlike wonder, and another thing after it has been more or less consciously manipulated by the poetic faculty. A mythology that broods over us in our cradles, that mingles with the lullaby of the nurse and the winter-evening legends of the chimney-corner, that brightens day with the possibility of divine encounters, and darkens night with intimations of demonic ambushes, is of other substance than one which we take down from our bookcase, sapless as the shelf it stood on, and remote from all present sympathy with man or nature as a town history. It is something like the difference between live metaphor and dead personification. Primarily, the action of the imagination is the same in the mythologizer and the poet, that is, it forces its own consciousness on the objects of the senses, and compels them to sympathize with its own momentary impressions. When Shakespeare in his "Lucrece" makes

"The threshold grate the door to have him heard,"

his mind is acting under the same impulse that first endowed with human feeling and then with human shape all the invisible forces of nature, and called into being those

"Fair humanities of old religion,"

whose loss the poets mourn. So also Shakespeare no doubt projected himself in his own creations; but those creations never became so perfectly disengaged from him, so objective, or, as they used to say, extrinsical, to him, as to react upon him like real and even alien existences. I mean permanently, for momentarily they may and must have done so. But before man's consciousness had wholly disentangled itself from outward objects, all nature was but a many-sided mirror which gave back to him a thousand images more or less beautified or distorted, magnified or diminished, of himself, till his imagination grew to look upon its own incorporations as having an independent being. Thus, by degrees, it became at last passive to its own creations. You may see imaginative children every day anthropomorphizing in this way, and the dupes of that superabundant vitality in themselves, which bestows qualities proper to itself on everything about them. There is a period of development in which grown men are childlike. In such a period the fables which endow beasts with human attributes first grew up; and we luckily read them so early as never to become suspicious of any absurdity in them. The Finnic epos of "Kalewala" is a curious illustration of the same fact. In that everything has the affections, passions, and consciousness of men. When the mother of Lemminkäinen is seeking her lost son, —

"Sought she many days the lost one,
Sought him ever without finding;
Then the roadways come to meet her,
And she asks them with beseeching:
'Roadways, ye whom God hath shapen,
Have ye not my son beholden,
Nowhere seen the golden apple,
Him, my darling staff of silver?'

Prudently they gave her answer,
Thus to her replied the roadways:
'For thy son we cannot plague us,
We have sorrows too, a many,
Since our own lot is a hard one
And our fortune is but evil,
By dog's feet to be run over,
By the wheel-tire to be wounded,
And by heavy heels down-trampled.'"

It is in this tendency of the mind under certain conditions to confound the objective with subjective, or rather to mistake the one for the other, that Mr. Tylor, in his "Early History of Mankind," is fain to seek the origin of the supernatural, as we somewhat vaguely call whatever transcends our ordinary experience. And this, no doubt, will in many cases account for the particular shapes assumed by certain phantasmal appearances, though I am inclined to doubt whether it be a sufficient explanation of the abstract phenomenon. It is easy for the arithmetician to make a key to the problems that he has devised to suit himself. An immediate and habitual confusion of the kind spoken of is insanity; and the hypochondriac is tracked by the black dog of his own mind. Disease itself is, of course, in one sense natural, as being the result of natural causes; but if we assume health as the mean representing the normal poise of all the mental faculties, we must be content to call hypochondria subternatural, because the tone of the instrument is lowered, and to designate as supernatural only those ecstasies in which the mind, under intense but not unhealthy excitement, is snatched sometimes above itself, as in poets and other persons of imaginative temperament. In poets this liability to be possessed by the creations of their own brains is limited and proportioned by the artistic sense, and the imagination thus truly becomes the shaping faculty, while in less regulated or coarser organizations it dwells forever in the *Nifelheim* of phantasmagoria and dream, a thaumaturge half cheat, half dupe. What Mr. Tylor has to say on this matter is ingenious and full of valuable suggestion, and to a certain extent solves our difficulties. Nightmare, for example, will explain the testimony of witnesses in trials for witchcraft, that they had been hag-ridden by the accused. But to prove the possibility, nay, the probability, of this confusion of objective with subjective is not enough. It accounts very well for such apparitions as those which appeared to Dion, to Brutus, and to Curtius Rufus. In such cases the imagination is undoubtedly its own *doppel-gänger*, and sees nothing more than the projection of its own deceit. But I am puzzled, I confess, to explain the appearance of the *first* ghost, especially among men who thought death to be the end-all here below. The thing once conceived of, it is easy, on Mr. Tylor's theory, to account for all after the first. If it was originally believed that only the spirits of those who had died violent deaths were permitted to wander,* the conscience of a remorseful murderer may have been haunted by the memory of his victim, till the imagination, infected in its turn, gave outward reality to the image on the inward eye. After putting to death Boëtius and Symmachus, it is said that Theodoric saw in the head of a

* Lucian, in his "Liars," puts this opinion into the mouth of Arignotus. The theory by which Lucretius seeks to explain apparitions, though materialistic, seems to allow some influence also to the working of imagination. It is hard otherwise to explain how his *simulacra* (which are not unlike the *astral spirits* of later times) should appear in dreams.

Quae simulacra . . . .
. . . . nobis vigilantibus obvia mentes
terrificant atque in somnis, cum saepe figuras
contuimur miras simulacraque luce carentum
quae nos horrifice languentis saepe sopore
excierunt.

De Rer. Nat. IV. 33 - 37, ed. Munro.

fish served at his dinner the face of Symmachus, grinning horribly and with flaming eyes, whereupon he took to his bed and died soon after in great agony of mind. It is not safe, perhaps, to believe all that is reported of an Arian; but supposing the story to be true, there is only a short step from such a delusion of the senses to the complete ghost of popular legend. But, in some of the most trustworthy stories of apparitions, they have shown themselves not only to persons who had done them no wrong in the flesh, but also to such as had never even known them. The *eidolon* of James Haddock appeared to a man named Taverner, that he might interest himself in recovering a piece of land unjustly kept from the dead man's infant son. If we may trust Defoe, Bishop Jeremy Taylor twice examined Taverner, and was convinced of the truth of his story. In this case, Taverner had formerly known Haddock. But the apparition of an old gentleman which entered the learned Dr. Scott's study, and directed him where to find a missing deed needful in settling what had lately been its estate in the West of England, chose for its attorney in the business an entire stranger, who had never even seen its original in the flesh.

Whatever its origin, a belief in spirits seems to have been common to all the nations of the ancient world who have left us any record of themselves. Ghosts began to walk early, and are walking still, in spite of the shrill cock-crow of *wir haben ja aufgeklärt.* Even the ghost in chains, which one would naturally take to be a fashion peculiar to convicts escaped from purgatory, is older than the belief in that reforming penitentiary. The younger Pliny tells a very good story to this effect: "There was at Athens a large and spacious house which lay under the disrepute of being haunted. In the dead of the night a noise resembling the clashing of iron was frequently heared, which, if you listened more attentively, sounded like the rattling of chains; at first it seemed at a distance, but approached nearer by degrees; immediately afterward a spectre appeared, in the form of an old man, extremely meagre and ghastly, with a long beard and dishevelled hair, rattling the chains on his feet and hands. . . . . By this means the house was at last deserted, being judged by everybody to be absolutely uninhabitable; so that it was now entirely abandoned to the ghost. However, in hopes that some tenant might be found who was ignorant of this great calamity which attended it, a bill was put up giving notice that it was either to be let or sold. It happened that the philosopher Athenodorus came to Athens at this time, and, reading the bill, inquired the price. The extraordinary cheapness raised his suspicion; nevertheless, when he heared the whole story, he was so far from being discouraged that he was more strongly inclined to hire it, and, in short, actually did so. When it grew towards evening, he ordered a couch to be prepared for him in the fore part of the house, and, after calling for a light, together with his pen and tablets, he directed all his people to retire. But that his mind might not, for want of employment, be open to the vain terrors of imaginary noises and spirits, he applied himself to writing with the utmost attention. The first part of the night passed with usual silence, when at length the chains began to rattle; however, he neither lifted up his eyes nor laid down his pen, but diverted his observation by pursuing his studies with greater earnestness. The noise increased, and advanced nearer, till it seemed at the door, and at last in the chamber. He looked up and saw the ghost exactly in the manner it had been described to him; it stood before him, beckoning with the finger. Athenodorus made a sign with his hand that it should wait a little, and threw his eyes again upon his papers; but the ghost still rattling his chains in his ears, he looked up and saw him beckoning as before. Upon this he immediately arose, and with the light in his hand followed it. The ghost slowly stalked along, as if encumbered with his chains, and, turning into the area of the house, suddenly vanished. Athenodorus, being thus deserted, made a mark with some grass and leaves where the spirit left him. The next day he gave information of this to the magistrates, and advised them to order that spot to be dug up. This was accordingly done, and the skeleton of a man in chains was there found; for the body, having lain a considerable time in the ground, was putrefied and mouldered away from the fetters. The bones, being collected together, were publicly buried, and thus, after the ghost was appeased by the proper ceremonies, the house was haunted no more."* This story has such a modern air as to be absolutely disheartening. Are ghosts, then, as incapable of invention as dramatic authors? But the demeanor of Athenodorus has the grand air of the classical period, of one *qui connaît son monde,* and feels the superiority of a living philosopher to a dead Philistine. How far above all modern armament is his prophylactic against his insubstantial fellow-lodger! Now-a-days men take pistols into haunted houses. Sterne, and after him Novalis, discovered that gunpowder made all men equally tall, but Athenodorus had found out that pen and ink establish a superiority in spiritual stature. As men of this world, we feel our dignity exalted by his keeping an ambassador from the other waiting till he had finished his paragraph. Never surely did authorship appear to greater advantage. Athenodorus seems to have been of Hamlet's mind:

* Pliny's Letters, VII. 27. Melmoth's translation.

"I do not set my life at a pin's fee,
And, for my soul, what can it do to that,
Being a thing immortal, as itself?" *

A superstition, as its name imports, is something that has been left to stand over, like unfinished business, from one session of the world's *witenagemot* to the next. The vulgar receive it implicitly on the principle of *omne ignotum pro possibili*, a theory acted on by a much larger number than is commonly supposed, and even the enlightened are too apt to consider it, if not proved, at least rendered probable by the hearsay evidence of popular experience. Particular superstitions are sometimes the embodiment by popular imagination of ideas that were at first mere poetic figments, but more commonly the degraded and distorted relics of religious beliefs. Dethroned gods, outlawed by the new dynasty, haunted the borders of their old dominions, lurking in forests and mountains, and venturing to show themselves only after nightfall. Grimm and others have detected old divinities skulking about in strange disguises, and living from hand to mouth on the charity of Gammer Grethel and Mère l'Oie. Cast out from Olympus and Asgard, they were thankful for the hospitality of the chimney-corner, and kept soul and body together by an illicit traffic between this world and the other. While Schiller was lamenting the Gods of Greece, some of them were nearer neighbors to him than

* Something like this is the speech of Don Juan, after the statue of Don Gonzales has gone out:

"Pero todas son ideas
Que da a la imaginacion
El temor; y temer muertos
Es muy villano temor.
Que si un cuerpo noble, vivo,
Con potencias y razon
Y con alma no se tema,
¿ Quien cuerpos muertos temió?"

El Burlador de Sevilla, A. iii. s. 15.

he dreamed; and Heine had the wit to turn them to delightful account, showing himself, perhaps, the wiser of the two in saving what he could from the shipwreck of the past for present use on this prosaic Juan Fernandez of a scientific age, instead of sitting down to bewail it. To make the pagan divinities hateful, they were stigmatized as cacodæmons; and as the human mind finds a pleasure in analogy and system, an infernal hierarchy gradually shaped itself as the convenient antipodes and counterpoise of the celestial one. Perhaps at the bottom of it all there was a kind of unconscious manicheism, and Satan, as Prince of Darkness, or of the Powers of the Air, became at last a sovereign, with his great feudatories and countless vassals, capable of maintaining a not unequal contest with the King of Heaven. He was supposed to have a certain power of bestowing earthly prosperity, but he was really, after all, nothing better than a James II. at St. Germains, who could make Dukes of Perth and confer titular fiefs and garters as much as he liked, without the unpleasant necessity of providing any substance behind the shadow. That there should have been so much loyalty to him, under these disheartening circumstances, seems to me, on the whole, creditable to poor human nature. In this case it is due, at least in part, to that instinct of the poor among the races of the North, where there was a long winter, and too often a scanty harvest, — and the poor have been always and everywhere a majority, — which made a deity of Wish. The *Acheronta-movebo* impulse must have been pardonably strong in old women starving with cold and hunger, and fathers with large families and a small winter stock of provision. Especially in the transition period from the old religion to the new, the temptation must have been great to try one's luck with the discrowned dynasty, when the intruder was deaf and blind to claims that seemed just enough, so long as it was still believed that God personally interfered in the affairs of men. On his death-bed, says Piers Plowman,

> "The poore dare plede and prove by reson
> To have allowance of his lord; by the law he it claimeth;
>
> . . . . .
>
> Thanne may beggaris as beestes after boote waiten
> That al hir lif han lyved in langour and in defaute
> But God sente hem som tyme som manere joye,
> Outher here or ellis where, kynde wolde it nevere."

He utters the common feeling when he says that it were against nature. But when a man has his choice between here and elsewhere, it may be feared that the other world will seem too desperately far away to be waited for when hungry ruin has him in the wind, and the chance on earth is so temptingly near. Hence the notion of a transfer of allegiance from God to Satan, sometimes by a written compact, sometimes with the ceremony by which homage is done to a feudal superior.

Most of the practices of witchcraft — such as the power to raise storms, to destroy cattle, to assume the shape of beasts by the use of certain ointments, to induce deadly maladies in men by waxen images, or love by means of charms and philtres — were inheritances from ancient paganism. But the theory of a compact was the product of later times, the result, no doubt, of the efforts of the clergy to inspire a horror of any lapse into heathenish rites by making devils of all the old gods. Christianity may be said to have invented the soul as an individual entity to be saved or lost; and thus grosser wits were led to conceive of it as a piece of property that could be transferred by deed of gift or sale, duly signed, sealed, and witnessed. The earliest legend of the kind is that of Theophilus, chancellor of the church of Adana in Cilicia some time during the sixth century. It is said to have been first written by Eutychianus, who had been a pupil of Theophilus, and who tells the story partly as an eyewitness, partly from the narration of his master. The nun Hroswitha first treated it dramatically in the latter half of the tenth century. Some four hundred years later Rutebeuf made it the theme of a French miracle-play. His treatment of it is not without a certain poetic merit. Theophilus has been deprived by his bishop of a lucrative office. In his despair he meets with Saladin, *qui parloit au deable quant il voloit.* Saladin tempts him to deny God and devote himself to the Devil, who, in return, will give him back all his old prosperity and more. He at last consents, signs and seals the contract required, and is restored to his old place by the bishop. But now remorse and terror come upon him; he calls on the Virgin, who, after some demur, compels Satan to bring back his deed from the infernal muniment-chest (which must have been fire-proof beyond any skill of our modern safe-makers), and the bishop having read it aloud to the awe-stricken congregation, Theophilus becomes his own man again. In this play, the theory of devilish compact is already complete in all its particulars. The paper must be signed with the blood of the grantor, who does feudal homage (*or joing tes mains, et si devien mes hom*), and engages to eschew good and do evil all the days of his life. The Devil, however, does not imprint any stigma upon his new vassal, as in the later stories of witch-compacts. The following passage from the opening speech of Theophilus will illustrate the conception to which I have alluded of God as a liege lord against whom one might seek revenge on sufficient provocation, — and the only revenge possible was to rob him of a subject by going over to the great Suzerain, his deadly foe: —

"N'est riens que por avoir ne face;
Ne pris riens Dieu et sa manace.
Irai me je noier ou pendre?
Ie ne m'en puis pas à Dieu prendre,
C'on ne puet à lui avenir.
. . . . .
Mès il s'est en si haut lieu mis,
Por eschiver ses anemis
C'on n'i puet trere ni lancier.
Se or pooie à lui tancier,
Et combattre et escrimir,
La char li feroie fremir.
Or est là sus en son solaz,
Laz! chetis! et je sui ès laz
De Povreté et de Soufrete." *

During the Middle Ages the story became a favorite topic with preachers, while carvings and painted windows tended still further to popularize it, and to render men's minds familiar with the idea which makes the nexus of its plot. The plastic hands of Calderon shaped it into a dramatic poem not surpassed, perhaps hardly equalled, in subtile imaginative quality by any other of modern times.

In proportion as a belief in the possibility of this damnable merchandising with hell became general, accusations of it grew more numerous. Among others, the memory of Pope Sylvester II. was blackened with the charge of having thus bargained away his soul. All learning fell under suspicion, till at length the very grammar itself (the last volume in the world, one would say, to conjure with) gave to English the word *gramary* (enchantment), and in French became a book of magic, under the alias of *Grimoire*. It is not at all unlikely that, in an age when the boundary between actual and possible was not very well defined, there were scholars who made experiments in this direction, and signed con-

* Théatre Français au Moyen Age (Monmerqué et Michel), pp. 139, 140.

tracts, though they never had a chance to complete their bargain by an actual delivery. I do not recall any case of witchcraft in which such a document was produced in court as evidence against the accused. Such a one, it is true, was ascribed to Grandier, but was not brought forward at his trial. It should seem that Grandier had been shrewd enough to take a bond to secure the fulfilment of the contract on the other side; for we have the document in fac-simile, signed and sealed by Lucifer, Beelzebub, Satan, Elimi, Leviathan, and Astaroth, duly witnessed by Baalberith, Secretary of the Grand Council of Demons. Fancy the competition such a state paper as this would arouse at a sale of autographs! Commonly no security appears to have been given by the other party to these arrangements but the bare word of the Devil, which was considered, no doubt, every whit as good as his bond. In most cases, indeed, he was the loser, and showed a want of capacity for affairs equal to that of an average giant of romance. Never was comedy acted over and over with such sameness of repetition as "The Devil is an Ass." How often must he have exclaimed (laughing in his sleeve): —

> "*I* to such blockheads set my wit,
> *I* damn such fools! — go, go, you 're bit!"

In popular legend he is made the victim of some equivocation so gross that any court of equity would have ruled in his favor. On the other hand, if the story had been dressed up by some mediæval Tract Society, the Virgin appears in person at the right moment *ex machina*, and compels him to give up the property he had honestly paid for. One is tempted to ask, Were there no attorneys, then, in the place he came from, of whom he might have taken advice beforehand? On the whole, he had rather hard measure, and it is a wonder he did not throw up the business in disgust. Sometimes, however, he was more lucky, as with the unhappy Dr. Faust; and even so lately as 1695, he came in the shape of a "tall fellow with black beard and periwig, respectable looking and well dressed," about two o'clock in the afternoon, to fly away with the Maréchal de Luxembourg, which, on the stroke of five, he punctually did as per contract, taking with him the window and its stone framing into the bargain. The clothes and wig of the involuntary aeronaut were, in the handsomest manner, left upon the bed, as not included in the bill of sale. In this case also we have a copy of the articles of agreement, twenty-eight in number, by the last of which the Maréchal renounces God and devotes himself to the enemy. This clause, sometimes the only one, always the most important in such compacts, seems to show that they first took shape in the imagination, while the struggle between Paganism and Christianity was still going on. As the converted heathen was made to renounce his false gods, none the less real for being false, so the renegade Christian must forswear the true Deity. It is very likely, however, that the whole thing may be more modern than the assumed date of Theophilus would imply, and if so, the idea of feudal allegiance gave the first hint, as it certainly modified the particulars, of the ceremonial.

This notion of a personal and private treaty with the Evil One has something of dignity about it that has made it perennially attractive to the most imaginative minds. It rather flatters than mocks our feeling of the dignity of man. As we come down to the vulgar parody of it in the confessions of wretched old women on the rack, our pity and indignation are mingled with disgust. One of the most particular of these confessions is that of Abel de la Rue, convicted in 1584. The accused was a novice in the Franciscan Convent at Meaux. Having been punished by the master of the novices for stealing some apples and nuts in the convent garden, the Devil appeared to him in the shape of a black dog, promising him his protection, and advising him to leave the convent. Not long after going into the sacristy, he saw a large volume fastened by a chain, and further secured by bars of iron. The name of this book was *Grimoire.* Thrusting his hands through the bars, he contrived to open it, and having read a sentence (which Bodin carefully suppresses), there suddenly appeared to him a man of middle stature, with a pale and very frightful countenance, clad in a long black robe of the Italian fashion, and with faces of men like his own on his breast and knees. As for his feet they were like those of cows. He could not have been the most agreeable of companions, *ayant le corps et haleine puante.* This man told him not to be afraid, to take off his habit, to put faith in him, and he would give him whatever he asked. Then laying hold of him below the arms, the unknown transported him under the gallows of Meaux, and then said to him with a trembling and broken voice, and having a visage as pale as that of a man who has been hanged, and a very stinking breath, that he should fear nothing, but have entire confidence in him, that he should never want for anything, that his own name was Maître Rigoux, and that he would like to be his master; to which De la Rue made answer that he would do whatever he commanded, and that he wished to be gone from the Franciscans. Thereupon Rigoux disappeared, but returning between seven and eight in the evening, took him round the waist and carried him back to the sacristy, promising to come again for him the next day. This he accordingly did, and told De la Rue to take off his habit, get him gone from the convent, and meet him near a great tree on the high-road from Meaux to Vaulx-Courtois. Rigoux met him there and took him to a certain Maître Pierre, who, after a few words exchanged in an undertone with Rigoux, sent De la Rue to the stable, after his return whence he saw no more of Rigoux. Thereupon Pierre and his wife made him good cheer, telling him that for the love of Maître Rigoux they would treat him well, and that he must obey the said Rigoux, which he promised to do. About two months after, Maître Pierre, who commonly took him to the fields to watch cattle, said to him there that they must go to the Assembly, because he (Pierre) was out of powders, to which he made answer that he was willing. Three days later, about Christmas eve, 1575, Pierre having sent his wife to sleep out of the house, set a long branch of broom in the chimney-corner, and bade De la Rue go to bed, but not to sleep. About eleven they heard a great noise as of an impetuous wind and thunder in the chimney: which hearing, Maître Pierre told him to dress himself, for it was time to be gone. Then Pierre took some grease from a little box and anointed himself under the arm-pits, and De la Rue on the palms of his hands, which incontinently felt as if on fire, and the said grease stank like a cat three weeks or a month dead. Then, Pierre and he bestriding the branch, Maître Rigoux took it by the butt and drew it up chimney as if the wind had lifted them. And, the night being dark, he saw suddenly a torch before them lighting them, and Maître Rigoux was gone unless he had changed himself into the said torch. Arrived at a grassy place some five leagues from Vaulx-Courtois, they found a company of some sixty people of all ages, none of whom he knew, except a certain Pierre of Dampmartin and an old woman who was executed, as he had heard, about five years ago for sorcery at Lagny. Then suddenly he noticed that all (except Rigoux, who was clad as before) were dressed in linen, though they had not changed their clothes. Then, at command of the eldest among them, who seemed about eighty years old, with a white beard and almost wholly bald, each swept the place in front of himself with his broom. Thereupon Rigoux changed into a great he-goat, black and stinking, around whom they all danced backward with their faces outward and their backs towards the goat. They danced about half an hour, and then his master told him they must adore the goat who was the Devil *et ce fait et dict, veit que ledict Bouc courba ses deux pieds de deuant et leua son cul en haut, et lors que certaines menues graines grosses comme testes d'espingles, qui se conuertissoient en poudres fort puantes, sentant le soulphre et poudre à canon et chair puant mesleés ensemble seroient tombeés sur plusieurs drappeaux en sept doubles.* Then the oldest, and so the rest in order, went forward on their knees and gathered up their cloths with the powders, but first each *se seroit incliné vers le Diable et iceluy baisé en la partie honteuse de son corps.* They went home on their broom, lighted as before. De la Rue confessed also that he was at another assembly on the eve of St. John Baptist. With the powders they could cause the death of men against whom they had a spite, or their cattle. Rigoux before long began to tempt him to drown himself, and, though he lay down, yet rolled him some distance towards the river. It is plain that the poor fellow was mad or half-witted or both. And yet Bodin, the author of the *De Republica*, reckoned one of the ablest books of that age, believed all this filthy nonsense, and prefixes it to his *Démonomanie*, as proof conclusive of the existence of sorcerers.

This was in 1587. Just a century later, Glanvil, one

of the most eminent men of his day, and Henry More, the Platonist, whose memory is still dear to the lovers of an imaginative mysticism, were perfectly satisfied with evidence like that which follows. Elizabeth Styles confessed, in 1664, "that the Devil about ten years since appeared to her in the shape of a handsome Man, and after of a black Dog. That he promised her Money, and that she should live gallantly, and have the pleasure of the World for twelve years, if she would with her Blood sign his Paper, which was to give her soul to him and observe his Laws and that he might suck her Blood. This after Four Solicitations, the Examinant promised him to do. Upon which he pricked the fourth Finger of her right hand, between the middle and upper Joynt (where the Sign at the Examination remained) and with a Drop or two of her Blood, she signed the Paper with an O. Upon this the Devil gave her sixpence and vanished with the Paper. That since he hath appeared to her in the Shape of a *Man*, and did so on *Wednesday* seven-night past, but more usually he appears in the Likeness of a *Dog*, and *Cat*, and a *Fly* like a Millar, in which last he usually sucks in the Poll about four of the Clock in the Morning, and did so *Jan.* 27, and that it is pain to her to be so suckt. That when she hath a desire to do harm she calls the Spirit by the name of *Robin*, to whom, when he appeareth, she useth these words, *O Sathan, give me my purpose.* She then tells him what she would have done. And that he should so appear to her was part of her Contract with him." The Devil in this case appeared as a black (dark-complexioned) man "in black clothes, with a little band," — a very clerical-looking personage. "Before they are carried to their meetings they anoint their Foreheads and Hand-Wrists with an Oyl the Spirit brings them (which smells raw) and then they are carried in a very short time, using these words as they pass, *Thout, tout a tout, throughout and about.* And when they go off from their Meetings they say, *Rentum, Tormentum.* That at every meeting before the Spirit vanisheth away, he appoints the next meeting place and time, and at his departure there is a foul smell. At their meeting they have usually Wine or good Beer, Cakes, Meat or the like. They eat and drink really when they meet, in their Bodies, dance also and have some Musick. The Man in black sits at the higher end, and *Anne Bishop* usually next him. He useth some words before meat, and none after; his Voice is audible but very low. The Man in black sometimes plays on a Pipe or Cittern, and the Company dance. At last the Devil vanisheth, and all are carried to their several homes in a short space. At their parting they say, *A Boy! merry meet, merry part!*" Alice Duke confessed "that Anne Bishop persuaded her to go with her into the Churchyard in the Night-time, and being come thither, to go backward round the Church, which they did three times. In their first round they met a Man in black Cloths who went round the second time with them; and then they met a thing in the Shape of a great black Toad which leapt up against the Examinant's Apron. In their third round they met somewhat in the shape of a Rat, which vanished away." She also received sixpence from the Devil, and "her Familiar did commonly suck her right Breast about seven at night in the shape of a little Cat of a dunnish Colour, which is as smooth as a Want [mole], and when she is suckt, she is in a kind of Trance." Poor Christian Green got only fourpence half-penny for her soul, but her bargain was made some years later than that of the others, and quotations, as the stock-brokers would say, ranged lower. Her familiar took the shape of a hedgehog. Julian Cox confessed that "she had been often tempted by the Devil to be a Witch, but never consented. That one Evening she walkt about a Mile from her own House and there came riding towards her three Persons upon three Broomstaves, born up about a yard and a half from the ground. Two of them she formerly knew, which was a Witch and a Wizzard that were hanged for Witchcraft several years before. The third person she knew not. He came in the shape of a black Man, and tempted her to give him her Soul, or to that effect, and to express it by pricking her Finger and giving her name in her Blood in token of it." On her trial Judge Archer told the jury, "he had heard that a Witch could not repeat that Petition in the Lord's Prayer, viz. *And lead us not into temptation*, and having this occasion, he would try the Experiment." The jury "were not in the least measure to guide their Verdict according to it, because it was not legal Evidence." Accordingly it was found that the poor old trot could say only, *Lead us into temptation*, or *Lead us not into no temptation.* Probably she used the latter form first, and, finding she had blundered, corrected herself by leaving out both the negatives. The old English double negation seems never to have been heard of by the court. Janet Douglass, a pretended dumb girl, by whose contrivance five persons had been burned at Paisley, in 1677, for having caused the sickness of Sir George Maxwell by means of waxen and other images, having recovered her speech shortly after, declared that she "had some smattering knowledge of the Lord's prayer, which she had heard the witches repeat, it seems, by her vision, in the presence of the Devil; and at his desire, which they observed, they added to the word *art* the letter *w*, which made it run, 'Our Father which wart in heaven,' by which means the Devil made the application of the prayer to himself." She also showed on the arm of a woman named Campbell "an *invisible* mark which she had gotten from the Devil." The wife of one Barton confessed that she had engaged "in the Devil's service. She renounced her baptism, and did prostrate her body to the foul spirit, and received his mark, and got a new name from him, and was called *Margaratus*. She was asked if she ever had any pleasure in his company? 'Never much,' says she, 'but one night going to a dancing upon Pentland Hills, in the likeness of a rough tanny [tawny] dog, playing on a pair of pipes; the spring he played,' says she, 'was *The silly bit chicken, gar cast it a pickle, and it will grow meikle.*'" * In 1670, near seventy of both sexes, among them fifteen children, were executed for witchcraft at the village of Mohra in Sweden. Thirty-six children, between the ages of nine and sixteen, were sentenced to be scourged with rods on the palms of their hands, once a week for a year. The evidence in this case against the accused seems to have been mostly that of children. "Being asked whether they were sure that they were at any time carried away by the Devil, they all declared they were, begging of the Commissioners that they might be freed from that intolerable slavery." They "used to go to a Gravel pit which lay hardby a Cross-way and there they put on a vest over their heads, and then danced round, and after ran to the Cross-way and called the Devil thrice, first with a still Voice, the second time somewhat louder, and the third time very loud, with these words, *Antecessour, come and carry us to Blockula.* Whereupon immediately he used to appear, but in different Habits; but for the most part they saw him in a gray Coat and red and blue Stockings. He had a red Beard, a highcrowned Hat, with linnen of divers

* "There sat Auld Nick in shape o' beast,
A towzy tyke, black, grim, an' large,
To gie them music was his charge."

Colours wrapt about it, and long Garters upon his Stockings." "They must procure some Scrapings of Altars and Filings of Church-Clocks [bells], and he gives them a Horn with some Salve in it wherewith they do anoint themselves." "Being asked whether they were sure of a real personal Transportation, and whether they were awake when it was done, they all answered in the Affirmative, and that the Devil sometimes laid something down in the Place that was very like them. But one of them confessed that he did only take away her Strength, and her Body lay still upon the Ground. Yet sometimes he took even her Body with him." "Till of late they never had that power to carry away Children, but only this year and the last, and the Devil did at this time force them to it. That heretofore it was sufficient to carry but one of their Children or a Stranger's Child, which yet happened seldom, but now he did plague them and whip them if they did not procure him Children, insomuch that they had no peace or quiet for him; and whereas formerly one Journey a Week would serve their turn from their own town to the place aforesaid, now they were forced to run to other Towns and Places for Children, and that they brought with them some fifteen, some sixteen Children every night. For their journey they made use of all sorts of Instruments, of Beasts, of Men, of Spits, and Posts, according as they had opportunity. If they do ride upon Goats and have many Children with them," they have a way of lengthening the goat with a spit, "and then are anointed with the aforesaid Ointment. A little Girl of Elfdale confessed, That, naming the name of JESUS, as she was carried away, she fell suddenly upon the Ground and got a great hole in her Side, which the Devil presently healed up again. The first thing they must do at Blockula was that they must deny all and devote themselves Body and

Soul to the Devil, and promise to serve him faithfully, and confirm all this with an Oath. Hereupon they cut their Fingers, and with their Bloud writ their Name in his Book. He caused them to be baptized by such Priests as he had there and made them confirm their Baptism with dreadful Oaths and Imprecations. Hereupon the Devil gave them a Purse, wherein their filings of Clocks [bells], with a Stone tied to it, which they threw into the Water, and then they were forced to speak these words: *As these filings of the Clock do never return to the Clock from which they are taken, so may my soul never return to Heaven.* The diet they did use to have there was Broth with Colworts and Bacon in it, Oatmeal-Bread spread with Butter, Milk, and Cheese. Sometimes it tasted very well, sometimes very ill. After Meals, they went to Dancing, and in the mean while Swore and Cursed most dreadfully, and afterward went to fighting one with another. The Devil had Sons and Daughters by them, which he did marry together, and they did couple and brought forth Toads and Serpents. If he hath a mind to be merry with them, he lets them all ride upon Spits before him, takes afterwards the Spits and beats them black and blue, and then laughs at them. They had seen sometimes a very great Devil like a Dragon, with fire about him and bound with an Iron Chain, and the Devil that converses with them tells them that, if they confess anything, he will let that great Devil loose upon them, whereby all *Sweedland* shall come into great danger. The Devil taught them to milk, which was in this wise: they used to stick a knife in the Wall and hang a kind of Label on it, which they drew and stroaked, and as long as this lasted the Persons that they had Power over were miserably plagued, and the Beasts were milked that way till sometimes they died of it. The minister of Elfdale declared that one Night these Witches were to his thinking upon the crown of his Head and that from thence he had had a long-continued Pain of the Head. One of the Witches confessed, too, that the Devil had sent her to torment the Minister, and that she was ordered to use a Nail and strike it into his Head, but it would not enter very deep. They confessed also that the Devil gives them a Beast about the bigness and shape of a young Cat, which they call a *Carrier*, and that he gives them a Bird too as big as a Raven, but white. And these two Creatures they can send anywhere, and wherever they come they take away all sorts of Victuals they can get. What the Bird brings they may keep for themselves; but what the Carrier brings they must reserve for the Devil. The Lords Commissioners were indeed very earnest and took great Pains to persuade them to show some of their Tricks, but to no Purpose; for they did all unanimously confess, that, since they had confessed all, they found that all their Witchcraft was gone, and that the Devil at this time appeared to them very terrible with Claws on his Hands and Feet, and with Horns on his Head and a long Tail behind." At Blockula "the Devil had a Church, such another as in the town of Mohra. When the Commissioners were coming, he told the Witches they should not fear them, for he would certainly kill them all. And they confessed that some of them had attempted to murther the Commissioners, but had not been able to effect it."

In these confessions we find included nearly all the particulars of the popular belief concerning witchcraft, and see the gradual degradation of the once superb Lucifer to the vulgar scarecrow with horns and tail. "The Prince of Darkness *was* a gentleman." From him who had not lost all his original brightness, to this dirty fellow who leaves a stench, sometimes of brimstone, behind him, the descent is a long one. For the dispersion of this foul odor Dr. Henry More gives an odd reason. "The Devil also, as in other stories, leaving an ill smell behind him, seems to imply the reality of the business, those adscititious particles he held together in his visible vehicle being loosened at his vanishing and so offending the nostrils by their floating and diffusing themselves in the open Air." In all the stories vestiges of Paganism are not indistinct. The three principal witch gatherings of the year were held on the days of great pagan festivals, which were afterwards adopted by the Church. Maury supposes the witches' Sabbath to be derived from the rites of Bacchus Sabazius, and accounts in this way for the Devil's taking the shape of a he-goat. But the name was more likely to be given from hatred of the Jews, and the goat may have a much less remote origin. Bodin assumes the identity of the Devil with Pan, and in the popular mythology both of Kelts and Teutons there were certain hairy wood-demons called by the former *Dus* and by the latter *Scrat*. Our common names of *Deuse* and *Old Scratch* are plainly derived from these, and possibly *Old Harry* is a corruption of *Old Hairy*. By Latinization they became Satyrs. Here, at any rate, is the source of the cloven hoof. The belief in the Devil's appearing to his worshippers as a goat is very old. Possibly the fact that this animal was sacred to Thor, the god of thunder, may explain it. Certain it is that the traditions of Vulcan, Thor, and Wayland * converged at last in Satan. Like Vulcan, he was hurled from heaven, and like him he still limps across the stage in Mephistopheles, though without knowing why. In Germany, he has a horse's and not a cloven foot,† because the

* Hence, perhaps, the name Valant applied to the Devil, about the origin of which Grimm is in doubt.

† One foot of the Greek Empusa was an ass's hoof.

horse was a frequent pagan sacrifice, and therefore associated with devil-worship under the new dispensation. Hence the horror of hippophagism which some French gastronomes are striving to overcome. Everybody who has read "Tom Brown," or Wordsworth's Sonnet on a German stove, remembers the Saxon horse sacred to Woden. The raven was also his peculiar bird, and Grimm is inclined to think this the reason why the witch's familiar appears so often in that shape. It is true that our *Old Nick* is derived from *Nikkar*, one of the titles of that divinity, but the association of the Evil One with the raven is older, and most probably owing to the ill-omened character of the bird itself. Already in the apocryphal gospel of the "Infancy," the demoniac Son of the Chief Priest puts on his head one of the swaddling-clothes of Christ which Mary has hung out to dry, and forthwith "the devils began to come out of his mouth and to fly away as *crows* and serpents."

It will be noticed that the witches underwent a form of baptism. As the system gradually perfected itself among the least imaginative of men, as the superstitious are apt to be, they could do nothing better than describe Satan's world as in all respects the reverse of that which had been conceived by the orthodox intellect as Divine. Have you an illustrated Bible of the last century? Very good. Turn it upside down, and you find the prints on the whole about as near nature as ever, and yet pretending to be something new by a simple device that saves the fancy a good deal of trouble. For, while it is true that the poetic fancy plays, yet the faculty which goes by that pseudonyme in prosaic minds (and it was by such that the details of this Satanic commerce were pieced together) is hard put to it for invention, and only too thankful for any labor-saving contrivance whatsoever. Accordingly, all it need take the trouble to do was to reverse the ideas of sacred things already engraved on its surface, and behold, a kingdom of hell with all the merit and none of the difficulty of originality! "Uti olim Deus populo suo Hierosolymis Synagogas erexit ut in iis ignarus legis divinæ populus erudiretur, voluntatemque Dei placitam ex verbo in iis prædicato hauriret; ita et Diabolus in omnibus omnino suis actionibus simiam Dei agens, gregi suo acherontico conventus et synagogas, quas satanica sabbata vocant, indicit. . . . . Atque de hisce Conventibus et Synagogis Lamiarum nullus Antorum quos quidem evolvi, imo nec ipse Lamiarum Patronus [here he glances at Wierus] scilicet ne dubiolum quidem movit. Adeo ut tuto affirmari liceat conventus a diabolo certo institui. Quos vel ipse, tanquam præses collegii, vel per dæmonem, qui ad cujuslibet sagæ custodiam constitutus est, ... vel per alios Magos aut sagas per unum aut duos dies antequam fiat congregatio denunciat. . . . . Loci in quibus solent a dæmone cœtus et conventicula malefica institui plerumque sunt sylvestres, occulti, subterranei, et ab hominum conversatione remoti. . . . . Evocatæ hoc modo et tempore Lamiæ, ... dæmon illis persuadet eas non posse conventiculis interesse nisi nudum corpus unguento ex corpusculis infantum ante baptismum necatorum præparato illinant, idque propterea solum illis persuadet ut ad quam plurimas infantum insontium cædes eas alliciat. . . . . Unctionis ritu peracto, abiturientes, ne forte a maritis in lectis desiderantur, vel per incantationem somnum, aurem nimirum vellicando dextra manu prius prædicto unguine illita, conciliant maritis ex quo non facile possunt excitari; vel dæmones personas quasdam dormientibus adumbrant, quas, si contigeret expergisci, suas uxores esse putarent; vel interea alius dæmon in forma succubi ad latus maritorum adjungitur qui loco uxoris est. . . . . Et ita sine omni remora insidentes baculo, furcæ, scopis, aut arundini vel tauro, equo, sui, hirco, aut cani, *quorum omnium exempla prodidit Remig.* L. I. c. 14, devehuntur a dæmone ad loca destinata. . . . . Ibi dæmon præses conventus in solio sedet magnifico, forma terrifica, ut plurimum hirci vel canis. Ad quem advenientes viri juxta ac mulieres accedunt reverentiæ exhibendæ et adorandi gratia, non tamen uno eodemque modo. Interdum complicatis genubus supplices; interdum obverso incedentes tergo et modo retrogrado, in oppositum directo illi reverentiæ quam nos præstare solemus. In signum homagii (sit honor castis auribus) Principem suum hircum in [obscænissimo quodam corporis loco] summa cum reverentia sacrilego ore osculantur. Quo facto, sacrificia dæmoni faciunt multis modis. Sæpe liberos suos ipsi offerunt. Sæpe communione sumpta benedictam hostiam in ore asservatam et extractam (horreo dicere) dæmoni oblatam coram eo pede conculcant. His et similibus flagitiis et abominationibus execrandis commissis, incipiunt mensis assidere et convivari de cibis insipidis, insulsis,* furtivis, quos dæmon suppeditat, vel quos singulæ attulere, inderdum tripudiant ante convivium, interdum post illud. . . . . Nec mensæ sua deest benedictio cœtu hoc digna, verbis constans plane blasphemis quibus ipsum Beelzebub et creatorem et datorem et conservatorem omnium profitentur. Eadem sententia est gratiarum actionis. Post convivium, dorsis invicem obversis . . . . choreas ducere et cantare fescenninos in honorem dæmonis obscænissimos, vel ad tympanum fistulamve sedentis alicujus in bifida arbore saltare . . . . tum suis amasiis dæmonibus fœdissime commisceri. Ultimo pulveribus (quos aliqui scribunt esse cineres hirci illis quem dæmon assumpserat et quem adorant subito coram illius flamma absumpti) vel venenis aliis acceptis, sæpe etiam cuique indicto nocendi

* Salt was forbidden at these witch-feasts.

penso, et pronunciato Pseudothei dæmonis decreto, ULCISCAMINI VOS, ALIOQUI MORIEMINI. Duabus aut tribus horis in hisce ludis exactis circa Gallicinium dæmon convivas suas dimittit." * Sometimes they were baptized anew. Sometimes they renounced the Virgin, whom they called in their rites *extensam mulierem.* If the Ave Mary bell should ring while the demon is conveying home his witch, he lets her drop. In the confession of Agnes Simpson the meeting place was North Berwick Kirk. "The Devil started up himself in the pulpit, like a meikle black man, and calling the row [roll] every one answered, *Here.* At his command they opened up three graves and cutted off from the dead corpses the joints of their fingers, toes, and nose, and parted them amongst them, and the said Agnes Simpson got for her part a winding-sheet and two joints. The Devil commanded them to keep the joints upon them while [till] they were dry, and then to make a powder of them to do evil withal." This confession is sadly memorable, for it was made before James I., then king of Scots, and is said to have convinced him of the reality of witchcraft. Hence the act passed in the first year of his reign in England, and not repealed till 1736, under which, perhaps in consequence of which, so many suffered.

The notion of these witch-gatherings was first suggested, there can be little doubt, by secret conventicles of persisting or relapsed pagans, or of heretics. Both, perhaps, contributed their share. Sometimes a mountain, as in Germany the Blocksberg,† sometimes a con-

* De Lamiis, p. 59 *et seq.*

† If the *Blokula* of the Swedish witches be a reminiscence of this, it would seem to point back to remote times and heathen ceremonies. But it is so impossible to distinguish what was put into the mind of those who confessed by their examining torturers from what may have been there before, the result of a common superstition, that perhaps,

spicuous oak or linden, and there were many such among both Gauls and Germans sacred of old to pagan rites, and later a lonely heath, a place where two roads crossed each other, a cavern, gravel-pit, or quarry, the gallows, or the churchyard, was the place appointed for their diabolic orgies. That the witch could be conveyed bodily to these meetings was at first admitted without any question. But as the husbands of accused persons sometimes testified that their wives had not left their beds on the alleged night of meeting, the witchmongers were put to strange shifts by way of accounting for it. Sometimes the Devil imposed on the husband by a *deceptio visus;* sometimes a demon took the place of the wife; sometimes the body was left and the spirit only transported. But the more orthodox opinion was in favor of corporeal deportation. Bodin appeals triumphantly to the cases of Habbakuk (now in the Apocrypha, but once making a part of the Book of Daniel), and of Philip in the Acts of the Apostles. "I find," he says, "this ecstatic ravishment they talk of much more wonderful than bodily transport. And if the Devil has this power, as they confess, of ravishing the spirit out of the body, is it not more easy to carry body and soul without separation or division of the reasonable part, than to withdraw and divide the one from the other without death?" The author of *De Lamiis* argues for the corporeal theory. "The evil Angels have the same superiority of natural power as the good, since by the Fall they lost none of the gifts of nature, but only those of grace." Now, as we know that good angels can thus transport men in the twinkling of an eye, it follows that evil ones may do the same. He fortifies his position by a recent example from secular history. "No one doubts about John Faust, who

after all, the meeting on mountains may have been suggested by what Pliny says of the dances of Satyrs on Mount Atlas.

dwelt at Wittenberg, in the time of the sainted Luther, and who, seating himself on his cloak with his companions, was conveyed away and borne by the Devil through the air to distant kingdoms." * Glanvin inclines rather to the spiritual than the material hypothesis, and suggests "that the Witch's anointing herself before she takes her flight may perhaps serve to keep the body tenantable and in fit disposition to receive the spirit at its return." Aubrey, whose "Miscellanies" were published in 1696, had no doubts whatever as to the physical asportation of the witch. He says that a gentleman of his acquaintance "was in Portugal *anno* 1655, when one was burnt by the inquisition for being brought thither from Goa, in East India, in the air, in an incredible short time." As to the conveyance of witches through crevices, keyholes, chimneys, and the like, Herr Walburger discusses the question with such comical gravity that we must give his argument in the undiminished splendor of its jurisconsult latinity. The first sentence is worthy of Magister Bartholomæus Kuckuk. "Hæc realis delatio trahit me quoque ad illam vulgo agitatam quæstionem : *An diabolus Lamias corpore per angusta foramina parietum, fenestrarum, portarum aut per cavernas ignifluas ferre queant ?*" (Surely if *tace* be good Latin for a candle, *caverna igniflua* should be flattering to a chimney.) "Resp. Lamiæ prædicto modo sæpius fatentur sese a diabolo per caminum aut alia loca angustiora scopis insidentes per ærem ad montem Bructerorum deferri. Verum deluduntur a Satana istæc mulieres hoc casu egregie nec revera rimulas istas penetrant, sed solummodo dæmon præcedens latenter aperit et claudit januas vel fenestras corporis earum capaces, per quas eas

* Wierus, whose book was published not long after Faust's death, apparently doubted the whole story, for he alludes to it with an *ut fertur*, and plainly looked on him as a mountebank.

intromittit quæ putant se formam animalculi parvi, mustelæ, catti, locustæ, et aliorum induisse. At si forte contingat ut per parietem se delatam confiteatur Saga, tunc, si non totum hoc præstigiosum est, dæmonem tamen maxima celeritate tot quot sufficiunt lapides eximere et sustinere aliosne ruant, et postea eadem celeritate iterum eos in suum locum reponere, existimo: cum hominum adspectus hanc tartarei latomi fraudem nequeat deprendere. Idem quoque judicium esse potest de translatione per caminum. Siquidem si caverna igniflua justæ amplitudinis est ut nullo impedimento et hæsitatione corpus humanum eam perrepere possit, diabolo impossibile non esse per eam eas educere. Si vero per inproportionatum (ut ita loquar) corporibus spatium eas educit tunc meras illusiones præstigiosas esse censeo, nec a diabolo hoc unquam effici posse. Ratio est, quoniam diabolus essentiam creaturæ seu lamiæ immutare non potest, multo minus efficere ut majus corpus penetret per spatium inproportionatum, alioquin corporum penetratio esset admittenda quod contra naturam et omne Physicorum principium est." This is fine reasoning, and the *ut ita loquar* thrown in so carelessly, as if with a deprecatory wave of the hand for using a less classical locution than usual, strikes me as a very delicate touch indeed.

Grimm tells us that he does not know when broomsticks, spits, and similar utensils were first assumed to be the canonical instruments of this nocturnal equitation. He thinks it comparatively modern, but I suspect it is as old as the first child that ever bestrode his father's staff, and fancied it into a courser shod with wind, like those of Pindar. Alas for the poverty of human invention! It cannot afford a hippogriff for an everyday occasion. The poor old crones, badgered by inquisitors into confessing they had been where they never were, were involved in the further necessity of explaining how the devil they got there. The only steed their parents had ever been rich enough to keep had been of this domestic sort, and they no doubt had ridden in this inexpensive fashion, imagining themselves the grand dames they saw sometimes flash by, in the happy days of childhood, now so far away. Forced to give a *how*, and unable to conceive of mounting in the air without something to sustain them, their bewildered wits naturally took refuge in some such simple subterfuge, and the broomstave, which might make part of the poorest house's furniture, was the nearest at hand. If youth and good spirits could put such life into a dead stick once, why not age and evil spirits now? Moreover, what so likely as an *emeritus* implement of this sort to become the staff of a withered beldame, and thus to be naturally associated with her image? I remember very well a poor half-crazed creature, who always wore a scarlet cloak and leaned on such a stay, cursing and banning after a fashion that would infallibly have burned her two hundred years ago. But apart from any adventitious associations of later growth, it is certain that a very ancient belief gave to magic the power of imparting life, or the semblance of it, to inanimate things, and thus sometimes making servants of them. The wands of the Egyptian magicians were turned to serpents. Still nearer to the purpose is the capital story of Lucian, out of which Goethe made his *Zauberlehrling*, of the stick turned water-carrier. The classical theory of the witch's flight was driven to no such vulgar expedients, the ointment turning her into a bird for the nonce, as in Lucian and Apuleius. In those days, too, there was nothing known of any camp-meeting of witches and wizards, but each sorceress transformed herself that she might fly to her paramour. According to some of the Scotch stories, the witch, after bestriding her broomstick, must repeat the magic formula, *Horse and Hattock!* The flitting of these ill-omened night-birds, like nearly all the general superstitions relating to witchcraft, mingles itself and is lost in a throng of figures more august.* Diana, Bertha, Holda, Abundia, Befana, once beautiful and divine, the bringers of blessing while men slept, became demons haunting the drear of darkness with terror and ominous suggestion. The process of disenchantment must have been a long one, and none can say how soon it became complete. Perhaps we may take Heine's word for it, that

> " Genau bei Weibern
> Weiss man niemals wo der Engel
> Aufhört und der Teufel anfängt."

Once goblinized, Herodias joins them, doomed still to bear about the Baptist's head; and Woden, who, first losing his identity in the Wild Huntsman, sinks by degrees into the mere *spook* of a Suabian baron, sinfully fond of field-sports, and therefore punished with an eternal phantasm of them, "the hunter and the deer a shade." More and more vulgarized, the infernal train snatches up and sweeps along with it every lawless shape and wild conjecture of distempered fancy, streaming away at last into a comet's tail of wild-haired hags, eager with unnatural hate and more unnatural lust, the nightmare breed of some exorcist's or inquisitor's surfeit, whose own lie has turned upon him in sleep.

As it is painfully interesting to trace the gradual degeneration of a poetic faith into the ritual of unimaginative Tupperism, so it is amusing to see pedantry clinging faithfully to the traditions of its prosaic nature, and holding sacred the dead shells that once housed a moral symbol. What a divine thing the *out*side always has been and continues to be! And how the cast clothes of the mind continue always to be in fashion! We turn

* See Grimm's D. M., under *Hexenfart*, *Wütendes Heer*, &c.

our coats without changing the cut of them. But was it possible for a man to change not only his skin but his nature? Were there such things as *versipelles, lycanthropi, werwolfs,* and *loupgarous?* In the earliest ages science was poetry, as in the later poetry has become science. The phenomena of nature, imaginatively represented, were not long in becoming myths. These the primal poets reproduced again as symbols, no longer of physical, but of moral truths. By and by the professional poets, in search of a subject, are struck by the fund of picturesque material lying unused in them, and work them up once more as narratives, with appropriate personages and decorations. Thence they take the further downward step into legend, and from that to superstition. How many metamorphoses between the elder Edda and the Nibelungen, between Arcturus and the "Idyls of the King"! Let a good, thorough-paced proser get hold of one of these stories, and he carefully desiccates them of whatever fancy may be left, till he has reduced them to the proper dryness of fact. King Lycaon, grandson by the spindleside of Oceanus, after passing through all the stages I have mentioned, becomes the ancestor of the werwolf. Ovid is put upon the stand as a witness, and testifies to the undoubted fact of the poor monarch's own metamorphosis: —

> "Territus ipse fugit, nactusque silentia ruris
> Exululat, frustraque loqui conatur."

Does any one still doubt that men may be changed into beasts? Call Lucian, call Apuleius, call Homer, whose story of the companions of Ulysses made swine of by Circe, says Bodin, *n'est pas fable.* If that arch-patron of sorcerers, Wierus, is still unconvinced, and pronounces the whole thing a delusion of diseased imagination, what does he say to Nebuchadnezzar? Nay, let St. Austin be subpœnaed, who declares that "in his time among the Alps sorceresses were common, who, by making travellers eat of a certain cheese, changed them into beasts of burden and then back again into men." Too confiding tourist, beware of *Gruyère*, especially at supper! Then there was the Philosopher Ammonius, whose lectures were constantly attended by an ass, — a phenomenon not without parallel in more recent times, and all the more credible to Bodin, who had been professor of civil law.

In one case we have fortunately the evidence of the ass himself. In Germany, two witches who kept an inn made an ass of a young actor, — not always a very prodigious transformation it will be thought by those familiar with the stage. In his new shape he drew customers by his amusing tricks, — *voluptates mille viatoribus exhibebat.* But one day making his escape (having overheard the secret from his mistresses), he plunged into the water and was disasinized to the extent of recovering his original shape. "Id Petrus Damianus, vir sua ætate inter primos numerandus, cum rem sciscitatus est diligentissime ex hero, *ex asino,* ex mulieribus sagis confessis factum, Leoni VII. Papæ narravit, et postquam diu in utramque partem coram Papa fuit disputatum, hoc tandem posse fieri fuit constitum." Bodin must have been delighted with this story, though perhaps as a Protestant he might have vilipended the infallible decision of the Pope in its favor. As for lycanthropy, that was too common in his own time to need any confirmation. It was notorious to all men. "In Livonia, during the latter part of December, a villain goes about summoning the sorcerers to meet at a certain place, and if they fail, the Devil scourges them thither with an iron rod, and that so sharply that the marks of it remain upon them. Their captain goes before; and they, to the number of several thousands, follow him across a river, which passed, they change into wolves, and, casting themselves upon men and flocks, do all manner of damage." This we have on the authority of Melancthon's son-in-law, Gaspar Peucerus. Moreover, many books published in Germany affirm "that one of the greatest kings in Christendom, not long since dead, was often changed into a wolf." But what need of words? The conclusive proof remains, that many in our own day, being put to the torture, have confessed the fact, and been burned alive accordingly. The maintainers of the reality of witchcraft in the next century seem to have dropped the *werwolf* by common consent, though supported by the same kind of evidence they relied on in other matters, namely, that of ocular witnesses, the confession of the accused, and general notoriety. So lately as 1765 the French peasants believed the "wild beast of the Gevaudan" to be a *loupgarou*, and that, I think, is his last appearance.

The particulars of the concubinage of witches with their familiars were discussed with a relish and a filthy minuteness worthy of Sanchez. Could children be born of these devilish amours? Of course they could, said one party; are there not plenty of cases in authentic history? Who was the father of Romulus and Remus? nay, not so very long ago, of Merlin? Another party denied the possibility of the thing altogether. Among these was Luther, who declared the children either to be supposititious, or else mere imps, disguised as innocent sucklings, and known as *Wechselkinder*, or changelings, who were common enough, as everybody must be aware. Of the intercourse itself Luther had no doubts.* A

* Some Catholics, indeed, affirmed that he himself was the son of a demon who lodged in his father's house under the semblance of a merchant. Wierus says that a bishop preached to that effect in 1565, and gravely refutes the story.

third party took a middle ground, and believed that vermin and toads might be the offspring of such amours. And how did the Demon, a mere spiritual essence, contrive himself a body? Some would have it that he entered into dead bodies, by preference, of course, those of sorcerers. It is plain, from the confession of De la Rue, that this was the theory of his examiners. This also had historical evidence in its favor. There was the well-known leading case of the Bride of Corinth, for example. And but yesterday, as it were, at Crossen in Silesia, did not Christopher Monig, an apothecary's servant, come back after being buried, and do duty, as if nothing particular had happened, putting up prescriptions as usual, and "pounding drugs in the mortar with a mighty noise"? Apothecaries seem to have been special victims of these Satanic pranks, for another appeared at Reichenbach not long before, affirming that, "he had poisoned several men with his drugs," which certainly gives an air of truth to the story. Accordingly the Devil is represented as being unpleasantly cold to the touch. "Caietan escrit qu'une sorciere demanda un iour au diable pourquoy il ne se rechauffoit, qui fist response qu'il faisoit ce qu'il pouuoit." Poor Devil! But there are cases in which the demon is represented as so hot that his grasp left a seared spot as black as charcoal. Perhaps some of them came from the torrid zone of their broad empire, and others from the thrilling regions of thick-ribbed ice. Those who were not satisfied with the dead-body theory contented themselves, like Dr. More, with that of "adscititious particles," which has, to be sure, a more metaphysical and scholastic flavor about it. That the demons really came, either corporeally or through some diabolic illusion that amounted to the same thing, and that the witch devoted herself to him body and soul, scarce anybody was bold enough to doubt.

To these familiars their venerable paramours gave endearing nicknames, such as My little Master, or My dear Martin, — the latter, probably, after the heresy of Luther, and when the rack was popish. The famous witch-finder Hopkins enables us to lengthen the list considerably. One witch whom he convicted, after being "kept from sleep two or three nights," called in five of her devilish servitors. The first was "*Holt*, who came in like a white kitling"; the second "*Jarmara*, like a fat spaniel without any legs at all"; the third, "*Vinegar Tom*, who was like a long-tailed greyhound with an head like an oxe, with a long tail and broad eyes, who, when this discoverer spoke to and bade him to the place provided for him and his angells, immediately transformed himself into the shape of a child of foure yeares old, without a head, and gave half a dozen turnes about the house and vanished at the doore"; the fourth, "*Sack and Sugar*, like a black rabbet"; the fifth, "*News*, like a polcat." Other names of his finding were Elemauzer, Pywacket, Peck-in-the-Crown, Grizzel, and Greedygut, "which," he adds, "no mortal could invent." The name of *Robin*, which we met with in the confession of Alice Duke, has, perhaps, wider associations than the woman herself dreamed of; for, through Robin des Bois and Robin Hood, it may be another of those scattered traces that lead us back to Woden. Probably, however, it is only our old friend Robin Goodfellow, whose namesake Knecht Ruprecht makes such a figure in the German fairy mythology. Possessed persons called in higher agencies, — Thrones, Dominations, Princedoms, Powers; and among the witnesses against Urbain Grandier we find the names of Leviathan, Behemoth, Isaacarum, Belaam, Asmodeus, and Beherit, who spoke French very well, but were remarkably poor Latinists, knowing, indeed, almost as little of the language as if their youth had been spent in writing Latin verses.* A shrewd Scotch physician tried them with Gaelic, but they could make nothing of it.

It was only when scepticism had begun to make itself uncomfortably inquisitive, that the Devil had any difficulty in making himself visible and even palpable. In simpler times, demons would almost seem to have made no inconsiderable part of the population. Trithemius tells of one who served as cook to the Bishop of Hildesheim (one shudders to think of the school where he had graduated as *Cordon bleu*), and who delectebatur esse cum hominibus, loquens, interrogans, respondens familiariter omnibus, aliquando visibiliter, aliquando invisibiliter apparens. This last feat of "appearing invisibly" would have been worth seeing. In 1554, the Devil came of a Christmas eve to Lawrence Doner, a parish priest in Saxony, and asked to be confessed. "Admissus, horrendas adversus Christum filium Dei blasphemias evomuit. Verum cum virtute verbi Dei a parocho victus esset, intolerabili post se relicto fœtore abiit." Splendidly dressed, with two companions, he frequented an honest man's house at Rothenberg. He brought with him a piper or fiddler, and contrived feasts and dances under pretext of wooing the goodman's daughter. He boasted that he was a foreign nobleman of immense wealth, and, for a time, was as successful as an Italian courier has been known to be at one of our fashionable watering-places. But the importunity of the guest and his friends at length displicuit patrifamilias, who accord-

* Melancthon, however, used to tell of a possessed girl in Italy who knew no Latin, but the Devil in her, being asked by Bonamico, a Bolognese professor, what was the best verse in Virgil, answered at once: —

"Discite justitiam moniti, et non temnere divos," —

a somewhat remarkable concession on the part of a fallen angel.

ingly one evening invited a minister of the Word to meet them at supper, and entered upon pious discourse with him from the word of God. Wherefore, seeking other matter of conversation, they said that there were many facetious things more suitable to exhilarate the supper-table than the interpretation of Holy Writ, and begged that they might be no longer bored with Scripture. Thoroughly satisfied by their singular way of thinking that his guests were diabolical, paterfamilias cries out in Latin worthy of Father Tom, "Apagite, vos scelerati nebulones!" This said, the tartarean impostor and his companions at once vanished with a great tumult, leaving behind them a most unpleasant fœtor and the bodies of three men who had been hanged. Perhaps if the clergyman-cure were faithfully tried upon the next fortune-hunting count with a large real estate in whiskers and an imaginary one in Barataria, he also might vanish, leaving a strong smell of barber's-shop, and taking with him a body that will come to the gallows in due time. It were worth trying. Luther tells of a demon who served as *famulus* in a monastery, fetching beer for the monks, and always insisting on honest measure for his money. There is one case on record where the Devil appealed to the courts for protection in his rights. A monk, going to visit his mistress, fell dead as he was passing a bridge. The good and bad angel came to litigation about his soul. The case was referred by agreement to Richard, Duke of Normandy, who decided that the monk's body should be carried back to the bridge, and his soul restored to it by the claimants. If he persevered in keeping his assignation, the Devil was to have him, if not, then the Angel. The monk, thus put upon his guard, turns back and saves his soul, such as it was.*

* This story seems mediæval and Gothic enough, but is hardly more so than bringing the case of the Furies *v.* Orestes before the Areopagus,

Perhaps the most impudent thing the Devil ever did was to open a school of magic in Toledo. The ceremony of graduation in this institution was peculiar. The senior class had all to run through a narrow cavern, and the venerable president was entitled to the hindmost, if he could catch him. Sometimes it happened that he caught only his shadow, and in that case the man who had been nimble enough to do what Goethe pronounces impossible, became the most profound magician of his year. Hence our proverb of *the Devil take the hindmost*, and Chamisso's story of Peter Schlemihl.

There is no end of such stories. They were repeated and believed by the gravest and wisest men down to the end of the sixteenth century; they were received undoubtingly by the great majority down to the end of the seventeenth. The Devil was an easy way of accounting for what was beyond men's comprehension. He was the simple and satisfactory answer to all the conundrums of Nature. And what the Devil had not time to bestow his personal attention upon, the witch was always ready to do for him. Was a doctor at a loss about a case? How could he save his credit more cheaply than by pronouncing it witchcraft, and turning it over to the parson to be exorcised? Did a man's cow die suddenly, or his horse fall lame? Witchcraft! Did one of those writers of controversial quartos, heavy as the stone of Diomed, feel a pain in the small of his back? Witchcraft! Unhappily there were always ugly old women; and if you crossed them in any way, or did them a wrong, they were given to scolding and banning. If, within a year

and putting Apollo in the witness-box, as Æschylus has done. The classics, to be sure, are always so classic! In the *Eumenides*, Apollo takes the place of the good angel. And why not? For though a demon, and a lying one, he has crept in to the calendar under his other name of Helios as St. Helias. Could any of his oracles have foretold this?

or two after, anything should happen to you or yours, why, of course, old Mother Bombie or Goody Blake must be at the bottom of it. For it was perfectly well known that there were witches, (does not God's law say expressly, "Suffer not a *witch* to live?") and that they could cast a spell by the mere glance of their eyes, could cause you to pine away by melting a waxen image, could give you a pain wherever they liked by sticking pins into the same, could bring sickness into your house or into your barn by hiding a Devil's powder under the threshold; and who knows what else? Worst of all, they could send a demon into your body, who would cause you to vomit pins, hair, pebbles, knives, — indeed, almost anything short of a cathedral, — without any fault of yours, utter through you the most impertinent things *verbi ministro*, and, in short, make you the most important personage in the parish for the time being. Meanwhile, you were an object of condolence and contribution to the whole neighborhood. What wonder if a lazy apprentice or servant-maid (Bekker gives several instances of the kind detected by him) should prefer being possessed, with its attendant perquisites, to drudging from morning till night? And to any one who has observed how common a thing in certain states of mind self-connivance is, and how near it is to self-deception, it will not be surprising that some were, to all intents and purposes, really possessed. Who has never felt an almost irresistible temptation, and seemingly not self-originated, to let himself go? to let his mind gallop and kick and curvet and roll like a horse turned loose? in short, as we Yankees say, "to speak out in meeting"? Who never had it suggested to him by the fiend to break in at a funeral with a real character of the deceased, instead of that Mrs. Grundyfied view of him which the clergyman is so painfully elaborating in his prayer? Remove the pendulum of conventional routine, and the mental machinery runs on with a whir that gives a delightful excitement to sluggish temperaments, and is, perhaps, the natural relief of highly nervous organizations. The tyrant Will is dethroned, and the sceptre snatched by his frolic sister Whim. This state of things, if continued, must become either insanity or imposture. But who can say precisely where consciousness ceases and a kind of automatic movement begins, the result of over-excitement? The subjects of these strange disturbances have been almost always young women or girls at a critical period of their development. Many of the most remarkable cases have occurred in convents, and both there and elsewhere, as in other kinds of temporary nervous derangement, have proved contagious. Sometimes, as in the affair of the nuns of Loudon, there seems every reason to suspect a conspiracy; but I am not quite ready to say that Grandier was the only victim, and that some of the energumens were not unconscious tools in the hands of priestcraft and revenge. One thing is certain: that in the dioceses of humanely sceptical prelates the cases of possession were sporadic only, and either cured, or at least hindered from becoming epidemic, by episcopal mandate. Cardinal Mazarin, when Papal vice-legate at Avignon, made an end of the trade of exorcism within his government.

But scepticism, down to the beginning of the eighteenth century, was the exception. Undoubting and often fanatical belief was the rule. It is easy enough to be astonished at it, still easier to misapprehend it. How could sane men have been deceived by such nursery-tales? Still more, how could they have suffered themselves, on what seems to us such puerile evidence, to consent to such atrocious cruelties, nay, to urge them on? As to the belief, we should remember that the human mind, when it sails by *dead reckoning*, without the possibility of a fresh observation, perhaps without the instruments necessary to take one, will sometimes bring up in very strange latitudes. Do we of the nineteenth century, then, always strike out boldly into the unlandmarked deep of speculation and shape our courses by the stars, or do we not sometimes con our voyage by what seem to us the firm and familiar headlands of truth, planted by God himself, but which may, after all, be no more than an insubstantial mockery of cloud or airy juggle of mirage? The refraction of our own atmosphere has by no means made an end of its tricks with the appearances of things in our little world of thought. The men of that day believed what they saw, or, as our generation would put it, what they *thought* they saw. Very good. The vast majority of men believe, and always will believe, on the same terms. When one comes along who can partly distinguish the thing seen from that travesty or distortion of it which the thousand disturbing influences within him and without him would *make* him see, we call him a great philosopher. All our intellectual charts are engraved according to his observations, and we steer contentedly by them till some man whose brain rests on a still more unmovable basis corrects them still further by eliminating what his predecessor thought *he* saw. We must account for many former aberrations in the moral world by the presence of more or less nebulous bodies of a certain gravity which modified the actual position of truth in its relation to the mind, and which, if they have now vanished, have made way, perhaps, for others whose influence will in like manner be allowed for by posterity in their estimate of us. In matters of faith, astrology has by no means yet given place to astronomy, nor alchemy become chemistry, which knows what to seek for and how to find it. In the days of witchcraft all science was still in the condition of *May-be;* it is only just bringing itself to find a higher satisfaction in the imperturbable *Must-be* of law. We should remember that what we call *natural* may have a very different meaning for one generation from that which it has for another. The boundary between the "other" world and this ran till very lately, and at some points runs still, through a vast tract of unexplored border-land of very uncertain tenure. Even now the territory which Reason holds firmly as Lord Warden of the marches during daylight, is subject to sudden raids of Imagination by night. But physical darkness is not the only one that lends opportunity to such incursions; and in midsummer 1692, when Ebenezer Bapson, looking out of the fort at Gloucester in broad day, saw shapes of men, sometimes in blue coats like Indians, sometimes in white waistcoats like Frenchmen, it seemed *more* natural to most men that they should be spectres than men of flesh and blood. Granting the assumed premises, as nearly every one did, the syllogism was perfect.

So much for the apparent reasonableness of the belief, since every man's logic is satisfied with a legitimate deduction from his own postulates. Causes for the cruelty to which the belief led are not further to seek. Toward no crime have men shown themselves so cold-bloodedly cruel as in punishing difference of belief, and the first systematic persecutions for witchcraft began with the inquisitors in the South of France in the thirteenth century. It was then and there that the charge of sexual uncleanness with demons was first devised. Persecuted heretics would naturally meet in darkness and secret, and it was easy to blacken such meetings with the accusation of deeds so foul as to shun the light of day and the eyes of men. They met to renounce God and worship the Devil. But this was not enough. To excite popular hatred and keep it fiercely alive, fear must be mingled with it; and this end was reached by making the heretic also a sorcerer, who, by the Devil's help, could and would work all manner of fiendish mischief. When by this means the belief in a league between witch and demon had become firmly established, witchcraft grew into a well-defined crime, hateful enough in itself to furnish pastime for the torturer and food for the fagot. In the fifteenth century, witches were burned by thousands, and it may well be doubted if all paganism together was ever guilty of so many human sacrifices in the same space of time. In the sixteenth, these holocausts were appealed to as conclusive evidence of the reality of the crime, terror was again aroused, the more vindictive that its sources were so vague and intangible, and cruelty was the natural consequence. Nothing but an abject panic, in which the whole use of reason, except as a mill to grind out syllogisms, was altogether lost, will account for some chapters in Bodin's *Démonomanie.* Men were surrounded by a forever-renewed conspiracy whose ramifications they could not trace, though they might now and then lay hold on one of its associates. Protestant and Catholic might agree in nothing else, but they were unanimous in their dread of this invisible enemy. If fright could turn civilized Englishmen into savage Iroquois during the imagined negro plots of New York in 1741 and of Jamaica in 1865, if the same invisible omnipresence of Fenianism shall be able to work the same miracle, as it perhaps will, next year in England itself, why need we be astonished that the blows should have fallen upon many an innocent head when men were striking wildly in self-defence, as they supposed, against the unindictable Powers of Darkness, against a plot which could be carried on by human agents, but with invisible accessories and by supernatural means? In the seventeenth century an element was added which pretty well supplied the place of heresy as a sharpener of hatred and an awakener of indefinable suspicion. Scepticism had been born into the world, almost more hateful than heresy, because it had the manners of good society and contented itself with a smile, a shrug, an almost imperceptible lift of the eyebrow, — a kind of reasoning especially exasperating to disputants of the old school, who still cared about victory, even when they did not about the principles involved in the debate.

The Puritan emigration to New England took place at a time when the belief in diabolic agency had been hardly called in question, much less shaken. The early adventurers brought it with them to a country in every way fitted, not only to keep it alive, but to feed it into greater vigor. The solitude of the wilderness (and solitude alone, by dis-furnishing the brain of its commonplace associations, makes it an apt theatre for the delusions of imagination), the nightly forest noises, the glimpse, perhaps, through the leaves, of a painted savage face, uncertain whether of redman or Devil, but more likely of the latter, above all, that measureless mystery of the unknown and conjectural stretching away illimitable on all sides and vexing the mind, somewhat as physical darkness does, with intimation and misgiving, — under all these influences, whatever seeds of superstition had in any way got over from the Old World would find an only too congenial soil in the New. The leaders of that emigration believed and taught that demons loved to dwell in waste and wooded places, that the Indians did homage to the bodily presence of the Devil, and that he was especially enraged against those who had planted an outpost of the true faith upon this continent hitherto all his own. In the third generation of the settlement, in proportion as living faith decayed, the clergy insisted all the more strongly on the traditions of the elders, and as they all placed the sources of goodness and religion in some inaccessible Other World rather than in the soul of man himself, they clung to every shred of the supernatural as proof of the existence of that Other World, and of its interest in the affairs of this. They had the countenance of all the great theologians, Catholic as well as Protestant, of the leaders of the Reformation, and in their own day of such men as More and Glanvil and Baxter.* If to all these causes, more or less operative in 1692, we add the harassing excitement of an Indian war (urged on by Satan in his hatred of the churches), with its daily and nightly apprehensions and alarms, we shall be less astonished that the delusion in Salem Village rose so high than that it subsided so soon.

I have already said that it was religious antipathy or clerical interest that first made heresy and witchcraft identical and cast them into the same expiatory fire. The invention was a Catholic one, but it is plain that Protestants soon learned its value and were not slow in making it a plague to the inventor. It was not till after the Reformation that there was any systematic hunting out of witches in England. Then, no doubt, the inno-

* Mr. Leckie, in his admirable chapter on Witchcraft, gives a little more credit to the enlightenment of the Church of England in this matter than it would seem fairly to deserve. More and Glanvil were faithful sons of the Church; and if the persecution of witches was especially rife during the ascendency of the Puritans, it was because they happened to be in power while there was a reaction against Sadducism. All the convictions were under the statute of James I., who was no Puritan. After the restoration, the reaction was the other way, and Hobbism became the fashion. It is more philosophical to say that the age believes this and that, than that the particular men who live in it do so.

cent charms and rhyming prayers of the old religion were regarded as incantations, and twisted into evidence against miserable beldames who mumbled over in their dotage what they had learned at their mother's knee. It is plain, at least, that this was one of Agnes Simpson's crimes.

But as respects the frivolity of the proof adduced, there was nothing to choose between Catholic and Protestant. Out of civil and canon law a net was woven through whose meshes there was no escape, and into it the victims were driven by popular clamor. Suspicion of witchcraft was justified by general report, by the ill-looks of the suspected, by being silent when accused, by her mother's having been a witch, by flight, by exclaiming when arrested, *I am lost!* by a habit of using imprecations, by the evidence of two witnesses, by the accusation of a man on his death-bed, by a habit of being away from home at night, by fifty other things equally grave. Anybody might be an accuser, — a personal enemy, an infamous person, a child, parent, brother, or sister. Once accused, the culprit was not to be allowed to touch the ground on the way to prison, was not to be left alone there lest she have interviews with the Devil and get from him the means of being insensible under torture, was to be stripped and shaved in order to prevent her concealing some charm, or to facilitate the finding of witch-marks. Her right thumb tied to her left great-toe, and *vice versa*, she was thrown into the water. If she floated, she was a witch; if she sank and was drowned, she was lucky. This trial, as old as the days of Pliny the Elder, was gone out of fashion, the author of *De Lamiis* assures us, in his day, everywhere but in Westphalia. "On halfproof or strong presumption," says Bodin, the judge may proceed to torture. If the witch did not shed tears under the rack, it was almost conclusive of guilt. On this topic of torture he grows eloquent. The rack does very well, but to thrust splinters between the nails and flesh of hands and feet "is the most excellent gehenna of all, and practised in Turkey." That of Florence, where they seat the criminal in a hanging chair so contrived that if he drop asleep it overturns and leaves him hanging by a rope which wrenches his arms backwards, is perhaps even better, "for the limbs are not broken, and without trouble or labor one gets out the truth." It is well in carrying the accused to the chamber of torture to cause some in the next room to shriek fearfully as if on the rack, that they may be terrified into confession. It is proper to tell them that their accomplices have confessed and accused them ("though they have done no such thing") that they may do the same out of revenge. The judge may also with a good conscience lie to the prisoner and tell her that if she admit her guilt, she may be pardoned. This is Bodin's opinion, but Walburger, writing a century later, concludes that the judge may go to any extent *citra mendacium*, this side of lying. He may tell the witch that he will be favorable, meaning to the Commonwealth; that he will see that she has a new house built for her, that is, a wooden one to burn her in; that her confession will be most useful in saving her life, to wit, her life eternal. There seems little difference between the German's white lies and the Frenchman's black ones. As to punishment, Bodin is fierce for burning. Though a Protestant, he quotes with evident satisfaction a decision of the magistrates that one "who had eaten flesh on a Friday should be burned alive unless he repented, and if he repented, yet he was hanged out of compassion." A child under twelve who will not confess meeting with the Devil should be put to death if convicted of the fact, though Bodin allows that Satan made no express compact with those who had not arrived at puberty. This he learned from the examination of Jeanne Harvillier, who deposed, "that, though her mother dedicated her to Satan so soon as she was born, yet she was not married to him, nor did he demand that, or her renunciation of God, till she had attained the age of twelve."

There is no more painful reading than this, except the trials of the witches themselves. These awaken, by turns, pity, indignation, disgust, and dread, — dread at the thought of what the human mind may be brought to believe not only probable, but proven. But it is well to be put upon our guard by lessons of this kind, for the wisest man is in some respects little better than a madman in a strait-waistcoat of habit, public opinion, prudence, or the like. Scepticism began at length to make itself felt, but it spread slowly and was shy of proclaiming itself. The orthodox party was not backward to charge with sorcery whoever doubted their facts or pitied their victims. Bodin says that it is good cause of suspicion against a judge if he turn the matter into ridicule, or incline toward mercy. The mob, as it always is, was orthodox. It was dangerous to doubt, it might be fatal to deny. In 1453 Guillaume de Lure was burned at Poitiers on his own confession of a compact with Satan, by which he agreed "to preach and did preach that everything told of sorcerers was mere fable, and that it was cruelly done to condemn them to death." This contract was found among his papers signed "with the Devil's own claw," as Howell says speaking of a similar case. It is not to be wondered at that the earlier doubters were cautious. There was literally a reign of terror, and during such *régimes* men are commonly found more eager to be informers and accusers than of counsel for the defence. Peter of Abano is reckoned among the earliest unbelievers who declared himself openly.* Chaucer was certainly a sceptic, as appears by the opening of the Wife of Bath's Tale. Wierus, a German physician, was the first to undertake (1563) a refutation of the facts and assumptions on which the prosecutions for witchcraft were based. His explanation of the phenomena is mainly physiological. Mr. Leckie hardly states his position correctly, in saying, "that he never dreamed of restricting the sphere of the supernatural." Wierus went as far as he dared. No one can read his book without feeling that he insinuates much more than he positively affirms or denies. He would have weakened his cause if he had seemed to disbelieve in demoniacal possession, since that had the supposed warrant of Scripture; but it may be questioned whether he uses the words *Satan* and *Demon* in any other way than that in which many people still use the word *Nature*. He was forced to accept certain premises of his opponents by the line of his argument. When he recites incredible stories without comment, it is not that he believes them, but that he thinks their absurdity obvious. That he wrote under a certain restraint is plain from the Colophon of his book, where he says: "Nihil autem hic ita assertum volo, quod æquiori judicio Catholicæ Christi Ecclesiæ non omnino submittam, palinodia mox spontanea emendaturus, si erroris alicubi convincar." A great deal of latent and timid scepticism seems to have been brought to the surface by his work. Many eminent persons wrote to him in gratitude and commendation. In the Preface to his shorter treatise *De Lamiis* (which is a

* I have no means of ascertaining whether he did or not. He was more probably charged with it by the inquisitors. Mr. Leckie seems to write of him only upon hearsay, for he calls him Peter "of Apono," apparently translating a French translation of the Latin "Aponus." The only book attributed to him that I have ever seen is itself a kind of manual of magic.

mere abridgment), he thanks God that his labors had "in many places caused the cruelty against innocent blood to slacken," and that "some more distinguished judges treat more mildly and even absolve from capital punishment the wretched old women branded with the odious name of witches by the populace." In the *Pseudomonarchia Dœmonum*, he gives a kind of census of the diabolic kingdom,* but evidently with secret intention of making the whole thing ridiculous, or it would not have so stirred the bile of Bodin. Wierus was saluted by many contemporaries as a Hercules who destroyed monsters, and himself not immodestly claimed the civic wreath for having saved the lives of fellow-citizens. Posterity should not forget a man who really did an honest life's work for humanity and the liberation of thought. From one of the letters appended to his book we learn that Jacobus Savagius, a physician of Antwerp, had twenty years before written a treatise with the same design, but confining himself to the medical argument exclusively. He was, however, prevented from publishing it by death. It is pleasant to learn from Bodin that Alciato, the famous lawyer and emblematist, was one of those who "laughed and made others laugh at the evidence relied on at the trials, insisting that witchcraft was a thing impossible and fabulous, and so softened the hearts of judges (in spite of the fact that an inquisitor had caused to burn more than a hundred sorcerers in Piedmont), that all the accused escaped." In England, Reginald Scot was the first to enter the lists in behalf of those who had no champion. His book, published in 1584, is full of manly sense and spirit, above all, of a tender humanity that gives it a warmth which we miss in every other written on the same side. In the dedica-

* "With the names and surnames," says Bodin, indignantly, "of seventy-two princes, and of seven million four hundred and five thousand nine hundred and twenty-six devils, *errors excepted.*"

tion to Sir Roger Manwood he says: "I renounce all protection and despise all friendship that might serve towards the suppressing or supplanting of truth." To his kinsman, Sir Thomas Scot, he writes: "My greatest adversaries are *young ignorance* and *old custom;* for what folly soever tract of time hath fostered, it is so superstitiously pursued of some, as though no error could be acquainted with custom." And in his Preface he thus states his motives: "God that knoweth my heart is witness, and you that read my book shall see, that my drift and purpose in this enterprise tendeth only to these respects. First, that the glory and power of God be not so abridged and abased as to be thrust into the hand or lip of a lewd old woman, whereby the work of the Creator should be attributed to the power of a creature. Secondly, that the religion of the Gospel may be seen to stand without such peevish trumpery. Thirdly, that lawful favor and Christian compassion be rather used towards these poor souls than rigor and extremity. Because they which are commonly accused of witchcraft are the least sufficient of all other persons to speak for themselves, as having the most base and simple education of all others, the extremity of their age giving them leave to dote, their poverty to beg, their wrongs to chide and threaten (as being void of any other way of revenge), their humor melancholical to be full of imaginations, from whence chiefly proceedeth the vanity of their confessions. . . . . And for so much as the mighty help themselves together, and the poor widow's cry, though it reach to Heaven, is scarce heard here upon earth, I thought good (according to my poor ability) to make intercession that some part of common rigor and some points of hasty judgment may be advised upon." . . . . The case is nowhere put with more point, or urged with more sense and eloquence, than by Scot, whose book contains also more curious matter, in the way of charms, incantations, exorcisms, and feats of legerdemain, than any other of the kind.

Other books followed on the same side, of which Bekker's, published about a century later, was the most important. It is well reasoned, learned, and tedious to a masterly degree. But though the belief in witchcraft might be shaken, it still had the advantage of being on the whole orthodox and respectable. Wise men, as usual, insisted on regarding superstition as of one substance with faith, and objected to any scouring of the shield of religion, lest, like that of Cornelius Scriblerus, it should suddenly turn out to be nothing more than "a paltry old sconce with the nozzle broke off." The Devil continued to be the only recognized Minister Resident of God upon earth. When we remember that one man's accusation on his death-bed was enough to constitute grave presumption of witchcraft, it might seem singular that dying testimonies were so long of no avail against the common credulity. But it should be remembered that men are mentally no less than corporeally gregarious, and that public opinion, the fetish even of the nineteenth century, makes men, whether for good or ill, into a mob, which either hurries the individual judgment along with it, or runs over and tramples it into insensibility. Those who are so fortunate as to occupy the philosophical position of spectators *ab extra* are very few in any generation.

There were exceptions, it is true, but the old cruelties went on. In 1610 a case came before the tribunal of the *Tourelle*, and when the counsel for the accused argued at some length that sorcery was ineffectual, and that the Devil could not destroy life, President Séguier told him that he might spare his breath, since the court had long been convinced on those points. And yet two years later the grand-vicars of the Bishop of Beauvais solemnly summoned Beelzebuth, Satan, Motelu, and Briffaut, with the four legions under their charge, to appear and sign an agreement never again to enter the bodies of reasonable or other creatures, under pain of excommunication! If they refused, they were to be given over to "the power of hell to be tormented and tortured more than was customary, three thousand years after the judgment." Under this proclamation they all came in, like reconstructed rebels, and signed whatever document was put before them. Toward the middle of the seventeenth century, the safe thing was still to believe, or at any rate to profess belief. Sir Thomas Browne, though he had written an exposure of "Vulgar Errors," testified in court to his faith in the possibility of witchcraft. Sir Kenelm Digby, in his "Observations on the Religio Medici," takes, perhaps, as advanced ground as any, when he says: "Neither do I deny there are witches; I only reserve my assent till I meet with stronger motives to carry it." The position of even enlightened men of the world in that age might be called semi-sceptical. La Bruyère, no doubt, expresses the average of opinion: "Que penser de la magie et du sortilége? La théorie en est obscurcie, les principes vagues, incertains, et qui approchent du visionnaire; mais il y a des faits embarrassants, affirmés par des hommes graves qui les ont vus; les admettre tous, ou les nier tous, paraît un égal inconvénient, et j'ose dire qu'en cela comme en toutes les choses extraordinaires et qui sortent des communes règles, il y a un parti à trouver entre les âmes crédules et les esprits forts." * Montaigne, to be sure, had long before declared his entire disbelief, and yet the Parliament of Bourdeaux, his own city, condemned a man to be burned

* Cited by Maury, p. 221, note 4.

as a *noüeur d'aiguillettes* so lately as 1718. Indeed, it was not, says Maury, till the first quarter of the eighteenth century that one might safely publish his incredulity in France. In Scotland, witches were burned for the last time in 1722. Garinet cites the case of a girl near Amiens possessed by three demons, — Mimi, Zozo, and Crapoulet, — in 1816.

The two beautiful volumes of Mr. Upham are, so far as I know, unique in their kind. It is, in some respects, a clinical lecture on human nature, as well as on the special epidemical disease under which the patient is laboring. He has written not merely a history of the so-called Salem Witchcraft, but has made it intelligible by a minute account of the place where the delusion took its rise, the persons concerned in it, whether as actors or sufferers, and the circumstances which led to it. By deeds, wills, and the records of courts and churches, by plans, maps, and drawings, he has recreated Salem Village as it was two hundred years ago, so that we seem wellnigh to talk with its people and walk over its fields, or through its cart-tracks and bridle-roads. We are made partners in parish and village feuds, we share in the chimney-corner gossip, and learn for the first time how many mean and merely human motives, whether consciously or unconsciously, gave impulse and intensity to the passions of the actors in that memorable tragedy which dealt the death-blow in this country to the belief in Satanic compacts. Mr. Upham's minute details, which give us something like a photographic picture of the in-door and out-door scenery that surrounded the events he narrates, help us materially to understand their origin and the course they inevitably took. In this respect his book is original and full of new interest. To know the kind of life these people led, the kind of place they dwelt in, and the tenor of their thought, makes much real to us that was conjectural before. The influences of outward nature, of remoteness from the main highways of the world's thought, of seclusion, as the foster-mother of traditionary beliefs, of a hard life and unwholesome diet in exciting or obscuring the brain through the nerves and stomach, have been hitherto commonly overlooked in accounting for the phenomena of witchcraft. The great persecutions for this imaginary crime have always taken place in lonely places, among the poor, the ignorant, and, above all, the ill-fed.

One of the best things in Mr. Upham's book is the portrait of Parris, the minister of Salem Village, in whose household the children who, under the assumed possession of evil spirits, became accusers and witnesses, began their tricks. He is shown to us pedantic and something of a martinet in church discipline and ceremony, somewhat inclined to magnify his office, fond of controversy as he was skilful and rather unscrupulous in the conduct of it, and glad of any occasion to make himself prominent. Was he the unconscious agent of his own superstition, or did he take advantage of the superstition of others for purposes of his own? The question is not an easy one to answer. Men will sacrifice everything, sometimes even themselves, to their pride of logic and their love of victory. Bodin loses sight of humanity altogether in his eagerness to make out his case, and display his learning in the canon and civil law. He does not scruple to exaggerate, to misquote, to charge his antagonists with atheism, sorcery, and insidious designs against religion and society, that he may persuade the jury of Europe to bring in a verdict of guilty.* Yet there is no reason to doubt

* There is a kind of compensation in the fact that he himself lived to be accused of sorcery and Judaism.

the sincerity of his belief. Was Parris equally sincere? On the whole, I think it likely that he was. But if we acquit Parris, what shall we say of the demoniacal girls? The probability seems to be that those who began in harmless deceit found themselves at length involved so deeply, that dread of shame and punishment drove them to an extremity where their only choice was between sacrificing themselves, or others to save themselves. It is not unlikely that some of the younger girls were so far carried along by imitation or imaginative sympathy as in some degree to "credit their own lie." Any one who has watched or made experiments in animal magnetism knows how easy it is to persuade young women of nervous temperaments that they are doing that by the will of another which they really do by an obscure volition of their own, under the influence of an imagination adroitly guided by the magnetizer. The marvellous is so fascinating, that nine persons in ten, if once persuaded that a thing is possible, are eager to believe it probable, and at last cunning in convincing themselves that it is proven. But it is impossible to believe that the possessed girls in this case did not know how the pins they vomited got into their mouths. Mr. Upham has shown, in the case of Anne Putnam, Jr., an hereditary tendency to hallucination, if not insanity. One of her uncles had seen the Devil by broad daylight in the novel disguise of a blue boar, in which shape, as a tavern sign, he had doubtless proved more seductive than in his more ordinary transfigurations. A great deal of light is let in upon the question of whether there was deliberate imposture or no, by the narrative of Rev. Mr. Turell of Medford, written in 1728, which gives us all the particulars of a case of pretended possession in Littleton, eight years before. The eldest of three sisters began the game, and found herself before long obliged to take the next in age into her confidence. By and by the youngest, finding her sisters pitied and caressed on account of their supposed sufferings while she was neglected, began to play off the same tricks. The usual phenomena followed. They were convulsed, they fell into swoons, they were pinched and bruised, they were found in the water, on the top of a tree or of the barn. To these places they said they were conveyed through the air, and there were those who had seen them flying, which shows how strong is the impulse which prompts men to conspire with their own delusion, where the marvellous is concerned. The girls did whatever they had heard or read that was common in such cases. They even accused a respectable neighbor as the cause of their torments. There were some doubters, but "so far as I can learn," says Turell, "the greater number believed and said they were under the evil hand, or possessed by Satan." But the most interesting fact of all is supplied by the confession of the elder sister, made eight years later under stress of remorse. Having once begun, they found returning more tedious than going o'er. To keep up their cheat made life a burden to them, but they could not stop. Thirty years earlier, their juggling might have proved as disastrous as that at Salem Village. There, parish and boundary feuds had set enmity between neighbors, and the girls, called on to say who troubled them, cried out upon those whom they had been wont to hear called by hard names at home. They probably had no notion what a frightful ending their comedy was to have; but at any rate they were powerless, for the reins had passed out of their hands into the sterner grasp of minister and magistrate. They were dragged deeper and deeper, as men always are by their own lie.

The proceedings at the Salem trials are sometimes spoken of as if they were exceptionally cruel. But, in fact, if compared with others of the same kind, they were exceptionally humane. At a time when Baxter could tell with satisfaction of a "*reading* parson" eighty years old, who, after being kept awake five days and nights, confessed his dealings with the Devil, it is rather wonderful that no mode of torture other than mental was tried at Salem. Nor were the magistrates more besotted or unfair than usual in dealing with the evidence. Now and then, it is true, a man more sceptical or intelligent than common had exposed some pretended demoniac. The Bishop of Orléans, in 1598, read aloud to Martha Brossier the story of the Ephesian Widow, and the girl, hearing Latin, and taking it for Scripture, went forthwith into convulsions. He found also that the Devil who possessed her could not distinguish holy from profane water. But that there were deceptions did not shake the general belief in the reality of possession. The proof in such cases could not and ought not to be subjected to the ordinary tests. "If many natural things," says Bodin, "are incredible and some of them incomprehensible, *a fortiori* the power of supernatural intelligences and the doings of spirits are incomprehensible. But error has risen to its height in this, that those who have denied the power of spirits and the doings of sorcerers have wished to dispute physically concerning supernatural or metaphysical things, which is a notable incongruity." That the girls were really possessed, seemed to Stoughton and his colleägues the most rational theory, — a theory in harmony with the rest of their creed, and sustained by the unanimous consent of pious men as well as the evidence of that most cunning and least suspected of all sorcerers, the Past, — and how confront or cross-examine invisible witnesses, especially witnesses whom it was a kind of impiety to doubt? Evidence that would have been convincing in ordinary cases was of no weight against the general prepossession. In 1659 the house of a man in Brightling, Sussex, was troubled by a demon, who set it on fire at various times, and was continually throwing things about. The clergy of the neighborhood held a day of fasting and prayer in consequence. A maid-servant was afterwards detected as the cause of the missiles. But this did not in the least stagger Mr. Bennet, minister of the parish, who merely says: "There was a *seeming blur* cast, though not on the whole, yet upon some part of it, for their servant-girl was at last found throwing some things," and goes off into a eulogium on the "efficacy of prayer."

In one respect, to which Mr. Upham first gives the importance it deserves, the Salem trials were distinguished from all others. Though some of the accused had been terrified into confession, yet not one persevered in it, but all died protesting their innocence, and with unshaken constancy, though an acknowledgment of guilt would have saved the lives of all. This martyr proof of the efficacy of Puritanism in the character and conscience may be allowed to outweigh a great many sneers at Puritan fanaticism. It is at least a testimony to the courage and constancy which a profound religious sentiment had made common among the people of whom these sufferers were average representatives. The accused also were not, as was commonly the case, abandoned by their friends. In all the trials of this kind there is nothing so pathetic as the picture of Jonathan Cary holding up the weary arms of his wife during her trial, and wiping away the sweat from her brow and the tears from her face. Another remarkable fact is this, that while in other countries the delusion was extinguished by the incredulity of the upper classes and the interference of authority, here the reaction took place among the people themselves, and here only was an attempt made at some legislative restitution, however inadequate. Mr. Upham's sincere and honest narrative, while it never condescends to a formal plea, is the best vindication possible of a community which was itself the greatest sufferer by the persecution which its credulity engendered.

If any lesson may be drawn from the tragical and too often disgustful history of witchcraft, it is not one of exultation at our superior enlightenment or shame at the shortcomings of the human intellect. It is rather one of charity and self-distrust. When we see what inhuman absurdities men in other respects wise and good have clung to as the corner-stone of their faith in immortality and a divine ordering of the world, may we not suspect that those who now maintain political or other doctrines which seem to us barbarous and unenlightened, may be, for all that, in the main as virtuous and clear-sighted as ourselves? While we maintain our own side with an honest ardor of conviction, let us not forget to allow for mortal incompetence in the other. And if there are men who regret the Good Old Times, without too clear a notion of what they were, they should at least be thankful that we are rid of that misguided energy of faith which justified conscience in making men unrelentingly cruel. Even Mr. Leckie softens a little at the thought of the many innocent and beautiful beliefs of which a growing scepticism has robbed us in the decay of supernaturalism. But we need not despair; for, after all, scepticism is first cousin of credulity, and we are not surprised to see the tough doubter Montaigne hanging up his offerings in the shrine of our Lady of Loreto. Scepticism commonly takes up the room left by defect of imagination, and is the very quality of mind most likely to seek for sensual proof of supersensual things. If one came from the dead, it could not believe; and yet it longs for such a witness, and will put up with a very dubious one. So long as night is left and the helplessness of dream, the wonderful will not cease from among men. While we are the solitary prisoners of darkness, the witch seats herself at the loom of thought, and weaves strange figures into the web that looks so familiar and ordinary in the dry light of every-day. Just as we are flattering ourselves that the old spirit of sorcery is laid, behold the tables are tipping and the floors drumming all over Christendom. The faculty of wonder is not defunct, but is only getting more and more emancipated from the unnatural service of terror, and restored to its proper function as a minister of delight. A higher mode of belief is the best exorciser, because it makes the spiritual at one with the actual world instead of hostile, or at best alien. It has been the grossly material interpretations of spiritual doctrine that have given occasion to the two extremes of superstition and unbelief. While the resurrection of the body has been insisted on, that resurrection from the body which is the privilege of all has been forgotten. Superstition in its baneful form was largely due to the enforcement by the Church of arguments that involved a *petitio principii*, for it is the miserable necessity of all false logic to accept of very ignoble allies. Fear became at length its chief expedient for the maintenance of its power; and as there is a beneficent necessity laid upon a majority of mankind to sustain and perpetuate the order of things they are born into, and to make all new ideas manfully prove their right, first, to be at all, and then to be heard, many even superior minds dreaded the tearing away of vicious accretions as dangerous to the whole edifice of religion and society. But if this old ghost be fading away in what we regard as the dawn of a better day, we may console ourselves by thinking that perhaps, after all, we are not so *much* wiser than our ancestors. The rappings, the trance mediums, the visions of hands without bodies, the sounding of musical instruments without visible fingers, the miraculous inscriptions on the naked flesh, the enlivenment of furniture, — we have invented none of them, they are all heirlooms. There is surely room for yet another schoolmaster, when a score of seers advertise themselves in Boston newspapers. And if the metaphysicians can never rest till they have taken their watch to pieces and have arrived at a happy positivism as to its structure, though at the risk of bringing it to a no-go, we may be sure that the majority will always take more satisfaction in seeing its hands mysteriously move on, even if they should err a little as to the precise time of day established by the astronomical observatories.

SHAKESPEARE ONCE MORE.

It may be doubted whether any language be rich enough to maintain more than one truly great poet, — and whether there be more than one period, and that very short, in the life of a language, when such a phenomenon as a great poet is possible. It may be reckoned one of the rarest pieces of good-luck that ever fell to the share of a race, that (as was true of Shakespeare) its most rhythmic genius, its acutest intellect, its profoundest imagination, and its healthiest understanding should have been combined in one man, and that he should have arrived at the full development of his powers at the moment when the material in which he was to work — that wonderful composite called English, the best result of the confusion of tongues — was in its freshest perfection. The English-speaking nations should build a monument to the misguided enthusiasts of the Plain of Shinar; for, as the mixture of many bloods seems to have made them the most vigorous of modern races, so has the mingling of divers speeches given them a language which is perhaps the noblest vehicle of poetic thought that ever existed.

Had Shakespeare been born fifty years earlier, he would have been cramped by a book-language not yet flexible enough for the demands of rhythmic emotion, not yet sufficiently popularized for the natural and familiar expression of supreme thought, not yet so rich in metaphysical phrase as to render possible that ideal representation of the great passions which is the aim and end of Art, not yet subdued by practice and general consent to a definiteness of accentuation essential to ease and congruity of metrical arrangement. Had he been born fifty years later, his ripened manhood would have found itself in an England absorbed and angry with the solution of political and religious problems, from which his whole nature was averse, instead of in that Elizabethan social system, ordered and planetary in functions and degrees as the angelic hierarchy of the Areopagite, where his contemplative eye could crowd itself with various and brilliant picture, and whence his impartial brain — one lobe of which seems to have been Normanly refined and the other Saxonly sagacious — could draw its morals of courtly and worldly wisdom, its lessons of prudence and magnanimity. In estimating Shakespeare, it should never be forgotten, that, like Goethe, he was essentially observer and artist, and incapable of partisanship. The passions, actions, sentiments, whose character and results he delighted to watch and to reproduce, are those of man in society as it existed; and it no more occurred to him to question the right of that society to exist than to criticise the divine ordination of the seasons. His business was with men as they were, not with man as he ought to be, — with the human soul as it is shaped or twisted into character by the complex experience of life, not in its abstract essence, as something to be saved or lost. During the first half of the seventeenth century, the centre of intellectual interest was rather in the other world than in this, rather in the region of thought and principle and conscience than in actual life. It was a generation in which the poet was, and felt himself, out of place. Sir Thomas Browne, our most imaginative mind since Shakespeare, found breathing-room, for a time, among the "*O altitudines!*" of religious speculation, but soon descended to occupy himself with the exactitudes of science. Jeremy Taylor, who half a century earlier would have been Fletcher's rival, compels his clipped fancy to the conventual discipline of prose, (Maid Marian turned nun,) and waters his poetic wine with doctrinal eloquence. Milton is saved from making total shipwreck of his large-utteranced genius on the desolate Noman's Land of a religious epic only by the lucky help of Satan and his colleagues, with whom, as foiled rebels and republicans, he cannot conceal his sympathy. As purely poet, Shakespeare would have come too late, had his lot fallen in that generation. In mind and temperament too exoteric for a mystic, his imagination could not have at once illustrated the influence of his epoch and escaped from it, like that of Browne; the equilibrium of his judgment, essential to him as an artist, but equally removed from propagandism, whether as enthusiast or logician, would have unfitted him for the pulpit; and his intellectual being was too sensitive to the wonder and beauty of outward life and Nature to have found satisfaction, as Milton's could, (and perhaps only by reason of his blindness,) in a world peopled by purely imaginary figures. We might fancy him becoming a great statesman, but he lacked the social position which could have opened that career to him. What we mean when we say *Shakespeare*, is something inconceivable either during the reign of Henry the Eighth, or the Commonwealth, and which would have been impossible after the Restoration.

All favorable stars seem to have been in conjunction at his nativity. The Reformation had passed the period of its vinous fermentation, and its clarified results remained as an element of intellectual impulse and exhilaration; there were small signs yet of the acetous and putrefactive stages which were to follow in the victory and decline of Puritanism. Old forms of belief and worship still lingered, all the more touching to Fancy, perhaps, that they were homeless and attainted; the light of sceptic day was baffled by depths of forest where superstitious shapes still cowered, creatures of immemorial wonder, the raw material of Imagination. The invention of printing, without yet vulgarizing letters, had made the thought and history of the entire past contemporaneous; while a crowd of translators put every man who could read in inspiring contact with the select souls of all the centuries. A new world was thus opened to intellectual adventure at the very time when the keel of Columbus had turned the first daring furrow of discovery in that unmeasured ocean which still girt the known earth with a beckoning horizon of hope and conjecture, which was still fed by rivers that flowed down out of primeval silences, and which still washed the shores of Dreamland. Under a wise, cultivated, and firm-handed monarch also, the national feeling of England grew rapidly more homogeneous and intense, the rather as the womanhood of the sovereign stimulated a more chivalric loyalty, — while the new religion, of which she was the defender, helped to make England morally, as it was geographically, insular to the continent of Europe.

If circumstances could ever make a great national poet, here were all the elements mingled at melting-heat in the alembic, and the lucky moment of projection was clearly come. If a great national poet could ever avail himself of circumstances, this was the occasion, — and, fortunately, Shakespeare was equal to it. Above all, we may esteem it lucky that he found words ready to his use, original and untarnished, — types of thought whose sharp edges were unworn by repeated impressions. In reading Hakluyt's Voyages, we are almost startled now and then to find that even common sailors could not tell the story of their wanderings without rising to an almost Odyssean strain, and habitually used a diction that we should be glad to buy back from desuetude at any cost. Those who look upon language only as anatomists of its structure, or who regard it as only a means of conveying abstract truth from mind to mind, as if it were so many algebraic formulæ, are apt to overlook the fact that its being alive is all that gives it poetic value. We do not mean what is technically called a living language, — the contrivance, hollow as a speaking-trumpet, by which breathing and moving bipeds, even now, sailing o'er life's solemn main, are enabled to hail each other and make known their mutual shortness of mental stores, — but one that is still hot from the hearts and brains of a people, not hardened yet, but moltenly ductile to new shapes of sharp and clear relief in the moulds of new thought. So soon as a language has become literary, so soon as there is a gap between the speech of books and that of life, the language becomes, so far as poetry is concerned, almost as dead as Latin, and (as in writing Latin verses) a mind in itself essentially original becomes in the use of such a medium of utterance unconsciously reminiscential and reflective, lunar and not solar, in expression and even in thought. For words and thoughts have a much more intimate and genetic relation, one with the other, than most men have any notion of; and it is one thing to use our mother-tongue as if it belonged to us, and another to be the puppets of an overmastering vocabulary. "Ye know not," says Ascham, "what hurt ye do to Learning, that care not for Words, but for Matter, and so make a Divorce betwixt the Tongue and the Heart." *Lingua Toscana in bocca Romana* is the Italian proverb; and that of poets should be, *The tongue of the people in the mouth of the scholar.* I imply here no assent to the early theory, or, at any rate, practice, of Wordsworth, who confounded plebeian modes of thought with rustic forms of phrase, and then atoned for his blunder by absconding into a diction more Latinized than that of any poet of his century.

Shakespeare was doubly fortunate. Saxon by the father and Norman by the mother, he was a representative Englishman. A country boy, he learned first the rough and ready English of his rustic mates, who knew how to make nice verbs and adjectives courtesy to their needs. Going up to London, he acquired the *lingua aulica* precisely at the happiest moment, just as it was becoming, in the strictest sense of the word, *modern*,—just as it had recruited itself, by fresh impressments from the Latin and Latinized languages, with new words to express the new ideas of an enlarging intelligence which printing and translation were fast making cosmopolitan, —words which, in proportion to their novelty, and to the fact that the mother-tongue and the foreign had not yet wholly mingled, must have been used with a more exact appreciation of their meaning.* It was in London, and chiefly by means of the stage, that a thorough amalgamation of the Saxon, Norman, and scholarly elements of English was brought about. Already, Puttenham, in his "Arte of English Poesy," declares that the practice of the capital and the country within sixty miles of it was the standard of correct diction, the *jus et norma loquendi.* Already Spenser had almost re-created English poetry,—and it is interesting to observe, that, scholar as he was, the archaic words which he was at first over-fond of introducing are often provincialisms of purely English original. Already Marlowe had brought the

* As where Ben Jonson is able to say,—

"Men may securely sin, but safely never."

English unrhymed pentameter (which had hitherto justified but half its name, by being always blank and never verse) to a perfection of melody, harmony, and variety which has never been surpassed. Shakespeare, then, found a language already to a certain extent *established*, but not yet fetlocked by dictionary and grammar mongers, — a versification harmonized, but which had not yet exhausted all its modulations, nor been set in the stocks by critics who deal judgment on refractory feet, that will dance to Orphean measures of which their judges are insensible. That the language was established is proved by its comparative uniformity as used by the dramatists, who wrote for mixed audiences, as well as by Ben Jonson's satire upon Marston's neologisms; that it at the same time admitted foreign words to the rights of citizenship on easier terms than now is in good measure equally true. What was of greater import, no arbitrary line had been drawn between high words and low; vulgar then meant simply what was common; poetry had not been aliened from the people by the establishment of an Upper House of vocables, alone entitled to move in the stately ceremonials of verse, and privileged from arrest while they forever keep the promise of meaning to the ear and break it to the sense. The hot conception of the poet had no time to cool while he was debating the comparative respectability of this phrase or that; but he snatched what word his instinct prompted, and saw no indiscretion in making a king speak as his country nurse might have taught him.* It was Waller who first learned in France that to talk in rhyme alone comported with the state of roy-

* "Vulgarem locutionem appellamus eam qua infantes adsuefiunt ab adsistentibus cum primitus distinguere voces incipiunt: vel, quod brevius dici potest, vulgarem locutionem asserimus *quam sine omni regula, nutricem imitantes, accepimus.* Dantes, *de Vulg. Eloquio*, Lib. I. cap. i.

alty. In the time of Shakespeare, the living tongue resembled that tree which Father Huc saw in Tartary, whose leaves were languaged, — and every hidden root of thought, every subtilest fibre of feeling, was mated by new shoots and leafage of expression, fed from those unseen sources in the common earth of human nature.

The Cabalists had a notion, that whoever found out the mystic word for anything attained to absolute mastery over that thing. The reverse of this is certainly true of poetic expression; for he who is thoroughly possessed of his thought, who imaginatively conceives an idea or image, becomes master of the word that shall most amply and fitly utter it. Heminge and Condell tell us, accordingly, that there was scarce a blot in the manuscripts they received from Shakespeare; and this is the natural corollary from the fact that such an imagination as his is as unparalleled as the force, variety, and beauty of the phrase in which it embodied itself.* We believe that Shakespeare, like all other great poets, instinctively used the dialect which he found current, and that his words are not more wrested from their ordinary meaning than followed necessarily from the unwonted weight of thought or stress of passion they were called on to

* Gray, himself a painful corrector, told Nicholls that "nothing was done so well as at the first concoction," — adding, as a reason, "We think in words." Ben Jonson said, it was a pity Shakespeare had not blotted more, for that he sometimes wrote nonsense, — and cited in proof of it the verse,

"Cæsar did never wrong but with just cause."

The last four words do not appear in the passage as it now stands, and Professor Craik suggests that they were stricken out in consequence of Jonson's criticism. This is very probable; but we suspect that the pen that blotted them was in the hand of Master Heminge or his colleague. The moral confusion in the idea was surely admirably characteristic of the general who had just accomplished a successful *coup d'état*, the condemnation of which he would fancy that he read in the face of every honest man he met, and which he would therefore be forever indirectly palliating.

support. He needed not to mask familiar thoughts in the weeds of unfamiliar phraseology; for the life that was in his mind could transfuse the language of every day with an intelligent vivacity, that makes it seem lambent with fiery purpose, and at each new reading a new creation. He could say with Dante, that "no word had ever forced him to say what he would not, though he had forced many a word to say what *it* would not," — but only in the sense that the mighty magic of his imagination had conjured out of it its uttermost secret of power or pathos. When I say that Shakespeare used the current language of his day, I mean only that he habitually employed such language as was universally comprehensible, — that he was not run away with by the hobby of any theory as to the fitness of this or that component of English for expressing certain thoughts or feelings. That the artistic value of a choice and noble diction was quite as well understood in his day as in ours is evident from the praises bestowed by his contemporaries on Drayton, and by the epithet "well-languaged" applied to Daniel, whose poetic style is as modern as that of Tennyson; but the endless absurdities about the comparative merits of Saxon and Norman-French, vented by persons incapable of distinguishing one tongue from the other, were as yet unheard of. Hasty generalizers are apt to overlook the fact, that the Saxon was never, to any great extent, a literary language. Accordingly, it held its own very well in the names of common things, but failed to answer the demands of complex ideas, derived from them. The author of "Piers Ploughman" wrote for the people, — Chaucer for the court. We open at random and count the Latin * words in ten verses of the "Vision" and ten of the "Romaunt

* We use the word *Latin* here to express words derived either mediately or immediately from that language.

of the Rose," (a translation from the French,) and find the proportion to be seven in the former and five in the latter.

The organs of the Saxon have always been unwilling and stiff in learning languages. He acquired only about as many British words as we have Indian ones, and I believe that more French and Latin was introduced through the pen and the eye than through the tongue and the ear. For obvious reasons, the question is one that must be decided by reference to prose-writers, and not poets; and it is, we think, pretty well settled that more words of Latin original were brought into the language in the century between 1550 and 1650 than in the whole period before or since, — and for the simple reason, that they were absolutely needful to express new modes and combinations of thought.* The language has gained immensely, by the infusion, in richness of synonyme and in the power of expressing nice shades of thought and feeling, but more than all in light-footed polysyllables that trip singing to the music of verse. There are certain cases, it is true, where the vulgar Saxon word is refined, and the refined Latin vulgar, in poetry, — as in *sweat* and *perspiration;* but there are vastly more in which the Latin bears the bell. Perhaps there might be a question between the old English *again-rising* and *resurrection;* but there can be no doubt that *conscience* is better than *inwit*, and *remorse* than *again-bite*. Should we translate the title of Wordsworth's famous ode, "Intimations of Immortality," into "Hints

* The prose of Chaucer (1390) and of Sir Thomas Malory (translating from the French, 1470) is less Latinized than that of Bacon, Browne, Taylor, or Milton. The glossary to Spenser's *Shepherd's Calendar* (1579) explains words of Teutonic and Romanic root in about equal proportions. The parallel but independent development of Scotch is not to be forgotten.

of Deathlessness," it would hiss like an angry gander. If, instead of Shakespeare's

> "Age cannot wither her,
> Nor custom stale her infinite variety,"

we should say, "her boundless manifoldness," the sentiment would suffer in exact proportion with the music. What homebred English could ape the high Roman fashion of such togated words as

> "The multitudinous sea incarnadine,"—

where the huddling epithet implies the tempest-tossed soul of the speaker, and at the same time pictures the wallowing waste of ocean more vividly than the famous phrase of Æschylus does its rippling sunshine? Again, *sailor* is less poetical than *mariner*, as Campbell felt, when he wrote,

> "Ye mariners of England,"

and Coleridge, when he chose

> "It was an ancient mariner,"

rather than

> "It was an elderly seaman";

for it is as much the charm of poetry that it suggest a certain remoteness and strangeness as familiarity; and it is essential not only that we feel at once the meaning of the words in themselves, but also their melodic meaning in relation to each other, and to the sympathetic variety of the verse. A word once vulgarized can never be rehabilitated. We might say now a *buxom* lass, or that a chambermaid was *buxom*, but we could not use the term, as Milton did, in its original sense of *bowsome*, — that is, *lithe, gracefully bending*.*

* I believe that for the last two centuries the Latin radicals of English have been more familiar and homelike to those who use them than the Teutonic. Even so accomplished a person as Professor Craik,

But the secret of force in writing lies not so much in the pedigree of nouns and adjectives and verbs, as in having something that you believe in to say, and making the parts of speech vividly conscious of it. It is when expression becomes an act of memory, instead of an unconscious necessity, that diction takes the place of warm and hearty speech. It is not safe to attribute special virtues (as Bosworth, for example, does to the Saxon) to words of whatever derivation, at least in poetry. Because Lear's "oak-cleaving thunderbolts," and "the all-dreaded thunder-stone" in "Cymbeline" are so fine, we would not give up Milton's Virgilian "fulmined over Greece," where the verb in English conveys at once the idea of flash and reverberation, but avoids that of riving and shattering. In the experiments made for casting the great bell for the Westminster Tower, it was found that the superstition which attrib-

in his *English of Shakespeare*, derives *head*, through the German *haupt*, from the Latin *caput!* I trust that its genealogy is nobler, and that it is of kin with *cœlum tueri*, rather than with the Greek κεφαλὴ, if Suidas be right in tracing the origin of that to a word meaning *vacuity*. Mr. Craik suggests, also, that *quick* and *wicked* may be etymologically identical, *because* he fancies a relationship between *busy* and the German *böse*, though *wicked* is evidently the participial form of A. S. *wacan*, (German *weichen*,) *to bend*, *to yield*, meaning *one who has given way to temptation*, while *quick* seems as clearly related to *wegan*, meaning *to move*, a different word, even if radically the same. In the "London Literary Gazette" for November 13, 1858, I find an extract from Miss Millington's "Heraldry in History, Poetry, and Romance," in which, speaking of the motto of the Prince of Wales, — *De par Houmout ich diene*, — she says: "The precise meaning of the former word [*Houmout*] has not, I think, been ascertained." The word is plainly the German *Hochmuth*, and the whole would read, *De par* (*Aus*) *Hochmuth ich diene*, — "Out of magnanimity I serve." So entirely lost is the Saxon meaning of the word *knave*, (A. S. *cnava*, German *knabe*,) that the name *navvie*, assumed by railway-laborers, has been transmogrified into *navigator*. I believe that more people could tell why the month of July was so called than could explain the origin of the names for our days of the week, and that it is oftener the Saxon than the French words in Chaucer that puzzle the modern reader.

uted the remarkable sweetness and purity of tone in certain old bells to the larger mixture of silver in their composition had no foundation in fact. It was the cunning proportion in which the ordinary metals were balanced against each other, the perfection of form, and the nice gradations of thickness, that wrought the miracle. And it is precisely so with the language of poetry. The genius of the poet will tell him what word to use (else what use in his being poet at all?); and even then, unless the proportion and form, whether of parts or whole, be all that Art requires and the most sensitive taste finds satisfaction in, he will have failed to make what shall vibrate through all its parts with a silvery unison, — in other words, a poem.

I think the component parts of English were in the latter years of Elizabeth thus exquisitely proportioned one to the other. Yet Bacon had no faith in his mother-tongue, translating the works on which his fame was to rest into what he called "the universal language," and affirming that "English would bankrupt all our books." He was deemed a master of it, nevertheless; and it is curious that Ben Jonson applies to him in prose the same commendation which he gave Shakespeare in verse, saying, that he "performed that in our tongue which may be compared or preferred either to *insolent Greece or haughty Rome*"; and he adds this pregnant sentence: "In short, within his view and about his time were all the wits born that could honor a language or help study. Now things daily fall: wits grow downwards, eloquence grows backwards." Ben had good reason for what he said of the wits. Not to speak of science, of Galileo and Kepler, the sixteenth century was a spendthrift of literary genius. An attack of immortality in a family might have been looked for then as scarlet-fever would be now. Montaigne, Tasso, and Cervantes were born within fourteen years of each other; and in England, while Spenser was still delving over the *propria quæ maribus,* and Raleigh launching paper navies, Shakespeare was stretching his baby hands for the moon, and the little Bacon, chewing on his coral, had discovered that impenetrability was one quality of matter. It almost takes one's breath away to think that "Hamlet" and the "Novum Organon" were at the risk of teething and measles at the same time. But Ben was right also in thinking that eloquence had grown backwards. He lived long enough to see the language of verse become in a measure traditionary and conventional. It was becoming so, partly from the necessary order of events, partly because the most natural and intense expression of feeling had been in so many ways satisfied and exhausted, — but chiefly because there was no man left to whom, as to Shakespeare, perfect conception gave perfection of phrase. Dante, among modern poets, his only rival in condensed force, says: "Optimis conceptionibus optima loquela conveniet; sed optimæ conceptiones non possunt esse nisi ubi scientia et ingenium est; . . . . et sic non omnibus versificantibus optima loquela convenit, cum plerique sine scientiâ et ingenio versificantur." *

Shakespeare must have been quite as well aware of the provincialism of English as Bacon was; but he knew that great poetry, being universal in its appeal to human nature, can make any language classic, and that the men whose appreciation is immortality will mine through any dialect to get at an original soul. He had as much confidence in his home-bred speech as Bacon had want of it, and exclaims: —

* *De Vulgari Eloquio*, Lib. II. cap. i. *ad finem.* I quote this treatise as Dante's, because the thoughts seem manifestly his; though I believe that in its present form it is an abridgment by some transcriber, who sometimes copies textually, and sometimes substitutes his own language for that of the original.

"Not marble nor the gilded monuments
Of princes shall outlive this powerful rhyme."

He must have been perfectly conscious of his genius, and of the great trust which he imposed upon his native tongue as the embodier and perpetuator of it. As he has avoided obscurities in his sonnets, he would do so *a fortiori* in his plays, both for the purpose of immediate effect on the stage and of future appreciation. Clear thinking makes clear writing, and he who has shown himself so eminently capable of it in one case is not to be supposed to abdicate intentionally in others. The difficult passages in the plays, then, are to be regarded either as corruptions, or else as phenomena in the natural history of Imagination, whose study will enable us to arrive at a clearer theory and better understanding of it.

While I believe that our language had two periods of culmination in poetic beauty, — one of nature, simplicity, and truth, in the ballads, which deal only with narrative and feeling, — another of Art, (or Nature as it is ideally reproduced through the imagination,) of stately amplitude, of passionate intensity and elevation, in Spenser and the greater dramatists, — and that Shakespeare made use of the latter as he found it, I by no means intend to say that he did not enrich it, or that any inferior man could have dipped the same words out of the great poet's inkstand. But he enriched it only by the natural expansion and exhilaration of which it was conscious, in yielding to the mastery of a genius that could turn and wind it like a fiery Pegasus, making it feel its life in every limb. He enriched it through that exquisite sense of music, (never approached but by Marlowe,) to which it seemed eagerly obedient, as if every word said to him,

"*Bid me* discourse, I will enchant thine ear," —

as if every latent harmony revealed itself to him as the

gold to Brahma, when he walked over the earth where it was hidden, crying, "Here am I, Lord! do with me what thou wilt!" That he used language with that intimate possession of its meaning possible only to the most vivid thought is doubtless true; but that he wantonly strained it from its ordinary sense, that he found it too poor for his necessities, and accordingly coined new phrases, or that, from haste or carelessness, he violated any of its received proprieties, I do not believe. I have said that it was fortunate for him that he came upon an age when our language was at its best; but it was fortunate also for us, because our costliest poetic phrase is put beyond reach of decay in the gleaming precipitate in which it united itself with his thought.

That the propositions I have endeavored to establish have a direct bearing in various ways upon the qualifications of whoever undertakes to edit the works of Shakespeare will, I think, be apparent to those who consider the matter. The hold which Shakespeare has acquired and maintained upon minds so many and so various, in so many vital respects utterly unsympathetic and even incapable of sympathy with his own, is one of the most noteworthy phenomena in the history of literature. That he has had the most inadequate of editors, that, as his own Falstaff was the cause of the wit, so he has been the cause of the foolishness that was in other men, (as where Malone ventured to discourse upon his metres, and Dr. Johnson on his imagination,) must be apparent to every one, — and also that his genius and its manifestations are so various, that there is no commentator but has been able to illustrate him from his own peculiar point of view or from the results of his own favorite studies. But to show that he was a good common lawyer, that he understood the theory of colors, that he was an accurate botanist, a master of the science of medicine, especially in its relation to mental disease, a profound metaphysician, and of great experience and insight in politics, — all these, while they may very well form the staple of separate treatises, and prove, that, whatever the extent of his learning, the range and accuracy of his knowledge were beyond precedent or later parallel, are really outside the province of an editor.

We doubt if posterity owe a greater debt to any two men living in 1623 than to the two obscure actors who in that year published the first folio edition of Shakespeare's plays. But for them, it is more than likely that such of his works as had remained to that time unprinted would have been irrecoverably lost, and among them were "Julius Cæsar," "The Tempest," and "Macbeth." But are we to believe them when they assert that they present to us the plays which they reprinted from stolen and surreptitious copies "cured and perfect of their limbs," and those which are original in their edition "absolute in their numbers as he [Shakespeare] conceived them"? Alas, we have read too many theatrical announcements, have been taught too often that the value of the promise was in an inverse ratio to the generosity of the exclamation-marks, too easily to believe that! Nay, we have seen numberless processions of healthy kine enter our native village unheralded save by the lusty shouts of drovers, while a wretched calf, cursed by stepdame Nature with two heads, was brought to us in a triumphal car, avant-couriered by a band of music as abnormal as itself, and announced as the greatest wonder of the age. If a double allowance of vituline brains deserve such honor, there are few commentators on Shakespeare that would have gone afoot, and the trumpets of Messieurs Heminge and Condell call up in our minds too many monstrous and deformed associations.

What, then, is the value of the first folio as an authority? For eighteen of the plays it is the only authority we have, and the only one also for four others in their complete form. It is admitted that in several instances Heminge and Condell reprinted the earlier quarto impressions with a few changes, sometimes for the better and sometimes for the worse; and it is most probable that copies of those editions (whether surreptitious or not) had taken the place of the original prompter's books, as being more convenient and legible. Even in these cases it is not safe to conclude that all or even any of the variations were made by the hand of Shakespeare himself. And where the players printed from manuscript, is it likely to have been that of the author? The probability is small that a writer so busy as Shakespeare must have been during his productive period should have copied out their parts for the actors himself, or that one so indifferent as he seems to have been to the immediate literary fortunes of his works should have given much care to the correction of copies, if made by others. The copies exclusively in the hands of Heminge and Condell were, it is manifest, in some cases, very imperfect, whether we account for the fact by the burning of the Globe Theatre or by the necessary wear and tear of years, and (what is worthy of notice) they are plainly more defective in some parts than in others. "Measure for Measure" is an example of this, and we are not satisfied with being told that its ruggedness of verse is intentional, or that its obscurity is due to the fact that Shakespeare grew more elliptical in his style as he grew older. Profounder in thought he doubtless became; though in a mind like his, we believe that this would imply only a more absolute supremacy in expression. But, from whatever original we suppose either the quartos or the first folio to have been printed, it is more than questionable whether the proof-sheets had the advantage of any revision other than that of the printing-office. Steevens was of opinion that authors in the time of Shakespeare never read their own proof-sheets; and Mr. Spedding, in his recent edition of Bacon, comes independently to the same conclusion.* We may be very sure that Heminge and Condell did not, as vicars, take upon themselves a disagreeable task which the author would have been too careless to assume.

Nevertheless, however strong a case may be made out against the Folio of 1623, whatever sins of omission we may lay to the charge of Heminge and Condell, or of commission to that of the printers, it remains the only text we have with any claims whatever to authenticity. It should be deferred to as authority in all cases where it does not make Shakespeare write bad sense, uncouth metre, or false grammar, of all which we believe him to have been more supremely incapable than any other man who ever wrote English. Yet we would not speak unkindly even of the blunders of the Folio. They have put bread into the mouth of many an honest editor, publisher, and printer for the last century and a half; and he who loves the comic side of human nature will find the serious notes of a *variorum* edition of Shakespeare as funny reading as the funny ones are serious.

* Vol. III. p. 348, *note*. He grounds his belief, not on the misprinting of words, but on the misplacing of whole paragraphs. We were struck with the same thing in the original edition of Chapman's "Biron's Conspiracy and Tragedy." And yet, in comparing two copies of this edition, I have found corrections which only the author could have made. One of the misprints which Mr. Spedding notices affords both a hint and a warning to the conjectural emendator. In the edition of "The Advancement of Learning" printed in 1605 occurs the word *dusinesse*. In a later edition this was conjecturally changed to *business*; but the occurrence of *vertigine* in the Latin translation enables Mr. Spedding to print rightly, *dizziness*.

Scarce a commentator of them all, for more than a hundred years, but thought, as Alphonso of Castile did of Creation, that, if he had only been at Shakespeare's elbow, he could have given valuable advice; scarce one who did not know off-hand that there was never a seaport in Bohemia, — as if Shakespeare's world were one which Mercator could have projected; scarce one but was satisfied that his ten finger-tips were a sufficient key to those astronomic wonders of poise and counterpoise, of planetary law and cometary seeming-exception, in his metres; scarce one but thought he could gauge like an ale-firkin that intuition whose edging shallows may have been sounded, but whose abysses, stretching down amid the sunless roots of Being and Consciousness, mock the plummet; scarce one but could speak with condescending approval of that prodigious intelligence so utterly without congener that our baffled language must coin an adjective to qualify it, and none is so audacious as to say Shakesperian of any other. And yet, in the midst of our impatience, we cannot help thinking also of how much healthy mental activity this one man has been the occasion, how much good he has indirectly done to society by withdrawing men to investigations and habits of thought that secluded them from baser attractions, for how many he has enlarged the circle of study and reflection; since there is nothing in history or politics, nothing in art or science, nothing in physics or metaphysics, that is not sooner or later taxed for his illustration. This is partially true of all great minds, open and sensitive to truth and beauty through any large arc of their circumference; but it is true in an unexampled sense of Shakespeare, the vast round of whose balanced nature seems to have been equatorial, and to have had a southward exposure and a summer sympathy at every point, so that life, society, statecraft, serve us at last but as commentaries on him, and whatever we have gathered of thought, of knowledge, and of experience, confronted with his marvellous page, shrinks to a mere foot-note, the stepping-stone to some hitherto inaccessible verse. We admire in Homer the blind placid mirror of the world's young manhood, the bard who escapes from his misfortune in poems all memory, all life and bustle, adventure and picture; we revere in Dante that compressed force of lifelong passion which could make a private experience cosmopolitan in its reach and everlasting in its significance; we respect in Goethe the Aristotelian poet, wise by weariless observation, witty with intention, the stately *Geheimerrath* of a provincial court in the empire of Nature. As we study these, we seem in our limited way to penetrate into their consciousness and to measure and master their methods; but with Shakespeare it is just the other way; the more we have familiarized ourselves with the operations of our own consciousness, the more do we find, in reading him, that he has been beforehand with us, and that, while we have been vainly endeavoring to find the door of his being, he has searched every nook and cranny of our own. While other poets and dramatists embody isolated phases of character and work inward from the phenomenon to the special law which it illustrates, he seems in some strange way unitary with human nature itself, and his own soul to have been the law and life-giving power of which his creations are only the phenomena. We justify or criticise the characters of other writers by our memory and experience, and pronounce them natural or unnatural; but he seems to have worked in the very stuff of which memory and experience are made, and we recognize his truth to Nature by an innate and unacquired sympathy, as if he alone possessed the secret of the "ideal form and universal mould," and embodied generic types rather than individuals. In this Cervantes alone has approached him; and Don Quixote and Sancho, like the men and women of Shakespeare, are the contemporaries of every generation, because they are not products of an artificial and transitory society, but because they are animated by the primeval and unchanging forces of that humanity which underlies and survives the forever-fickle creeds and ceremonials of the parochial corners which we who dwell in them sublimely call The World.

That Shakespeare did not edit his own works must be attributed, we suspect, to his premature death. That he should not have intended it is inconceivable. Is there not something of self-consciousness in the breaking of Prospero's wand and burying his book, — a sort of sad prophecy, based on self-knowledge of the nature of that man who, after such thaumaturgy, could go down to Stratford and live there for years, only collecting his dividends from the Globe Theatre, lending money on mortgage, and leaning over his gate to chat and bandy quips with neighbors? His mind had entered into every phase of human life and thought, had embodied all of them in living creations; — had he found all empty, and come at last to the belief that genius and its works were as phantasmagoric as the rest, and that fame was as idle as the rumor of the pit? However this may be, his works have come down to us in a condition of manifest and admitted corruption in some portions, while in others there is an obscurity which may be attributed either to an idiosyncratic use of words and condensation of phrase, to a depth of intuition for a proper coalescence with which ordinary language is inadequate, to a concentration of passion in a focus that consumes the lighter links which bind together the clauses of a sentence or of a process of reasoning in common parlance, or to a sense of music which mingles music and meaning without essentially confounding them. We should demand for a perfect editor, then, first, a thorough glossological knowledge of the English contemporary with Shakespeare; second, enough logical acuteness of mind and metaphysical training to enable him to follow recondite processes of thought; third, such a conviction of the supremacy of his author as always to prefer his thought to any theory of his own; fourth, a feeling for music, and so much knowledge of the practice of other poets as to understand that Shakespeare's versification differs from theirs as often in kind as in degree; fifth, an acquaintance with the world as well as with books; and last, what is, perhaps, of more importance than all, so great a familiarity with the working of the imaginative faculty in general, and of its peculiar operation in the mind of Shakespeare, as will prevent his thinking a passage dark with excess of light, and enable him to understand fully that the Gothic Shakespeare often superimposed upon the slender column of a single word, that seems to twist under it, but does not, — like the quaint shafts in cloisters, — a weight of meaning which the modern architects of sentences would consider wholly unjustifiable by correct principle.

Many years ago, while yet Fancy claimed that right in me which Fact has since, to my no small loss, so successfully disputed, I pleased myself with imagining the play of Hamlet published under some *alias*, and as the work of a new candidate in literature. Then I *played*, as the children say, that it came in regular course before some well-meaning doer of criticisms, who had never read the original, (no very wild assumption, as things go,) and endeavored to conceive the kind of way in which he would be likely to take it. I put myself in his place, and tried to write such a perfunctory notice as I thought would be likely, in filling his column, to satisfy his conscience. But it was a *tour de force* quite beyond my power to execute without grimace. I could not arrive at that artistic absorption in my own conception which would enable me to be natural, and found myself, like a bad actor, continually betraying my self-consciousness by my very endeavor to hide it under caricature. The path of Nature is indeed a narrow one, and it is only the immortals that seek it, and, when they find it, do not find themselves cramped therein. My result was a dead failure, — satire instead of comedy. I could not shake off that strange accumulation which we call self, and report honestly what I saw and felt even to myself, much less to others.

Yet I have often thought, that, unless we can so far free ourselves from our own prepossessions as to be capable of bringing to a work of art some freshness of sensation, and receiving from it in turn some new surprise of sympathy and admiration, — some shock even, it may be, of instinctive distaste and repulsion, — though we may praise or blame, weighing our *pros* and *cons* in the nicest balances, sealed by proper authority, yet we shall not criticise in the highest sense. On the other hand, unless we admit certain principles as fixed beyond question, we shall be able to render no adequate judgment, but only to record our impressions, which may be valuable or not, according to the greater or less ductility of the senses on which they are made. Charles Lamb, for example, came to the old English dramatists with the feeling of a discoverer. He brought with him an alert curiosity, and everything was delightful simply because it was strange. Like other early adventurers, he sometimes mistook shining sand for gold; but he had the great advantage of not feeling himself responsible for the manners of the inhabitants he found there, and not thinking it needful to make them square with any Westminster Catechism of æsthetics. Best of all, he did not feel compelled to compare them with the Greeks, about whom he knew little, and cared less. He took them as he found them, described them in a few pregnant sentences, and displayed his specimens of their growth and manufacture. When he arrived at the dramatists of the Restoration, so far from being shocked, he was charmed with their pretty and unmoral ways; and what he says of them reminds us of blunt Captain Dampier, who, in his account of the island of Timor, remarks, as a matter of no consequence, that the natives "take as many wives as they can maintain, and as for religion, they have none."

Lamb had the great advantage of seeing the elder dramatists as they were; it did not lie within his province to point out what they were not. Himself a fragmentary writer, he had more sympathy with imagination where it gathers into the intense focus of passionate phrase than with that higher form of it, where it is the faculty that shapes, gives unity of design and balanced gravitation of parts. And yet it is only this higher form of it which can unimpeachably assure to any work the dignity and permanence of a classic; for it results in that exquisite something called Style, which, like the grace of perfect breeding, everywhere pervasive and nowhere emphatic, makes itself felt by the skill with which it effaces itself, and masters us at last with a sense of indefinable completeness. On a lower plane we may detect it in the structure of a sentence, in the limpid expression that implies sincerity of thought; but it is only where it combines and organizes, where it eludes observation in particulars to give the rarer delight of perfection as a whole, that it belongs to art. Then it is truly ideal, the *forma mentis æterna*, not as a passive mould into which the thought is poured, but as the conceptive energy which finds all material plastic to its preconceived design. Mere vividness of expression, such as makes quotable passages, comes of the complete surrender of self to the impression, whether spiritual or sensual, of the moment. It is a quality, perhaps, in which the young poet is richer than the mature, his very inexperience making him more venturesome in those leaps of language that startle us with their rashness only to bewitch us the more with the happy ease of their accomplishment. For this there are no existing laws of rhetoric, for it is from such felicities that the rhetoricians deduce and codify their statutes. It is something which cannot be improved upon or cultivated, for it is immediate and intuitive. But this power of expression is subsidiary, and goes only a little way toward the making of a great poet. Imagination, where it is truly creative, is a faculty, and not a quality; it looks before and after, it gives the form that makes all the parts work together harmoniously toward a given end, its seat is in the higher reason, and it is efficient only as a servant of the will. Imagination, as it is too often misunderstood, is mere fantasy, the image-making power, common to all who have the gift of dreams, or who can afford to buy it in a vulgar drug as De Quincey bought it.

The true poetic imagination is of one quality, whether it be ancient or modern, and equally subject to those laws of grace, of proportion, of design, in whose free service, and in that alone, it can become art. Those laws are something which do not

> "Alter when they alteration find,
> And bend with the remover to remove."

And they are more clearly to be deduced from the eminent examples of Greek literature than from any other source. It is the advantage of this select company of ancients that their works are defecated of all turbid mixture of contemporaneousness, and have become to us pure *literature*, our judgment and enjoyment of which cannot be vulgarized by any prejudices of time or place. This is why the study of them is fitly called a liberal education, because it emancipates the mind from every narrow provincialism whether of egoism or tradition, and is the apprenticeship that every one must serve before becoming a free brother of the guild which passes the torch of life from age to age. There would be no dispute about the advantages of that Greek culture which Schiller advocated with such generous eloquence, if the great authors of antiquity had not been degraded from teachers of thinking to drillers in grammar, and made the ruthless pedagogues of root and inflection, instead of companions for whose society the mind must put on her highest mood. The discouraged youth too naturally transfers the epithet of *dead* from the languages to the authors that wrote in them. What concern have we with the shades of dialect in Homer or Theocritus, provided they speak the spiritual *lingua franca* that abolishes all alienage of race, and makes whatever shore of time we land on hospitable and homelike? There is much that is deciduous in books, but all that gives them a title to rank as literature in the highest sense is perennial. Their vitality is the vitality not of one or another blood or tongue, but of human nature; their truth is not topical and transitory, but of universal acceptation; and thus all great authors seem the coevals not only of each other, but of whoever reads them, growing wiser with him as he grows wise, and unlocking to him one secret after another as his own life and experience give him the key, but on no other condition. Their meaning is absolute, not conditional; it is a property of *theirs*, quite irrespective of manners or creed; for the highest culture, the development of the individual by observation, reflection, and study, leads to one result, whether in Athens or in London. The more we know of ancient literature, the more we are struck with its modernness, just as the more we study the maturer dramas of Shakespeare, the more we feel his nearness in certain primary qualities to the antique and classical. Yet even in saying this, I tacitly make the admission that it is the Greeks who must furnish us with our standard of comparison. Their stamp is upon all the allowed measures and weights of æsthetic criticism. Nor does a consciousness of this, nor a constant reference to it, in any sense reduce us to the mere copying of a bygone excellence; for it is the test of excellence in any department of art, that it can never be bygone, and it is not mere difference from antique models, but the *way* in which that difference is shown, the direction it takes, that we are to consider in our judgment of a modern work. The model is not there to be copied merely, but that the study of it may lead us insensibly to the same processes of thought by which its purity of outline and harmony of parts were attained, and enable us to feel that strength is consistent with repose, that multiplicity is not abundance, that grace is but a more refined form of power, and that a thought is none the less profound that the limpidity of its expression allows us to measure it at a glance. To be possessed with this conviction gives us at least a determinate point of view, and enables us to appeal a case of taste to a court of final judicature, whose decisions are guided by immutable principles. When we hear of certain productions, that they are feeble in design, but masterly in parts, that they are incoherent, to be sure, but have great merits of style, we know that it cannot be true; for in the highest examples we have, the master is revealed by his plan, by his power of making all accessories, each in its due relation, subordinate to it, and that to limit style to the rounding of a period or a distich is wholly to misapprehend its truest and highest function. Donne is full of salient verses that would take the rudest March winds of criticism with their beauty, of thoughts that first tease us like charades and then delight us with the felicity of their solution; but these have not saved him. He is exiled to the limbo of the formless and the fragmentary. To take a more recent instance, — Wordsworth had, in some respects, a deeper insight, and a more adequate utterance of it, than any man of his generation. But it was a piece-meal insight and utterance; his imagination was feminine, not masculine, receptive, and not creative. His longer poems are Egyptian sand-wastes, with here and there an oasis of exquisite greenery, a grand image, Sphinx-like, half buried in drifting commonplaces, or the solitary Pompey's Pillar of some towering thought. But what is the fate of a poet who owns the quarry, but cannot build the poem? Ere the century is out he will be nine parts dead, and immortal only in that tenth part of him which is included in a thin volume of "beauties." Already Moxon has felt the need of extracting this essential oil of him; and his memory will be kept alive, if at all, by the precious material rather than the workmanship of the vase that contains his heart. And what shall we forebode of so many modern poems, full of splendid passages, beginning everywhere and leading nowhere, reminding us of nothing so much as the amateur architect who planned his own house, and forgot the staircase that should connect one floor with another, putting it as an afterthought on the outside?

Lichtenberg says somewhere, that it was the advantage of the ancients to write before the great art of writing ill had been invented; and Shakespeare may be said to have had the good luck of coming after Spenser (to whom the debt of English poetry is incalculable) had reinvented the art of writing well. But Shakespeare arrived at a mastery in this respect which sets him above all other poets. He is not only superior in degree, but he is also different in kind. In that less purely artistic sphere of style which concerns the matter rather than the form his charm is often unspeakable. How perfect his style is may be judged from the fact that it never curdles into mannerism, and thus absolutely eludes imitation. Though here, if anywhere, the style is the man, yet it is noticeable only, like the images of Brutus, by its absence, so thoroughly is he absorbed in his work, while he fuses thought and word indissolubly together, till all the particles cohere by the best virtue of each. With perfect truth he has said of himself that he writes

"All one, ever the same,
Putting invention in a noted weed,
That every word doth almost tell his name."

And yet who has so succeeded in imitating him as to remind us of him by even so much as the gait of a single verse?* Those magnificent crystallizations of feeling and phrase, basaltic masses, molten and interfused by the primal fires of passion, are not to be reproduced by the slow experiments of the laboratory striving to parody creation with artifice. Mr. Matthew Arnold seems to think that Shakespeare has damaged English poetry. I wish he had! It is true he lifted Dryden above himself in "All

* "At first sight, Shakespeare and his contemporary dramatists seem to write in styles much alike; nothing so easy as to fall into that of Massinger and the others; whilst no one has ever yet produced one scene conceived and expressed in the Shakespearian idiom. I suppose it is because Shakespeare is universal, and, in fact, has no *manner*." — *Coleridge's Tabletalk*, 214.

for Love"; but it was Dryden who said of him, by instinctive conviction rather than judgment, that within his magic circle none dared tread but he. Is he to blame for the extravagances of modern diction, which are but the reaction of the brazen age against the degeneracy of art into artifice, that has characterized the silver period in every literature? We see in them only the futile effort of misguided persons to torture out of language the secret of that inspiration which should be in themselves. We do not find the extravagances in Shakespeare himself. We never saw a line in any modern poet that reminded us of him, and will venture to assert that it is only poets of the second class that find successful imitators. And the reason seems to us a very plain one. The genius of the great poet seeks repose in the expression of itself, and finds it at last in style, which is the establishment of a perfect mutual understanding between the worker and his material.* The secondary intellect, on the other hand, seeks for excitement in expression, and stimulates itself into mannerism, which is the wilful obtrusion of self, as style is its unconscious abnegation. No poet of the first class has ever left a school, because his imagination is incommunicable; while, just as surely as the thermometer tells of the neighborhood of an iceberg, you may detect the presence of a genius of the second class in any generation by the influence of his mannerism, for that, being an artificial thing, is capable of reproduction. Dante, Shakespeare, Goethe, left no heirs either to the form or mode of their expression; while Milton, Sterne, and Wordsworth left behind them whole regiments uniformed with all their external characteristics. We do not mean that great

* Pheidias said of one of his pupils that he had an inspired thumb, because the modelling-clay yielded to its careless sweep a grace of curve which it refused to the utmost pains of others.

poetic geniuses may not have influenced thought, (though we think it would be difficult to show how Shakespeare had done so, directly and wilfully,) but that they have not infected contemporaries or followers with mannerism. The quality in him which makes him at once so thoroughly English and so thoroughly cosmopolitan is that aëration of the understanding by the imagination which he has in common with all the greater poets, and which is the privilege of genius. The modern school, which mistakes violence for intensity, seems to catch its breath when it finds itself on the verge of natural expression, and to say to itself, "Good heavens! I had almost forgotten I was inspired!" But of Shakespeare we do not even suspect that he ever remembered it. He does not always speak in that intense way that flames up in Lear and Macbeth through the rifts of a soil volcanic with passion. He allows us here and there the repose of a commonplace character, the consoling distraction of a humorous one. He knows how to be equable and grand without effort, so that we forget the altitude of thought to which he has led us, because the slowly receding slope of a mountain stretching downward by ample gradations gives a less startling impression of height than to look over the edge of a ravine that makes but a wrinkle in its flank.

Shakespeare has been sometimes taxed with the barbarism of profuseness and exaggeration. But this is to measure him by a Sophoclean scale. The simplicity of the antique tragedy is by no means that of expression, but is of form merely. In the utterance of great passions, something must be indulged to the extravagance of Nature; the subdued tones to which pathos and sentiment are limited cannot express a tempest of the soul. The range between the piteous "no more but so," in which Ophelia compresses the heart-break whose compression was to make her mad, and that sublime appeal of Lear to the elements of Nature, only to be matched, if matched at all, in the "Prometheus," is a wide one, and Shakespeare is as truly simple in the one as in the other. The simplicity of poetry is not that of prose, nor its clearness that of ready apprehension merely. To a subtile sense, a sense heightened by sympathy, those sudden fervors of phrase, gone ere one can say it lightens, that show us Macbeth groping among the complexities of thought in his conscience-clouded mind, and reveal the intricacy rather than enlighten it, while they leave the eye darkened to the literal meaning of the words, yet make their logical sequence, the grandeur of the conception, and its truth to Nature clearer than sober daylight could. There is an obscurity of mist rising from the undrained shallows of the mind, and there is the darkness of thunder-cloud gathering its electric masses with passionate intensity from the clear element of the imagination, not at random or wilfully, but by the natural processes of the creative faculty, to brood those flashes of expression that transcend rhetoric, and are only to be apprehended by the poetic instinct.

In that secondary office of imagination, where it serves the artist, not as the reason that shapes, but as the interpreter of his conceptions into words, there is a distinction to be noticed between the higher and lower mode in which it performs its function. It may be either creative or pictorial, may body forth the thought or merely image it forth. With Shakespeare, for example, imagination seems immanent in his very consciousness; with Milton, in his memory. In the one it sends, as if without knowing it, a fiery life into the verse,

> "Sei die Braut das Wort,
> Bräutigam der Geist";

in the other it elaborates a certain pomp and elevation. Accordingly, the bias of the former is toward over-intensity, of the latter toward over-diffuseness. Shakespeare's temptation is to push a willing metaphor beyond its strength, to make a passion over-inform its tenement of words; Milton cannot resist running a simile on into a fugue. One always fancies Shakespeare *in* his best verses, and Milton at the key-board of his organ. Shakespeare's language is no longer the mere vehicle of thought, it has become part of it, its very flesh and blood. The pleasure it gives us is unmixed, direct, like that from the smell of a flower or the flavor of a fruit. Milton sets everywhere his little pitfalls of bookish association for the memory. I know that Milton's manner is very grand. It is slow, it is stately, moving as in triumphal procession, with music, with historic banners, with spoils from every time and every region, and captive epithets, like huge Sicambrians, thrust their broad shoulders between us and the thought whose pomp they decorate. But it is manner, nevertheless, as is proved by the ease with which it is parodied, by the danger it is in of degenerating into mannerism whenever it forgets itself. Fancy a parody of Shakespeare, — I do not mean of his words, but of his *tone*, for that is what distinguishes the master. You might as well try it with the Venus of Melos. In Shakespeare it is always the higher thing, the thought, the fancy, that is pre-eminent; it is Cæsar that draws all eyes, and not the chariot in which he rides, or the throng which is but the reverberation of his supremacy. If not, how explain the charm with which he dominates in all tongues, even under the disenchantment of translation? Among the most alien races he is as solidly at home as a mountain seen from different sides by many lands, itself superbly solitary, yet the companion of all thoughts and domesticated in all imaginations.

In description Shakespeare is especially great, and in that instinct which gives the peculiar quality of any object of contemplation in a single happy word that colors the impression on the sense with the mood of the mind. Most descriptive poets seem to think that a hogshead of water caught at the spout will give us a livelier notion of a thunder-shower than the sullen muttering of the first big drops upon the roof. They forget that it is by suggestion, not cumulation, that profound impressions are made upon the imagination. Milton's parsimony (so rare in him) makes the success of his

> "Sky lowered, and, muttering thunder, some sad drops
> Wept at completion of the mortal sin."

Shakespeare understood perfectly the charm of indirectness, of making his readers seem to discover for themselves what he means to show them. If he wishes to tell that the leaves of the willow are gray on the under side, he does not make it a mere fact of observation by bluntly saying so, but makes it picturesquely reveal itself to us as it might in Nature: —

> "There is a willow grows athwart the flood,
> That shows his *hoar* leaves in the glassy stream."

Where he goes to the landscape for a comparison, he does not ransack wood and field for specialties, as if he were gathering simples, but takes one image, obvious, familiar, and makes it new to us either by sympathy or contrast with his own immediate feeling. He always looked upon Nature with the eyes of the mind. Thus he can make the melancholy of autumn or the gladness of spring alike pathetic: —

> "That time of year thou mayst in me behold,
> When yellow leaves, or few, or none, do hang
> Upon those boughs that shake against the cold,
> Bare ruined choirs where late the sweet birds sang."

Or again: —

> "From thee have I been absent in the spring,
> When proud-pied April, dressed in all his trim,
> Hath put a spirit of youth in everything,
> That heavy Saturn leaped and laughed with him."

But as dramatic poet, Shakespeare goes even beyond this, entering so perfectly into the consciousness of the characters he himself has created, that he sees everything through their peculiar mood, and makes every epithet, as if unconsciously, echo and re-echo it. Theseus asks Hermia, —

> "Can you endure the livery of a nun,
> For aye to be in shady cloister mewed,
> To live a *barren* sister all your life,
> Chanting faint hymns to the *cold fruitless* moon?"

When Romeo must leave Juliet, the private pang of the lovers becomes a property of Nature herself, and

> "*Envious* streaks
> Do lace the *severing* clouds in yonder east."

But even more striking is the following instance from Macbeth: —

> "The raven himself is hoarse
> That croaks the fatal enterance of Duncan
> Under your battlements."

Here Shakespeare, with his wonted tact, makes use of a vulgar superstition, of a type in which mortal presentiment is already embodied, to make a common ground on which the hearer and Lady Macbeth may meet. After this prelude we are prepared to be possessed by her emotion more fully, to feel in her ears the dull tramp of the blood that seems to make the raven's croak yet hoarser than it is, and to betray the stealthy advance of the mind to its fell purpose. For Lady Macbeth hears not so much the voice of the bodeful bird as of her own premeditated murder, and we are thus made her shuddering accomplices before the fact. Every image receives the color of the mind, every word throbs with the pulse of one controlling passion. The epithet *fatal* makes us feel the implacable resolve of the speaker, and shows us that she is tampering with her conscience by putting off the crime upon the prophecy of the Weird Sisters to which she alludes. In the word *battlements*, too, not only is the fancy led up to the perch of the raven, but a hostile image takes the place of a hospitable; for men commonly speak of receiving a guest under their roof or within their doors. That this is not over-ingenuity, seeing what is not to be seen, nor meant to be seen, is clear to me from what follows. When Duncan and Banquo arrive at the castle, their fancies, free from all suggestion of evil, call up only gracious and amiable images. The raven was but the fantastical creation of Lady Macbeth's over-wrought brain.

> "This castle hath a pleasant seat, the air
> Nimbly and sweetly doth commend itself
> Unto our gentle senses.
> This *guest* of summer,
> The *temple-haunting* martlet, doth approve
> By his *loved mansionry* that the heaven's breath
> Smells *wooingly* here; no jutty, frieze,
> Buttress, or coigne of vantage, but this bird
> Hath made his pendent bed and procreant cradle."

The contrast here cannot but be as intentional as it is marked. Every image is one of welcome, security, and confidence. The summer, one may well fancy, would be a very different hostess from her whom we have just seen expecting *them*. And why *temple-haunting*, unless because it suggests sanctuary? *O immaginativa, che si ne rubi delle cose di fuor*, how infinitely more precious are the inward ones thou givest in return! If all this be accident, it is at least one of those accidents of which only this man was ever capable. I divine something like it now and then in Æschylus, through the mists of a language which will not let me be sure of what I see, but nowhere else. Shakespeare, it is true, had, as I have said, as respects English, the privilege which only first-comers enjoy. The language was still fresh from those sources at too great a distance from which it becomes fit only for the service of prose. Wherever he dipped, it came up clear and sparkling, undefiled as yet by the drainage of literary factories, or of those dye-houses where the machine-woven fabrics of sham culture are colored up to the last desperate style of sham sentiment. Those who criticise his diction as sometimes extravagant should remember that in poetry language is something more than merely the vehicle of thought, that it is meant to convey the sentiment as much as the sense, and that, if there is a beauty of use, there is often a higher use of beauty.

What kind of culture Shakespeare had is uncertain; how much he had is disputed; that he had as much as he wanted, and of whatever kind he wanted, must be clear to whoever considers the question. Dr. Farmer has proved, in his entertaining essay, that he got everything at second-hand from translations, and that, where his translator blundered, he loyally blundered too. But Goethe, the man of widest acquirement in modern times, did precisely the same thing. In his character of poet he set as little store by useless learning as Shakespeare did. He learned to write hexameters, not from Homer, but from Voss, and Voss found them faulty; yet somehow *Hermann und Dorothea* is more readable than *Luise.* So far as all the classicism then attainable was concerned, Shakespeare got it as cheap as Goethe did, who always bought it ready-made. For such purposes of mere æsthetic nourishment Goethe always milked other minds, — if minds those ruminators and digesters of antiquity into asses' milk may be called. There were plenty of professors who were forever assiduously browsing in vales of Enna and on Pentelican slopes among the vestiges of antiquity, slowly secreting lacteous facts, and not one of them would have raised his head from that exquisite pasturage, though Pan had made music through his pipe of reeds. Did Goethe wish to work up a Greek theme? He drove out Herr Böttiger, for example, among that fodder delicious to him for its very dryness, that sapless Arcadia of scholiasts, let him graze, ruminate, and go through all other needful processes of the antiquarian organism, then got him quietly into a corner and milked him. The product, after standing long enough, mantled over with the rich Goethean cream, from which a butter could be churned, if not precisely classic, quite as good as the ancients could have made out of the same material. But who has ever read the *Achilleis*, correct in all *un*essential particulars as it probably is?

It is impossible to conceive that a man, who, in other respects, made such booty of the world around him, whose observation of manners was so minute, and whose insight into character and motives, as if he had been one of God's spies, was so unerring that we accept it without question, as we do Nature herself, and find it more consoling to explain his confessedly immense superiority by attributing it to a happy instinct rather than to the conscientious perfecting of exceptional powers till practice made them seem to work independently of the will which still directed them, — it is impossible that such a man should not also have profited by the converse of the cultivated and quick-witted men in whose familiar society he lived, that he should not have over and over again discussed points of criticism and art with them, that he should not have had his curiosity, so alive to everything else, excited about those ancients whom university men then, no doubt, as now, extolled without too much knowledge of what they really were, that he should not have heard too much rather than too little.

of Aristotle's *Poetics*, Quinctilian's *Rhetoric*, Horace's *Art of Poetry*, and the *Unities*, especially from Ben Jonson, — in short, that he who speaks of himself as

"Desiring this man's art and that man's scope,
With what he most enjoyed contented least,"

and who meditated so profoundly on every other topic of human concern, should never have turned his thought to the principles of that art which was both the delight and business of his life, the bread-winner alike for soul and body. Was there no harvest of the ear for him whose eye had stocked its garners so full as wellnigh to forestall all after-comers? Did he who could so counsel the practisers of an art in which he never arrived at eminence, as in Hamlet's advice to the players, never take counsel with himself about that other art in which the instinct of the crowd, no less than the judgment of his rivals, awarded him an easy pre-eminence? If he had little Latin and less Greek, might he not have had enough of both for every practical purpose on this side pedantry? The most extraordinary, one might almost say contradictory, attainments have been ascribed to him, and yet he has been supposed incapable of what was within easy reach of every boy at Westminster School. There is a knowledge that comes of sympathy as living and genetic as that which comes of mere learning is sapless and unprocreant, and for this no profound study of the languages is needed.

If Shakespeare did not know the ancients, I think they were at least as unlucky in not knowing him. But is it incredible that he may have laid hold of an edition of the Greek tragedians, *Graecè et Latinè*, and then, with such poor wits as he was master of, contrived to worry some considerable meaning out of them? There are at least one or two coincidences which, whether accidental or not, are curious, and which I do not remember to have seen noticed. In the *Electra* of Sophocles, which is almost identical in its leading motive with *Hamlet*, the Chorus consoles Electra for the supposed death of Orestes in the same commonplace way which Hamlet's uncle tries with him.

Θνητοῦ πέφυκας πατρός, Ἠλέκτρα, φρόνει·
Θνητὸς δ' Ὀρέστης· ὥστε μὴ λίαν στένε,
Πᾶσιν γὰρ ἡμῖν τοῦτ' ὀφείλεται παθεῖν.

"Your father lost a father;
That father lost, lost his. . . . .
But to persévер
In obstinate condolement is a course
Of impious stubbornness. . . . .
'T is common; all that live must die."

Shakespeare expatiates somewhat more largely, but the sentiment in both cases is almost verbally identical. The resemblance is probably a chance one, for commonplace and consolation were always twin sisters, whom always to escape is given to no man; but it is nevertheless curious. Here is another, from the *Œdipus Coloneus*: —

Τοῖς τοι δικαίοις χὠ βραχὺς νικᾷ μέγαν,
"Thrice is he armed that hath his quarrel just."

Hamlet's "prophetic soul" may be matched with the *πρόμαντις θυμός* of Peleus, (Eurip. Androm. 1075,) and his "sea of troubles," with the *κακῶν πέλαγος* of Theseus in the *Hippolytus*, or of the Chorus in the *Hercules Furens*. And, for manner and tone, compare the speeches of Pheres in the *Alcestis*, and Jocasta in the *Phœnissæ*, with those of Claudio in *Measure for Measure*, and Ulysses in *Troilus and Cressida*.

The Greek dramatists were somewhat fond of a trick of words in which there is a reduplication of sense as well as of assonance, as in the *Electra*: —

Ἄλεκτρα γηράσκουσαν ἀνυμέναιά τε.

So Shakespeare: —

"Unhouseled, disappointed, unaneled";

and Milton after him, or, more likely, after the Greek: —

"Unrespited, unpitied, unreprieved." *

I mention these trifles, in passing, because they have interested me, and therefore may interest others. I lay no stress upon them, for, if once the conductors of Shakespeare's intelligence had been put in connection with those Attic brains, he would have reproduced their message in a form of his own. They would have inspired, and not enslaved him. His resemblance to them is that of consanguinity, more striking in expression than in mere resemblance of feature. The likeness between the Clytemnestra — *γυναικὸς ἀνδρόβουλον ἐλπίζον κέαρ* — of Æschylus and the Lady Macbeth of Shakespeare was too remarkable to have escaped notice. That between the two poets in their choice of epithets is as great, though more difficult of proof. Yet I think an attentive student of Shakespeare cannot fail to be reminded of something familiar to him in such phrases as "flame-eyed fire," "flax-winged ships," "star-neighboring peaks," the rock Salmydessus,

"Rude jaw of the sea,
Harsh hostess of the seaman, step-mother
Of ships,"

and the beacon with its "*speaking eye* of fire." Surely there is more than a verbal, there is a genuine, similarity between the *ἀνήριθμον γέλασμα* and "the unnumbered beach" and "multitudinous sea." Æschylus, it seems to me, is willing, just as Shakespeare is, to risk the prosperity of a verse upon a lucky throw of words, which may come up the sices of hardy metaphor or the ambs-

* The best instance I remember is in the *Frogs*, where Bacchus pleads his inexperience at the oar, and says he is

ἄπειρος, ἀθαλάττωτος, ἀσαλαμίνιος,

which might be rendered,

Unskilled, unsea-soned, and un-Salamised.

ace of conceit. There is such a difference between far-reaching and far-fetching! Poetry, to be sure, is always that daring one step beyond, which brings the right man to fortune, but leaves the wrong one in the ditch, and its law is, Be bold once and again, yet be not over-bold. It is true, also, that masters of language are a little apt to play with it. But whatever fault may be found with Shakespeare in this respect will touch a tender spot in Æschylus also. Does he sometimes overload a word, so that the language not merely, as Dryden says, bends under him, but fairly gives way, and lets the reader's mind down with the shock as of a false step in taste? He has nothing worse than πέλαγος ἀνθοῦν νεκροῖς. A criticism, shallow in human nature, however deep in Campbell's Rhetoric, has blamed him for making persons, under great excitement of sorrow, or whatever other emotion, parenthesize some trifling play upon words in the very height of their passion. Those who make such criticisms have either never felt a passion or seen one in action, or else they forget the exaltation of sensibility during such crises, so that the attention, whether of the senses or the mind, is arrested for the moment by what would be overlooked in ordinary moods. The more forceful the current, the more sharp the ripple from any alien substance interposed. A passion that looks forward, like revenge or lust or greed, goes right to its end, and is straightforward in its expression; but a tragic passion, which is in its nature unavailing, like disappointment, regret of the inevitable, or remorse, is reflective, and liable to be continually diverted by the suggestions of fancy. The one is a concentration of the will, which intensifies the character and the phrase that expresses it; in the other, the will is helpless, and, as in insanity, while the flow of the mind sets imperatively in one direction, it is liable to almost ludicrous interruptions and diversions upon the most trivial hint of involuntary association. I am ready to grant that Shakespeare sometimes allows his characters to spend time, that might be better employed, in carving some cherry-stone of a quibble;* that he is sometimes tempted away from the natural by the quaint; that he sometimes forces a partial, even a verbal, analogy between the abstract thought and the sensual image into an absolute identity, giving us a kind of serious pun. In a pun our pleasure arises from a gap in the logical nexus too wide for the reason, but which the ear can bridge in an instant. "Is that your own hare, or a wig?" The fancy is yet more tickled where logic is treated with a mock ceremonial of respect.

"His head was turned, *and so* he chewed
His pigtail till he died."

Now when this kind of thing is done in earnest, the result is one of those ill-distributed syllogisms which in rhetoric are called conceits.

"Hard was the hand that struck the blow,
Soft was the heart that bled."

I have seen this passage from Warner cited for its beauty, though I should have thought nothing could be worse, had I not seen General Morris's

"Her heart and morning broke together
In tears."

Of course, I would not rank with these Gloucester's

"What! will the aspiring blood of Lancaster
Sink in the ground? I thought it would have mounted";

though as mere rhetoric it belongs to the same class.†

* So Euripides (copied by Theocritus, Id. xxvii.):—

Πενθεὺς δ' ὅπως μὴ πένθος εἰσοίσει δόμοις. (*Bacchæ*, 363.)
'Εσωφρόνησεν ουκ ἔχουσα σωφρονεῖν. (*Hippol.*, 1037.)

So Calderon: "Y apenas llega, cuando llega á penas."

† I have taken the first passage in point that occurred to my memory. It may not be Shakespeare's, though probably his. The question of authorship is, I think, settled, so far as criticism can do it, in Mr. Grant White's admirable essay appended to the Second Part of Henry VI.

It might be defended as a bit of ghastly humor characteristic of the speaker. But at any rate it is not without precedent in the two greater Greek tragedians. In a chorus of the *Seven against Thebes* we have : —

> ἐν δὲ γαίᾳ
> Ζωὰ φονορυτῷ
> Μέμικται, κάρτα δ' εἶσ' ὅμαιμοι.

And does not Sophocles make Ajax in his despair quibble upon his own name quite in the Shakespearian fashion, under similar circumstances? Nor does the coarseness with which our great poet is reproached lack an Æschylean parallel. Even the Nurse in *Romeo and Juliet* would have found a true gossip in her of the *Agamemnon*, who is so indiscreet in her confidences concerning the nursery life of Orestes. Whether Raleigh is right or not in warning historians against following truth too close upon the heels, the caution is a good one for poets as respects truth to Nature. But it is a mischievous fallacy in historian or critic to treat as a blemish of the man what is but the common tincture of his age. It is to confound a spatter of mud with a moral stain.

But I have been led away from my immediate purpose. I did not intend to compare Shakespeare with the ancients, much less to justify his defects by theirs. Shakespeare himself has left us a pregnant satire on dogmatical and categorical æsthetics (which commonly in discussion soon lose their ceremonious tails and are reduced to the internecine dog and cat of their bald first syllables) in the cloud-scene between Hamlet and Polonius, suggesting exquisitely how futile is any attempt at a cast-iron definition of those perpetually metamorphic impressions of the beautiful whose source is as much in the man who looks as in the thing he sees. In the fine arts a thing is either good in itself or it is nothing. It neither gains nor loses by having it shown that another good thing was also good in itself, any more than a bad thing profits by comparison with another that is worse. The final judgment of the world is intuitive, and is based, not on proof that a work possesses some of the qualities of another whose greatness is acknowledged, but on the immediate feeling that it carries to a high point of perfection certain qualities proper to itself. One does not flatter a fine pear by comparing it to a fine peach, nor learn what a fine peach is by tasting ever so many poor ones. The boy who makes his first bite into one does not need to ask his father if or how or why it is good. Because continuity is a merit in some kinds of writing, shall we refuse ourselves to the authentic charm of Montaigne's want of it? I have heard people complain of French tragedies because they were so very French. This, though it may not be to some particular tastes, and may from one point of view be a defect, is from another and far higher a distinguished merit. It is their flavor, as direct a telltale of the soil whence they drew it as that of French wines is. Suppose we should tax the Elgin marbles with being too Greek? When will people, nay, when will even critics, get over this self-defrauding trick of cheapening the excellence of one thing by that of another, this conclusive style of judgment which consists simply in belonging to the other parish? As one grows older, one loses many idols, perhaps comes at last to have none at all, though he may honestly enough uncover in deference to the worshippers before any shrine. But for the seeming loss the compensation is ample. These saints of literature descend from their canopied remoteness to be even more precious as men like ourselves, our companions in field and street, speaking the same tongue, though in many dialects, and owning one creed under the most diverse masks of form.

Much of that merit of structure which is claimed for the ancient tragedy is due, if I am not mistaken, to circumstances external to the drama itself, — to custom, to convention, to the exigencies of the theatre. It is formal rather than organic. The *Prometheus* seems to me one of the few Greek tragedies in which the whole creation has developed itself in perfect proportion from one central germ of living conception. The motive of the ancient drama is generally outside of it, while in the modern (at least in the English) it is necessarily within. Goethe, in a thoughtful essay,* written many years later than his famous criticism of Hamlet in *Wilhelm Meister,* says that the distinction between the two is the difference between *sollen* and *wollen,* that is, between *must* and *would.* He means that in the Greek drama the catastrophe is foreordained by an inexorable Destiny, while the element of Freewill, and consequently of choice, is the very axis of the modern. The definition is conveniently portable, but it has its limitations. Goethe's attention was too exclusively fixed on the Fate tragedies of the Greeks, and upon Shakespeare among the moderns. In the Spanish drama, for example, custom, loyalty, honor, and religion are as imperative and as inevitable as doom. In the *Antigone,* on the other hand, the crisis lies in the character of the protagonist. In this sense it is modern, and is the first example of true character-painting in tragedy. But, from whatever cause, that exquisite analysis of complex motives, and the display of them in action and speech, which constitute for us the abiding charm of fiction, were quite unknown to the ancients. They reached their height in Cervantes and Shakespeare, and, though on a lower plane, still belong to the upper region of art in Le Sage, Molière, and Fielding. The personages of the Greek

* Shakspeare und kein Ende.

tragedy seem to be commonly rather types than individuals. In the modern tragedy, certainly in the four greatest of Shakespeare's tragedies, there is still something very like Destiny, only the place of it is changed. It is no longer above man, but in him; yet the catastrophe is as sternly foredoomed in the characters of Lear, Othello, Macbeth, and Hamlet as it could be by an infallible oracle. In Macbeth, indeed, the Weird Sisters introduce an element very like Fate; but generally it may be said that with the Greeks the character is involved in the action, while with Shakespeare the action is evolved from the character. In the one case, the motive of the play controls the personages; in the other, the chief personages are in themselves the motive to which all else is subsidiary. In any comparison, therefore, of Shakespeare with the ancients, we are not to contrast him with them as unapproachable models, but to consider whether he, like them, did not consciously endeavor, under the circumstances and limitations in which he found himself, to produce the most excellent thing possible, a model also in its own kind, — whether higher or lower in degree is another question. The only fair comparison would be between him and that one of his contemporaries who endeavored to anachronize himself, so to speak, and to subject his art, so far as might be, to the laws of classical composition. Ben Jonson was a great man, and has sufficiently proved that he had an eye for the external marks of character; but when he would make a whole of them, he gives us instead either a bundle of humors or an incorporated idea. With Shakespeare the plot is an interior organism, in Jonson an external contrivance. It is the difference between man and tortoise. In the one the osseous structure is out of sight, indeed, but sustains the flesh and blood that envelop it, while the other is boxed up and imprisoned in his bones.

I have been careful to confine myself to what may be called Shakespeare's ideal tragedies. In the purely historical or chronicle plays, the conditions are different, and his imagination submits itself to the necessary restrictions on its freedom of movement. Outside the tragedies also, the *Tempest* makes an exception worthy of notice. If I read it rightly, it is an example of how a great poet should write allegory, — not embodying metaphysical abstractions, but giving us ideals abstracted from life itself, suggesting an under-meaning everywhere, forcing it upon us nowhere, tantalizing the mind with hints that imply so much and tell so little, and yet keep the attention all eye and ear with eager, if fruitless, expectation. Here the leading characters are not merely typical, but symbolical, — that is, they do not illustrate a class of persons, they belong to universal Nature. Consider the scene of the play. Shakespeare is wont to take some familiar story, to lay his scene in some place the name of which, at least, is familiar, — well knowing the reserve of power that lies in the familiar as a background, when things are set in front of it under a new and unexpected light. But in the *Tempest* the scene is laid nowhere, or certainly in no country laid down on any map. Nowhere, then? At once nowhere and anywhere, — for it is in the soul of man, that still vexed island hung between the upper and the nether world, and liable to incursions from both. There is scarce a play of Shakespeare's in which there is such variety of character, none in which character has so little to do in the carrying on and development of the story. But consider for a moment if ever the Imagination has been so embodied as in Prospero, the Fancy as in Ariel, the brute Understanding as in Caliban, who, the moment his poor wits are warmed with the glorious liquor of Stephano, plots rebellion against his natural lord, the higher Reason. Miranda is mere abstract Womanhood, as truly so before she sees Ferdinand as Eve before she was wakened to consciousness by the echo of her own nature coming back to her, the same, and yet not the same, from that of Adam. Ferdinand, again, is nothing more than Youth, compelled to drudge at something he despises, till the sacrifice of will and abnegation of self win him his ideal in Miranda. The subordinate personages are simply types; Sebastian and Antonio, of weak character and evil ambition; Gonzalo, of average sense and honesty; Adrian and Francisco, of the walking gentlemen who serve to fill up a world. They are not characters in the same sense with Iago, Falstaff, Shallow, or Leontius; and it is curious how every one of them loses his way in this enchanted island of life, all the victims of one illusion after another, except Prospero, whose ministers are purely ideal. The whole play, indeed, is a succession of illusions, winding up with those solemn words of the great enchanter who had summoned to his service every shape of merriment or passion, every figure in the great tragi-comedy of life, and who was now bidding farewell to the scene of his triumphs. For in Prospero shall we not recognize the Artist himself, —

> "That did not better for his life provide
> Than public means which public manners breeds,
> Whence comes it that his name receives a brand," —

who has forfeited a shining place in the world's eye by devotion to his art, and who, turned adrift on the ocean of life in the leaky carcass of a boat, has shipwrecked on that Fortunate Island (as men always do who find their true vocation) where he is absolute lord, making all the powers of Nature serve him, but with Ariel and Caliban as special ministers? Of whom else could he have been thinking, when he says, —

> "Graves, at my command,
> Have waked their sleepers, oped, and let them forth,
> By my so potent art"?

Was this man, so extraordinary from whatever side we look at him, who ran so easily through the whole scale of human sentiment, from the homely common-sense of, "When two men ride of one horse, one *must* ride behind," to the transcendental subtilty of,

> "No, Time, thou shalt not boast that I do change;
> Thy pyramids, built up with newer might,
> To me are nothing novel, nothing strange;
> They are but dressings of a former sight,"—

was he alone so unconscious of powers, some part of whose magic is recognized by all mankind, from the school-boy to the philosopher, that he merely sat by and saw them go without the least notion what they were about? Was he an inspired idiot, *vôtre bizarre Shakespeare?* a vast, irregular genius? a simple rustic, warbling his *native* wood-notes wild, in other words, insensible to the benefits of culture? When attempts have been made at various times to prove that this singular and seemingly contradictory creature, not one, but all mankind's epitome, was a musician, a lawyer, a doctor, a Catholic, a Protestant, an atheist, an Irishman, a discoverer of the circulation of the blood, and finally, that he was not himself, but somebody else, is it not a little odd that the last thing anybody should have thought of proving him was an artist? Nobody believes any longer that immediate inspiration is possible in modern times (as if God had grown old),—at least, nobody believes it of the prophets of those days, of John of Leyden, or Reeves, or Muggleton,—and yet everybody seems to take it for granted of this one man Shakespeare. He, somehow or other, without knowing it, was able to do what none of the rest of them, though knowing it all too perfectly well, could begin to do. Everybody seems to get afraid of him in turn. Voltaire plays gentleman usher for him to his countrymen, and then, perceiving that his countrymen find a flavor in him beyond that of *Zaïre* or *Mahomet*, discovers him to be a *Sauvage ivre, sans le moindre étincelle de bon goût, et sans le moindre connoissance des règles.* Goethe, who tells us that *Götz von Berlichingen* was written in the Shakespearian manner, — and we certainly should not have guessed it, if he had not blabbed, — comes to the final conclusion, that Shakespeare was a poet, but not a dramatist. Châteaubriand thinks that he has corrupted art. "If, to attain," he says, "the height of tragic art, it be enough to heap together disparate scenes without order and without connection, to dovetail the burlesque with the pathetic, to set the water-carrier beside the monarch and the huckster-wench beside the queen, who may not reasonably flatter himself with being the rival of the greatest masters? Whoever should give himself the trouble to retrace a single one of his days, ... to keep a journal from hour to hour, would have made a drama in the fashion of the English poet." But there journals and journals, as the French say, and what goes into them depends on the eye that gathers for them. It is a long step from St. Simon to Dangeau, from Pepys to Thoresby, from Shakespeare even to the Marquis de Châteaubriand. M. Hugo alone, convinced that, as founder of the French Romantic School, there is a kind of family likeness between himself and Shakespeare, stands boldly forth to prove the father as extravagant as the son. Calm yourself, M. Hugo, you are no more a child of his than Will Davenant was! But, after all, is it such a great crime to produce something absolutely new in a world so tedious as ours, and so apt to tell its old stories over again? I do not mean new in substance, but in the manner of presentation. Surely the highest office of a great poet is to show us how much variety, freshness, and opportunity abides in the obvious and familiar. He invents nothing, but seems rather to *re*-discover the world about him, and his penetrating vision gives to things of daily encounter something of the strangeness of new creation. Meanwhile the changed conditions of modern life demand a change in the method of treatment. The ideal is not a strait-waistcoat. Because *Alexis and Dora* is so charming, shall we have no *Paul and Virginia?* It was the idle endeavor to reproduce the old enchantment in the old way that gave us the pastoral, sent to the garret now with our grandmothers' achievements of the same sort in worsted. Every age says to its poets, like a mistress to her lover, "Tell me what I am like"; and he who succeeds in catching the evanescent expression that reveals character — which is as much as to say, what is intrinsically human — will be found to have caught something as imperishable as human nature itself. Aristophanes, by the vital and essential qualities of his humorous satire, is already more nearly our contemporary than Molière; and even the *Trouvères*, careless and trivial as they mostly are, could fecundate a great poet like Chaucer, and are still delightful reading.

The Attic tragedy still keeps its hold upon the loyalty of scholars through their imagination, or their pedantry, or their feeling of an exclusive property, as may happen, and, however alloyed with baser matter, this loyalty is legitimate and well bestowed. But the dominion of the Shakespearian is even wider. It pushes forward its boundaries from year to year, and moves no landmark backward. Here Alfieri and Lessing own a common allegiance; and the loyalty to him is one not of guild or tradition, but of conviction and enthusiasm. Can this be said of any other modern? of robust Corneille? of tender Racine? of Calderon even, with his tropical warmth and vigor of production? The Greeks and he are alike and alone in this, and for the same reason, that both are unapproachably the highest in their kind. Call him Gothic, if you like, but the inspiring mind that presided over the growth of these clustered masses of arch and spire and pinnacle and buttress is neither Greek nor Gothic, — it is simply genius lending itself to embody the new desire of man's mind, as it had embodied the old. After all, to be delightful is to be classic, and the chaotic never pleases long. But manifoldness is not confusion, any more than formalism is simplicity. If Shakespeare rejected the unities, as I think he who complains of "Art made tongue-tied by Authority" might very well deliberately do, it was for the sake of an imaginative unity more intimate than any of time and place. The antique in itself is not the ideal, though its remoteness from the vulgarity of everyday associations helps to make it seem so. The true ideal is not opposed to the real, nor is it any artificial heightening thereof, but lies *in* it, and blessed are the eyes that find it! It is the *mens divinior* which hides within the actual, transfiguring matter-of-fact into matter-of-meaning for him who has the gift of second-sight. In this sense Hogarth is often more truly ideal than Raphael, Shakespeare often more truly so than the Greeks. I think it is a more or less conscious perception of this ideality, as it is a more or less well-grounded persuasion of it as respects the Greeks, that assures to him, as to them, and with equal justice, a permanent supremacy over the minds of men. This gives to his characters their universality, to his thought its irradiating property, while the artistic purpose running through and combining the endless variety of scene and character will alone account for his power of dramatic effect.

Goethe affirmed, that, without Schröder's prunings and adaptations, Shakespeare was too undramatic for the German theatre, — that, if the theory that his plays should be represented textually should prevail, he would be driven from the boards. The theory has prevailed, and he not only holds his own, but is acted oftener than ever. It is not irregular genius that can do this, for surely Germany need not go abroad for what her own Werners could more than amply supply her with.

But I would much rather quote a fine saying than a bad prophecy of a man to whom I owe so much. Goethe, in one of the most perfect of his shorter poems, tells us that a poem is like a painted window. Seen from without, (and he accordingly justifies the Philistine, who never looks at them otherwise,) they seem dingy and confused enough; but enter, and then

"Da ist's auf einmal farbig helle,
Geschicht' und Zierath glänzt in Schnelle."

With the same feeling he says elsewhere in prose, that "there is a destructive criticism and a productive. The former is very easy; for one has only to set up in his mind any standard, any model, however narrow" (let us say the Greeks), "and then boldly assert that the work under review does not match with it, and therefore is good for nothing, — the matter is settled, and one must at once deny its claim. Productive criticism is a great deal more difficult; it asks, What did the author propose to himself? Is what he proposes reasonable and comprehensible? and how far has he succeeded in carrying it out?" It is in applying this latter kind of criticism to Shakespeare that the Germans have set us an example worthy of all commendation. If they have been sometimes over-subtile, they at least had the merit of first looking at his works as wholes, as something that very likely contained an idea, perhaps conveyed a moral, if we could get at it. The illumination lent us by most of the English commentators reminds us of the candles which guides hold up to show us a picture in a dark place, the smoke of which gradually makes the work of the artist invisible under its repeated layers. Lessing, as might have been expected, opened the first glimpse in the new direction; Goethe followed with his famous exposition of Hamlet; A. W. Schlegel took a more comprehensive view in his Lectures, which Coleridge worked over into English, adding many fine criticisms of his own on single passages; and finally, Gervinus has devoted four volumes to a comment on the plays, full of excellent matter, though pushing the moral exegesis beyond all reasonable bounds.* With the help of all these, and especially of the last, I shall apply this theory of criticism to Hamlet, not in the hope of saying anything new, but of bringing something to the support of the thesis, that, if Shakespeare was skilful as a playwright, he was even greater as a dramatist, — that, if his immediate business was to fill the theatre, his higher object was to create something which, by fulfilling the conditions and answering the requirements of modern life, should as truly deserve to be called a work of art as others had deserved it by doing the same thing in former times and under other circumstances. Supposing him to have accepted — consciously or not is of little importance — the new terms of the problem which makes character the pivot of dramatic action, and consequently the key of dramatic unity, how far did he succeed?

Before attempting my analysis, I must clear away a little rubbish. Are such anachronisms as those of which Voltaire accuses Shakespeare in Hamlet, such as the introduction of cannon before the invention of gunpowder,

* I do not mention Ulrici's book, for it seems to me unwieldy and dull, — zeal without knowledge.

and making Christians of the Danes three centuries too soon, of the least bearing æsthetically? I think not; but as they are of a piece with a great many other criticisms upon the great poet, it is worth while to dwell upon them a moment.

The first demand we make upon whatever claims to be a work of art (and we have a right to make it) is that it shall be *in keeping*. Now this propriety is of two kinds, either extrinsic or intrinsic. In the first I should class whatever relates rather to the body than the soul of the work, such as fidelity to the facts of history, (wherever that is important,) congruity of costume, and the like, — in short, whatever might come under the head of *picturesque* truth, a departure from which would shock too rudely our preconceived associations. I have seen an Indian chief in French boots, and he seemed to me almost tragic; but, put upon the stage in tragedy, he would have been ludicrous. Lichtenberg, writing from London in 1775, tells us that Garrick played Hamlet in a suit of the French fashion, then commonly worn, and that he was blamed for it by some of the critics; but, he says, one hears no such criticism during the play, nor on the way home, nor at supper afterwards, nor indeed till the emotion roused by the great actor has had time to subside. He justifies Garrick, though we should not be able to endure it now. Yet nothing would be gained by trying to make Hamlet's costume true to the assumed period of the play, for the scene of it is laid in a Denmark that has no dates.

In the second and more important category, I should put, first, co-ordination of character, that is, a certain variety in harmony of the personages of a drama, as in the attitudes and coloring of the figures in a pictorial composition, so that, while mutually relieving and setting off each other, they shall combine in the total impression; second, that subordinate truth to Nature which makes each character coherent in itself; and, third, such propriety of costume and the like as shall satisfy the superhistoric sense, to which, and to which alone, the higher drama appeals. All these come within the scope of *imaginative* truth. To illustrate my third head by an example. Tieck criticises John Kemble's dressing for Macbeth in a modern Highland costume, as being ungraceful without any countervailing merit of historical exactness. I think a deeper reason for his dissatisfaction might be found in the fact, that this garb, with its purely modern and British army associations, is out of place on Fores Heath, and drags the Weird Sisters down with it from their proper imaginative remoteness in the gloom of the past to the disenchanting glare of the foot-lights. It is not the antiquarian, but the poetic conscience, that is wounded. To this, exactness, so far as concerns ideal representation, may not only not be truth, but may even be opposed to it. Anachronisms and the like are in themselves of no account, and become important only when they make a gap too wide for our illusion to cross unconsciously, that is, when they are anacoluthons to the imagination. The aim of the artist is psychologic, not historic truth. It is comparatively easy for an author to *get up* any period with tolerable minuteness in externals, but readers and audiences find more difficulty in getting them down, though oblivion swallows scores of them at a gulp. The saving truth in such matters is a truth to essential and permanent characteristics. The Ulysses of Shakespeare, like the Ulysses of Dante and Tennyson, more or less harmonizes with our ideal conception of the wary, long-considering, though adventurous son of Laertes, yet Simon Lord Lovat is doubtless nearer the original type. In Hamlet, though there is no Denmark of the ninth century, Shakespeare has suggested the prevailing rudeness of manners quite enough for his purpose. We see it in the single combat of Hamlet's father with the elder Fortinbras, in the vulgar wassail of the king, in the English monarch being expected to hang Rosencrantz and Guildenstern out of hand merely to oblige his cousin of Denmark, in Laertes, sent to Paris to be made a gentleman of, becoming instantly capable of any the most barbarous treachery to glut his vengeance. We cannot fancy Ragnar Lodbrog or Eric the Red matriculating at Wittenberg, but it was essential that Hamlet should be a scholar, and Shakespeare sends him thither without more ado. All through the play we get the notion of a state of society in which a savage nature has disguised itself in the externals of civilization, like a Maori deacon, who has only to strip and he becomes once more a tattooed pagan with his mouth watering for a spare-rib of his pastor. Historically, at the date of Hamlet, the Danes were in the habit of burning their enemies alive in their houses, with as much of their family about them as might be to make it comfortable. Shakespeare seems purposely to have dissociated his play from history by changing nearly every name in the original legend. The motive of the play — revenge as a religious duty — belongs only to a social state in which the traditions of barbarism are still operative, but, with infallible artistic judgment, Shakespeare has chosen, not untamed Nature, as he found it in history, but the period of transition, a period in which the times are always out of joint, and thus the irresolution which has its root in Hamlet's own character is stimulated by the very incompatibility of that legacy of vengeance he has inherited from the past with the new culture and refinement of which he is the representative. One of the few books which Shakespeare is known to have possessed was Florio's Montaigne, and he might well have transferred the Frenchman's motto, *Que sçais je?* to the front of his tragedy; nor can I help fancying something more than accident in the fact that Hamlet has been a student at Wittenberg, whence those new ideas went forth, of whose results in unsettling men's faith, and consequently disqualifying them for promptness in action, Shakespeare had been not only an eye-witness, but which he must actually have experienced in himself.

One other objection let me touch upon here, especially as it has been urged against Hamlet, and that is the introduction of low characters and comic scenes in tragedy. Even Garrick, who had just assisted at the Stratford Jubilee, where Shakespeare had been pronounced divine, was induced by this absurd outcry for the proprieties of the tragic stage to omit the grave-diggers' scene from Hamlet. Leaving apart the fact that Shakespeare would not have been the representative poet he is, if he had not given expression to this striking tendency of the Northern races, which shows itself constantly, not only in their literature, but even in their mythology and their architecture, the grave-diggers' scene always impresses me as one of the most pathetic in the whole tragedy. That Shakespeare introduced such scenes and characters with deliberate intention, and with a view to artistic relief and contrast, there can hardly be a doubt. We must take it for granted that a man whose works show everywhere the results of judgment sometimes acted with forethought. I find the springs of the profoundest sorrow and pity in this hardened indifference of the grave-diggers, in their careless discussion as to whether Ophelia's death was by suicide or no, in their singing and jesting at their dreary work.

> "A pickaxe and a spade, a spade,
> For — and a shrouding-sheet:

O, a pit of clay for to be made
For such a guest is meet!"

We know who is to be the guest of this earthen hospitality, — how much beauty, love, and heartbreak are to be covered in that pit of clay. All we remember of Ophelia reacts upon us with tenfold force, and we recoil from our amusement at the ghastly drollery of the two delvers with a shock of horror. That the unconscious Hamlet should stumble on *this* grave of all others, that it should be *here* that he should pause to muse humorously on death and decay, — all this prepares us for the revulsion of passion in the next scene, and for the frantic confession, —

"I loved Ophelia; forty thousand brothers
Could not with all *their* quantity of love
Make up my sum!"

And it is only here that such an asseveration would be true even to the feeling of the moment; for it is plain from all we know of Hamlet that he could not so have loved Ophelia, that he was incapable of the self-abandonment of a true passion, that he would have analyzed this emotion as he does all others, would have peeped and botanized upon it till it became to him a mere matter of scientific interest. All this force of contrast, and this horror of surprise, were necessary so to intensify his remorseful regret that he should believe himself for once in earnest. The speech of the King, "O, he is mad, Laertes," recalls him to himself, and he at once begins to rave: —

"Zounds! show me what thou 'lt do!
Woul't weep? woul't fight? woul't fast? woul't tear thyself?
Woul't drink up eysil? eat a crocodile?"

It is easy to see that the whole plot hinges upon the character of Hamlet, that Shakespeare's conception of this was the ovum out of which the whole organism was hatched. And here let me remark, that there is a kind of genealogical necessity in the character,—a thing not altogether strange to the attentive reader of Shakespeare. Hamlet seems the natural result of the mixture of father and mother in his temperament, the resolution and persistence of the one, like sound timber wormholed and made shaky, as it were, by the other's infirmity of will and discontinuity of purpose. In natures so imperfectly mixed it is not uncommon to find vehemence of intention the prelude and counterpoise of weak performance, the conscious nature striving to keep up its self-respect by a triumph in words all the more resolute that it feels assured beforehand of inevitable defeat in action. As in such slipshod housekeeping men are their own largest creditors, they find it easy to stave off utter bankruptcy of conscience by taking up one unpaid promise with another larger, and at heavier interest, till such self-swindling becomes habitual and by degrees almost painless. How did Coleridge discount his own notes of this kind with less and less specie as the figures lengthened on the paper! As with Hamlet, so it is with Ophelia and Laertes. The father's feebleness comes up again in the wasting heartbreak and gentle lunacy of the daughter, while the son shows it in a rashness of impulse and act, a kind of crankiness, of whose essential feebleness we are all the more sensible as contrasted with a nature so steady on its keel, and drawing so much water, as that of Horatio,—the foil at once, in different ways, to both him and Hamlet. It was natural, also, that the daughter of self-conceited old Polonius should have her softness stiffened with a fibre of obstinacy; for there are two kinds of weakness, that which breaks, and that which bends. Ophelia's is of the former kind; Hero is her counterpart, giving way before calamity, and rising again so soon as the pressure is removed.

I find two passages in Dante that contain the exactest possible definition of that habit or quality of Hamlet's mind which justifies the tragic turn of the play, and renders it natural and unavoidable from the beginning. The first is from the second canto of the *Inferno:*—

> "E quale è quei che disvuol ciò che volle,
> E per nuovi pensier cangia proposta,
> Si che del cominciar tutto si tolle;
> Tal mi fec' io in quella oscura costa:
> Perchè pensando consumai la impresa
> Che fu nel cominciar cotanto tosta."

> "And like the man who unwills what he willed,
> And for new thoughts doth change his first intent,
> So that he cannot anywhere begin,
> Such became I upon that slope obscure,
> Because with thinking I consumed resolve,
> That was so ready at the setting out."

Again, in the fifth of the *Purgatorio:*—

> "Che sempre l' uomo in cui pensier rampoglia
> Sovra pensier, da sè dilunga il segno,
> Perchè la foga l' un dell' altro insolla."

> "For always he in whom one thought buds forth
> Out of another farther puts the goal,
> For each has only force to mar the other."

Dante was a profound metaphysician, and as in the first passage he describes and defines a certain quality of mind, so in the other he tells us its result in the character and life, namely, indecision and failure,—the goal *farther* off at the end than at the beginning. It is remarkable how close a resemblance of thought, and even of expression, there is between the former of these quotations and a part of Hamlet's famous soliloquy:—

> "Thus conscience [i. e. consciousness] doth make cowards of us all:
> And thus the native hue of resolution
> Is sicklied o'er with the pale cast of thought,
> And enterprises of great pitch and moment
> With this regard their currents turn awry,
> And lose the name of action!"

It is an inherent peculiarity of a mind like Hamlet's that it should be conscious of its own defect. Men of his type are forever analyzing their own emotions and motives. They cannot do anything, because they always see two ways of doing it. They cannot determine on any course of action, because they are always, as it were, standing at the cross-roads, and see too well the disadvantages of every one of them. It is not that they are incapable of resolve, but somehow the band between the motive power and the operative faculties is relaxed and loose. The engine works, but the machinery it should drive stands still. The imagination is so much in overplus, that thinking a thing becomes better than doing it, and thought with its easy perfection, capable of everything because it can accomplish everything with ideal means, is vastly more attractive and satisfactory than deed, which must be wrought at best with imperfect instruments, and always falls short of the conception that went before it. "If to do," says Portia in the *Merchant of Venice*, — "if to do were as easy as to know what 't were good to do, chapels had been churches, and poor men's cottages princes' palaces." Hamlet knows only too well what 't were good to do, but he palters with everything in a double sense: he sees the grain of good there is in evil, and the grain of evil there is in good, as they exist in the world, and, finding that he can make those feather-weighted accidents balance each other, infers that there is little to choose between the essences themselves. He is of Montaigne's mind, and says expressly that "there is nothing good or ill, but thinking makes it so." He dwells so exclusively in the world of ideas that the world of facts seems trifling, nothing is worth the while; and he has been so long objectless and purposeless, so far as actual life is concerned, that, when at last an object and an aim are forced upon him, he cannot deal with them, and gropes about vainly for a motive outside of himself that shall marshal his thoughts for him and guide his faculties into the path of action. He is the victim not so much of feebleness of will as of an intellectual indifference that hinders the will from working long in any one direction. He wishes to will, but never wills. His continual iteration of resolve shows that he has no resolution. He is capable of passionate energy where the occasion presents itself suddenly from without, because nothing is so irritable as conscious irresolution with a duty to perform. But of deliberate energy he is not capable; for there the impulse must come from within, and the blade of his analysis is so subtile that it can divide the finest hair of motive 'twixt north and northwest side, leaving him desperate to choose between them. The very consciousness of his defect is an insuperable bar to his repairing it; for the unity of purpose, which infuses every fibre of the character with will available whenever wanted, is impossible where the mind can never rest till it has resolved that unity into its component elements, and satisfied itself which on the whole is of greater value. A critical instinct so insatiable that it must turn upon itself, for lack of something else to hew and hack, becomes incapable at last of originating anything except indecision. It becomes infallible in what *not* to do. How easily he might have accomplished his task is shown by the conduct of Laertes. When *he* has a death to avenge, he raises a mob, breaks into the palace, bullies the king, and proves how weak the usurper really was.

The world is the victim of splendid parts, and is slow to accept a rounded whole, because that is something which is long in completing, still longer in demonstrating its completion. We like to be surprised into admiration, and not logically convinced that we ought to admire. We are willing to be delighted with success, though we are somewhat indifferent to the homely qualities which insure it. Our thought is so filled with the rocket's burst of momentary splendor so far above us, that we forget the poor stick, useful and unseen, that made its climbing possible. One of these homely qualities is continuity of character, and it escapes present applause because it tells chiefly, in the long run, in results. With his usual tact, Shakespeare has brought in such a character as a contrast and foil to Hamlet. Horatio is the only complete *man* in the play, — solid, well-knit, and true; a noble, quiet nature, with that highest of all qualities, judgment, always sane and prompt; who never drags his anchors for any wind of opinion or fortune, but grips all the closer to the reality of things. He seems one of those calm, undemonstrative men whom we love and admire without asking to know why, crediting them with the capacity of great things, without any test of actual achievement, because we feel that their manhood is a constant quality, and no mere accident of circumstance and opportunity. Such men are always sure of the presence of their highest self on demand. Hamlet is continually drawing bills on the future, secured by his promise of himself to himself, which he can never redeem. His own somewhat feminine nature recognizes its complement in Horatio, and clings to it instinctively, as naturally as Horatio is attracted by that fatal gift of imagination, the absence of which makes the strength of his own character, as its overplus does the weakness of Hamlet's. It is a happy marriage of two minds drawn together by the charm of unlikeness. Hamlet feels in Horatio the solid steadiness which he misses in himself; Horatio in Hamlet that need of service and sustainment to render which gives him a consciousness of his own value. Hamlet fills the place of a woman to Horatio, revealing him to himself not only in what he says, but by a constant claim upon his strength of nature; and there is great psychological truth in making suicide the first impulse of this quiet, undemonstrative man, after Hamlet's death, as if the very reason for his being were taken away with his friend's need of him. In his grief, he for the first and only time speaks of himself, is first made conscious of himself by his loss. If this manly reserve of Horatio be true to Nature, not less so are the communicativeness of Hamlet, and his tendency to soliloquize. If self-consciousness be alien to the one, it is just as truly the happiness of the other. Like a musician distrustful of himself, he is forever tuning his instrument, first overstraining this cord a little, and then that, but unable to bring them into unison, or to profit by it if he could.

We do not believe that Horatio ever thought he "was not a pipe for Fortune's finger to play what stop she please," till Hamlet told him so. That was Fortune's affair, not his; let her try it, if she liked. He is unconscious of his own peculiar qualities, as men of decision commonly are, or they would not be men of decision. When there is a thing to be done, they go straight at it, and for the time there is nothing for them in the whole universe but themselves and their object. Hamlet, on the other hand, is always studying himself. This world and the other, too, are always present to his mind, and there in the corner is the little black kobold of a doubt making mouths at him. He breaks down the bridges before him, not behind him, as a man of action would do; but there is something more than this. He is an ingrained sceptic; though his is the scepticism, not of reason, but of feeling, whose root is want of faith in himself. In him it is passive, a malady rather than a function of the mind. We might call him insincere: not that he was in any sense a hypocrite, but only that he never was and never could be in earnest. Never could be, because no man without intense faith in something ever can. Even if he only believed in himself, that were better than nothing; for it will carry a man a great way in the outward successes of life, nay, will even sometimes give him the Archimedean fulcrum for moving the world. But Hamlet doubts everything. He doubts the immortality of the soul, just after seeing his father's spirit, and hearing from its mouth the secrets of the other world. He doubts Horatio even, and swears him to secrecy on the cross of his sword, though probably he himself has no assured belief in the sacredness of the symbol. He doubts Ophelia, and asks her, "Are you honest?" He doubts the ghost, after he has had a little time to think about it, and so gets up the play to test the guilt of the king. And how coherent the whole character is! With what perfect tact and judgment Shakespeare, in the advice to the players, makes him an exquisite critic! For just here that part of his character which would be weak in dealing with affairs is strong. A wise scepticism is the first attribute of a good critic. He must not believe that the fire-insurance offices will raise their rates of premium on Charles River, because the new volume of poems is printing at Riverside or the University Press. He must not believe so profoundly in the ancients as to think it wholly out of the question that the world has still vigor enough in its loins to beget some one who will one of these days be as good an ancient as any of them.

Another striking quality in Hamlet's nature is his perpetual inclination to irony. I think this has been generally passed over too lightly, as if it were something external and accidental, rather assumed as a mask than part of the real nature of the man. It seems to me to go deeper, to be something innate, and not merely factitious. It is nothing like the grave irony of Socrates, which was the weapon of a man thoroughly in earnest, — the *boomerang* of argument, which one throws in the opposite direction of what he means to hit, and which seems to be flying away from the adversary, who will presently find himself knocked down by it. It is not like the irony of Timon, which is but the wilful refraction of a clear mind twisting awry whatever enters it, — or of Iago, which is the slime that a nature essentially evil loves to trail over all beauty and goodness to taint them with distrust: it is the half-jest, half-earnest of an inactive temperament that has not quite made up its mind whether life is a reality or no, whether men were not made in jest, and which amuses itself equally with finding a deep meaning in trivial things and a trifling one in the profoundest mysteries of being, because the want of earnestness in its own essence infects everything else with its own indifference. If there be now and then an unmannerly rudeness and bitterness in it, as in the scenes with Polonius and Osrick, we must remember that Hamlet was just in the condition which spurs men to sallies of this kind: dissatisfied, at one neither with the world nor with himself, and accordingly casting about for something out of himself to vent his spleen upon. But even in these passages there is no hint of earnestness, of any purpose beyond the moment; they are mere cat's-paws of vexation, and not the deep-raking groundswell of passion, as we see it in the sarcasm of Lear.

The question of Hamlet's madness has been much discussed and variously decided. High medical authority has pronounced, as usual, on both sides of the question. But the induction has been drawn from too narrow premises, being based on a mere diagnosis of the *case*, and not on an appreciation of the character in its completeness. We have a case of pretended madness in the Edgar of *King Lear;* and it is certainly true that that is a charcoal sketch, coarsely outlined, compared with the delicate drawing, the lights, shades, and half-tints of the portraiture in Hamlet. But does this tend to prove that the madness of the latter, because truer to the recorded observation of experts, is real, and meant to be real, as the other to be fictitious? Not in the least, as it appears to me. Hamlet, among all the characters of Shakespeare, is the most eminently a metaphysician and psychologist. He is a close observer, continually analyzing his own nature and that of others, letting fall his little drops of acid irony on all who come near him, to make them show what they are made of. Even Ophelia is not too sacred, Osrick not too contemptible for experiment. If such a man assumed madness, he would play his part perfectly. If Shakespeare himself, without going mad, could so observe and remember all the abnormal symptoms as to be able to reproduce them in Hamlet, why should it be beyond the power of Hamlet to reproduce them in himself? If you deprive Hamlet of reason, there is no truly tragic motive left. He would be a fit subject for Bedlam, but not for the stage. We might have pathology enough, but no pathos. Ajax first becomes tragic when he recovers his wits. If Hamlet is irresponsible, the whole play is a chaos. That he is not so might be proved by evidence enough, were it not labor thrown away.

This feigned madness of Hamlet's is one of the few points in which Shakespeare has kept close to the old story on which he founded his play; and as he never decided without deliberation, so he never acted without unerring judgment. Hamlet *drifts* through the whole tragedy. He never keeps on one tack long enough to get steerage-way, even if, in a nature like his, with those electric streamers of whim and fancy forever wavering across the vault of his brain, the needle of judgment would point in one direction long enough to strike a course by. The scheme of simulated insanity is precisely the one he would have been likely to hit upon, because it enabled him to follow his own bent, and to drift with an apparent purpose, postponing decisive action by the very means he adopts to arrive at its accomplishment, and satisfying himself with the show of doing something that he may escape so much the longer the dreaded necessity of really doing anything at all. It enables him to *play* with life and duty, instead of taking them by the rougher side, where alone any firm grip is possible, —to feel that he is on the way toward accomplishing somewhat, when he is really paltering with his own irresolution. Nothing, I think, could be more finely imagined than this. Voltaire complains that he goes mad without any sufficient object or result. Perfectly true, and precisely what was most natural for him to do, and, accordingly, precisely what Shakespeare meant that he should do. It was delightful to him to indulge his imagination and humor, to prove his capacity for something by playing a part: the one thing he could not do was to bring himself to *act*, unless when surprised by a sudden impulse of suspicion, — as where he kills Polonius, and there he could not see his victim. He discourses admirably of suicide, but does not kill himself; he talks daggers, but uses none. He puts by the chance to kill the king with the excuse that he will not do it while he is praying, lest his soul be saved thereby, though it is more than doubtful whether he believed it himself. He allows himself to be packed off to England, without any motive except that it would for the time take him farther from a present duty: the more disagreeable to a nature like his because it *was* present, and not a mere matter for speculative consideration. When Goethe made his famous comparison of the acorn planted in a vase which it bursts with its growth, and says that in like manner Hamlet is a nature which breaks down under the weight of a duty too great for it to bear, he seems to have considered the character too much from one side. Had Hamlet actually killed himself to escape his too onerous commission, Goethe's conception of him would have been satisfactory enough. But Hamlet was hardly a sentimentalist, like Werther; on the contrary, he saw things only too clearly in the dry north-light of the intellect. It is chance that at last brings him to his end. It would appear rather that Shakespeare intended to show us an imaginative temperament brought face to face with actualities, into any clear relation of sympathy with which it cannot bring itself. The very means that Shakespeare makes use of to lay upon him the obligation of acting — the ghost — really seems to make it all the harder for him to act; for the spectre but gives an additional excitement to his imagination and a fresh topic for his scepticism.

I shall not attempt to evolve any high moral significance from the play, even if I thought it possible; for that would be aside from the present purpose. The scope of the higher drama is to represent life, not every-day life, it is true, but life lifted above the plane of bread-and-butter associations, by nobler reaches of language, by the influence at once inspiring and modulating of verse, by an intenser play of passion condensing that misty mixture of feeling and reflection which makes the ordinary atmosphere of existence into flashes of thought and phrase whose brief, but terrible, illumination prints the outworn landscape of every-day upon our brains, with its little motives and mean results, in lines of telltale fire. The moral office of tragedy is to show us our own weaknesses idealized in grander figures and more awful results, — to teach us that what we pardon in ourselves as venial faults, if they seem to have but slight influence on our immediate fortunes, have arms as long as those of kings, and reach forward to the catastrophe of our lives, that they are dry-rotting the very fibre of will and conscience, so that, if we should be brought to the test of a great temptation or a stringent emergency, we must be involved in a ruin as sudden and complete as that we shudder at in the unreal scene of the theatre. But the primary *object* of a tragedy is not to inculcate a formal moral. Representing life, it teaches, like life, by indirection, by those nods and winks that are thrown away on us blind horses in such profusion. We may learn, to be sure, plenty of lessons from Shakespeare. We are not likely to have kingdoms to divide, crowns foretold us by weird sisters, a father's death to avenge, or to kill our wives from jealousy; but Lear may teach us to draw the line more clearly between a wise generosity and a loose-handed weakness of giving; Macbeth, how one sin involves another, and forever another, by a fatal parthenogenesis, and that the key which unlocks forbidden doors to our will or passion leaves a stain on the hand, that may not be so dark as blood, but that will not out; Hamlet, that all the noblest gifts of person, temperament, and mind slip like sand through the grasp of an infirm purpose; Othello, that the perpetual silt of some one weakness, the eddies of a suspicious temper depositing their one impalpable layer after another, may build up a shoal on which an heroic life and an otherwise magnanimous nature may bilge and go to pieces. All this we may learn, and much more, and Shakespeare was no doubt well aware of all this and more; but I do not believe that he wrote his plays with any such didactic purpose. He knew human nature too well not to know that one thorn of experience is worth a whole wilderness of warning, — that, where one man shapes his life by precept and example, there are a thousand who have it shaped for them by impulse and by circumstances. He did not mean his great tragedies for scarecrows, as if the nailing of one hawk to the barn-door would prevent the next from coming down souse into the hen-yard. No, it is not the poor bleaching victim hung up to moult its draggled feathers in the rain that he wishes to show us. He loves the hawk-nature as well as the hen-nature ; and if he is unequalled in anything, it is in that sunny breadth of view, that impregnability of reason, that looks down all ranks and conditions of men, all fortune and misfortune, with the equal eye of the pure artist.

Whether I have fancied anything into Hamlet which the author never dreamed of putting there I do not greatly concern myself to inquire. Poets are always entitled to a royalty on whatever we find in their works ; for these fine creations as truly build themselves up in the brain as they are built up with deliberate forethought. Praise art as we will, that which the artist did not mean to put into his work, but which found itself there by some generous process of Nature of which he was as unaware as the blue river is of its rhyme with the blue sky, has somewhat in it that snatches us into sympathy with higher things than those which come by plot and observation. Goethe wrote his *Faust* in its earliest form without a thought of the deeper meaning which the exposition of an age of criticism was to find in it : without foremeaning it, he had impersonated in Mephistopheles the genius of his century. Shall this subtract from the debt we owe him ? Not at all. If originality were conscious of itself, it would have lost its right to be original. I believe that Shakespeare intended to impersonate in Hamlet not a mere metaphysical entity, but a man of flesh and blood : yet it is certainly curious how prophetically typical the character is of that introversion of mind which is so constant a phenomenon of these latter days, of that over-consciousness which wastes itself in analyzing the motives of action instead of acting.

The old painters had a rule, that all compositions should be pyramidal in form, — a central figure, from which the others slope gradually away on the two sides. Shakespeare probably had never heard of this rule, and, if he had, would not have been likely to respect it more than he has the so-called classical unities of time and place. But he understood perfectly the artistic advantages of gradation, contrast, and relief. Taking Hamlet as the key-note, we find in him weakness of character, which, on the one hand, is contrasted with the feebleness that springs from overweening conceit in Polonius and with frailty of temperament in Ophelia, while, on the other hand, it is brought into fuller relief by the steady force of Horatio and the impulsive violence of Laertes, who is resolute from thoughtlessness, just as Hamlet is irresolute from overplus of thought.

If we must draw a moral from Hamlet, it would seem to be, that Will is Fate, and that, Will once abdicating, the inevitable successor in the regency is Chance. Had Hamlet acted, instead of musing how good it would be to act, the king might have been the only victim. As it is, all the main actors in the story are the fortuitous sacrifice of his irresolution. We see how a single great vice of character at last draws to itself as allies and confederates all other weaknesses of the man, as in civil wars the timid and the selfish wait to throw themselves upon the stronger side.

"In Life's small things be resolute and great
To keep thy muscles trained: know'st thou when Fate
Thy measure takes? or when she'll say to thee,
'I find thee worthy, do this thing for me'?"

I have said that it was doubtful if Shakespeare had any conscious moral intention in his writings. I meant only that he was purely and primarily poet. And while he was an English poet in a sense that is true of no other, his method was thoroughly Greek, yet with this remarkable difference, — that, while the Greek dramatists took purely national themes and gave them a universal interest by their mode of treatment, he took what may be called cosmopolitan traditions, legends of human nature, and nationalized them by the infusion of his perfectly Anglican breadth of character and solidity of understanding. Wonderful as his imagination and fancy are, his perspicacity and artistic discretion are more so. This country tradesman's son, coming up to London, could set high-bred wits, like Beaumont, uncopiable lessons in drawing gentlemen such as are seen nowhere else but on the canvas of Titian; he could take Ulysses away from Homer and expand the shrewd and crafty islander into a statesman whose words are the pith of history. But what makes him yet more exceptional was his utterly unimpeachable judgment, and that poise of character which enabled him to be at once the greatest of poets and so unnoticeable a good citizen as to leave no incidents for biography. His material was never far-sought; (it is still disputed whether the fullest head of which we have record were cultivated beyond the range of grammar-school precedent!) but he used it with a poetic instinct which we cannot parallel, identified himself with it, yet remained always its born and questionless master. He finds the Clown and Fool upon the stage, — he makes them the tools of his pleasantry, his satire, and even his pathos; he finds a fading rustic superstition, and shapes out of it ideal Pucks, Titanias, and Ariels, in whose existence statesmen and scholars believe forever. Always poet, he subjects all to the ends of his art, and gives in Hamlet the churchyard ghost, but with the cothurnus on, — the messenger of God's revenge against murder; always philosopher, he traces in Macbeth the metaphysics of apparitions, painting the shadowy Banquo only on the o'erwrought brain of the murderer, and staining the hand of his wife-accomplice (because she was the more refined and higher nature) with the disgustful blood-spot that is not there. We say he had no moral intention, for the reason, that, as artist, it was not his to deal with the realities, but only with the shows of things; yet, with a temperament so just, an insight so inevitable as his, it was impossible that the moral reality, which underlies the *mirage* of the poet's vision, should not always be suggested. His humor and satire are never of the destructive kind; what he does in that way is suggestive only, — not breaking bubbles with Thor's hammer, but puffing them away with the breath of a Clown, or shivering them with the light laugh of a genial cynic. Men go about to prove the existence of a God! Was it a bit of phosphorus, that brain whose creations are so real, that, mixing with them, we feel as if we ourselves were but fleeting magic-lantern shadows?

But higher even than the genius we rate the character of this unique man, and the grand impersonality of what he wrote. What has he told us of himself? In our self-exploiting nineteenth century, with its melancholy liver-complaint, how serene and high he seems! If he had sorrows, he has made them the woof of everlasting consolation to his kind; and if, as poets are wont to whine, the outward world was cold to him, its biting air did but trace itself in loveliest frost-work of fancy on the many windows of that self-centred and cheerful soul.

NEW ENGLAND TWO CENTURIES AGO.*

THE history of New England is written imperishably on the face of a continent, and in characters as beneficent as they are enduring. In the Old World national pride feeds itself with the record of battles and conquests; — battles which proved nothing and settled nothing; conquests which shifted a boundary on the map, and put one ugly head instead of another on the coin which the people paid to the tax-gatherer. But wherever the New-Englander travels among the sturdy commonwealths which have sprung from the seed of the Mayflower, churches, schools, colleges, tell him where the men of his race have been, or their influence penetrated; and an intelligent freedom is the monument of conquests whose results are not to be measured in square miles. Next to the fugitives whom Moses led out of Egypt, the little ship-load of outcasts who landed at Plymouth two centuries and a half ago are destined to influence the future of the world. The spiritual thirst of mankind has for ages been quenched at Hebrew fountains; but the embodiment in human institutions of

* History of New England during the Stuart Dynasty. By JOHN GORHAM PALFREY. Vol. III. Boston: Little, Brown, & Co. 1864. pp. xxii, 648.

Collections of the Massachusetts Historical Society. Third Series, Vols. IX. and X. Fourth Series, Vols. VI. and VII.

truths uttered by the Son of man eighteen centuries ago was to be mainly the work of Puritan thought and Puritan self-devotion. Leave New England out in the cold! While you are plotting it, she sits by every fireside in the land where there is piety, culture, and free thought.

Faith in God, faith in man, faith in work, — this is the short formula in which we may sum up the teaching of the founders of New England, a creed ample enough for this life and the next. If their municipal regulations smack somewhat of Judaism, yet there can be no nobler aim or more practical wisdom than theirs; for it was to make the law of man a living counterpart of the law of God, in their highest conception of it. Were they too earnest in the strife to save their souls alive? That is still the problem which every wise and brave man is lifelong in solving. If the Devil take a less hateful shape to us than to our fathers, he is as busy with us as with them; and if we cannot find it in our hearts to break with a gentleman of so much worldly wisdom, who gives such admirable dinners, and whose manners are so perfect, so much the worse for us.

Looked at on the outside, New England history is dry and unpicturesque. There is no rustle of silks, no waving of plumes, no clink of golden spurs. Our sympathies are not awakened by the changeful destinies, the rise and fall, of great families, whose doom was in their blood. Instead of all this, we have the homespun fates of Cephas and Prudence repeated in an infinite series of peaceable sameness, and finding space enough for record in the family Bible; we have the noise of axe and hammer and saw, an apotheosis of dogged work, where, reversing the fairy-tale, nothing is left to luck, and, if there be any poetry, it is something that cannot be helped, — the waste of the water over the dam. Extrinsically, it is prosaic and plebeian; intrinsically, it is poetic and noble; for it is, perhaps, the most perfect incarnation of an idea the world has ever seen. That idea was not to found a democracy, nor to charter the city of New Jerusalem by an act of the General Court, as gentlemen seem to think whose notions of history and human nature rise like an exhalation from the good things at a Pilgrim Society dinner. Not in the least. They had no faith in the Divine institution of a system which gives Teague, because he can dig, as much influence as Ralph, because he can think, nor in personal at the expense of general freedom. Their view of human rights was not so limited that it could not take in human relations and duties also. They would have been likely to answer the claim, "I am as good as anybody," by a quiet "Yes, for some things, but not for others; as good, doubtless, in your place, where all things are good." What the early settlers of Massachusetts *did* intend, and what they accomplished, was the founding here of a *new* England, and a better one, where the political superstitions and abuses of the old should never have leave to take root. So much, we may say, they deliberately intended. No nobles, either lay or cleric, no great landed estates, and no universal ignorance as the seed-plot of vice and unreason; but an elective magistracy and clergy, land for all who would till it, and reading and writing, will ye nill ye, instead. Here at last, it would seem, simple manhood is to have a chance to play his stake against Fortune with honest dice, uncogged by those three hoary sharpers, Prerogative, Patricianism, and Priestcraft. Whoever has looked into the pamphlets published in England during the Great Rebellion cannot but have been struck by the fact, that the principles and practice of the Puritan Colony had begun to react with considerable force on the mother country; and the policy of the retrograde party there, after the Restoration, in its dealings with New England, finds a curious parallel as to its motives (time will show whether as to its results) in the conduct of the same party towards America during the last four years.* This influence and this fear alike bear witness to the energy of the principles at work here.

We have said that the details of New England history were essentially dry and unpoetic. Everything is near, authentic, and petty. There is no mist of distance to soften outlines, no mirage of tradition to give characters and events an imaginative loom. So much downright work was perhaps never wrought on the earth's surface in the same space of time as during the first forty years after the settlement. But mere work is unpicturesque, and void of sentiment. Irving instinctively divined and admirably illustrated in his "Knickerbocker" the humorous element which lies in this nearness of view, this clear, prosaic daylight of modernness, and this poverty of stage properties, which makes the actors and the deeds they were concerned in seem ludicrously small when contrasted with the semimythic grandeur in which we have clothed them, as we look backward from the crowned result, and fancy a cause as majestic as our conception of the effect. There was, indeed, one poetic side to the existence otherwise so narrow and practical; and to have conceived this, however partially, is the one original and American thing in Cooper. This diviner glimpse illumines the lives of our Daniel Boones, the man of civilization and old-world ideas confronted with our forest solitudes, — confronted, too, for the first time, with his real self, and so led gradually to disentangle the original substance of his manhood from the artificial results of culture. Here

* Written in December, 1864.

was our new Adam of the wilderness, forced to name anew, not the visible creation of God, but the invisible creation of man, in those forms that lie at the base of social institutions, so insensibly moulding personal character and controlling individual action. Here is the protagonist of our New World epic, a figure as poetic as that of Achilles, as ideally representative as that of Don Quixote, as romantic in its relation to our homespun and plebeian mythus as Arthur in his to the mailed and plumed cycle of chivalry. We do not mean, of course, that Cooper's "Leatherstocking" is all this or anything like it, but that the character typified in him is ideally and potentially all this and more.

But whatever was poetical in the lives of the early New-Englanders had something shy, if not sombre, about it. If their natures flowered, it was out of sight, like the fern. It was in the practical that they showed their true quality, as Englishmen are wont. It has been the fashion lately with a few feeble-minded persons to undervalue the New England Puritans, as if they were nothing more than gloomy and narrow-minded fanatics. But all the charges brought against these large-minded and far-seeing men are precisely those which a really able fanatic, Joseph de Maistre, lays at the door of Protestantism. Neither a knowledge of human nature nor of history justifies us in confounding, as is commonly done, the Puritans of Old and New England, or the English Puritans of the third with those of the fifth decade of the seventeenth century. Fanaticism, or, to call it by its milder name, enthusiasm, is only powerful and active so long as it is aggressive. Establish it firmly in power, and it becomes conservatism, whether it will or no. A sceptre once put in the hand, the grip is instinctive; and he who is firmly seated in authority soon learns to think security, and not progress, the highest lesson of statecraft. From the summit of power men no longer turn their eyes upward, but begin to look about them. Aspiration sees only one side of every question; possession, many. And the English Puritans, after their revolution was accomplished, stood in even a more precarious position than most successful assailants of the prerogative of whatever *is* to continue in being. They had carried a political end by means of a religious revival. The fulcrum on which they rested their lever to overturn the existing order of things (as history always placidly calls the particular forms of *dis*order for the time being) was in the soul of man. They could not renew the fiery gush of enthusiasm, when once the molten metal had begun to stiffen in the mould of policy and precedent. The religious element of Puritanism became insensibly merged in the political; and, its one great man taken away, it died, as passions have done before, of possession. It was one thing to shout with Cromwell before the battle of Dunbar, "Now, Lord, arise, and let thine enemies be scattered!" and to snuffle, "Rise, Lord, and keep us safe in our benefices, our sequestered estates, and our five per cent!" Puritanism meant something when Captain Hodgson, riding out to battle through the morning mist, turns over the command of his troop to a lieutenant, and stays to hear the prayer of a cornet, there was "so much of God in it." Become traditional, repeating the phrase without the spirit, reading the present backward as if it were written in Hebrew, translating Jehovah by "I was" instead of "I am," — it was no more like its former self than the hollow drum made of Zisca's skin was like the grim captain whose soul it had once contained. Yet the change was inevitable, for it is not safe to confound the things of Cæsar with the things of God. Some honest republicans, like Ludlow, were never able to comprehend the chilling contrast between the ideal aim and the material fulfilment, and looked askance on the strenuous reign of Oliver, — that rugged boulder of primitive manhood lying lonely there on the dead level of the century, — as if some crooked changeling had been laid in the cradle instead of that fair babe of the Commonwealth they had dreamed. Truly there is a tide in the affairs of men, but there is no gulf-stream setting forever in one direction; and those waves of enthusiasm on whose crumbling crests we sometimes see nations lifted for a gleaming moment are wont to have a gloomy trough before and behind.

But the founders of New England, though they must have sympathized vividly with the struggles and triumphs of their brethren in the mother country, were never subjected to the same trials and temptations, never hampered with the same lumber of usages and tradition. They were not driven to win power by doubtful and desperate ways, nor to maintain it by any compromises of the ends which make it worth having. From the outset they were builders, without need of first pulling down, whether to make room or to provide material. For thirty years after the colonization of the Bay, they had absolute power to mould as they would the character of their adolescent commonwealth. During this time a whole generation would have grown to manhood who knew the Old World only by report, in whose habitual thought kings, nobles, and bishops would be as far away from all present and practical concern as the figures in a fairy-tale, and all whose memories and associations, all their unconscious training by eye and ear, were New English wholly. Nor were the men whose influence was greatest in shaping the framework and the policy of the Colony, in any true sense of the word, fanatics. Enthusiasts, perhaps, they were, but with them the fermentation had never gone further than the ripeness of the vinous stage. Disappointment had never made it acetous, nor had it ever putrefied into the turbid zeal of Fifth Monarchism and sectarian whimsey. There is no better ballast for keeping the mind steady on its keel, and saving it from all risk of *crankiness*, than business. And they were business men, men of facts and figures no less than of religious earnestness. The sum of two hundred thousand pounds had been invested in their undertaking, — a sum, for that time, truly enormous as the result of private combination for a doubtful experiment. That their enterprise might succeed, they must show a balance on the right side of the counting-house ledger, as well as in their private accounts with their own souls. The liberty of praying when and how they would, must be balanced with an ability of paying when and as they ought. Nor is the resulting fact in this case at variance with the *a priori* theory. They succeeded in making their thought the life and soul of a body politic, still powerful, still benignly operative, after two centuries; a thing which no mere fanatic ever did or ever will accomplish. Sober, earnest, and thoughtful men, it was no Utopia, no New Atlantis, no realization of a splendid dream, which they had at heart, but the establishment of the divine principle of Authority on the common interest and the common consent; the making, by a contribution from the free-will of all, a power which should curb and guide the free-will of each for the general good. If they were stern in their dealings with sectaries, it should be remembered that the Colony was in fact the private property of the Massachusetts Company, that unity was essential to its success, and that John of Leyden had taught them how unendurable by the nostrils of honest men is the corruption of the right of private judgment in the evil and selfish hearts of men when no thorough mental training has developed the understanding and given the judgment its needful means of comparison and correction. They knew that liberty in the hands of feeble-minded and unreasoning persons (and all the worse if they are honest) means nothing more than the supremacy of their particular form of imbecility; means nothing less, therefore, than downright chaos, a Bedlam-chaos of monomaniacs and bores. What was to be done with men and women, who bore conclusive witness to the fall of man by insisting on walking up the broad-aisle of the meeting-house in a costume which that event had put forever out of fashion? About their treatment of witches, too, there has been a great deal of ignorant babble. Puritanism had nothing whatever to do with it. They acted under a delusion, which, with an exception here and there (and those mainly medical men, like Wierus and Webster), darkened the understanding of all Christendom. Dr. Henry More was no Puritan; and his letter to Glanvil, prefixed to the third edition of the "Sadducismus Triumphatus," was written in 1678, only fourteen years before the trials at Salem. Bekker's "Bezauberte Welt" was published in 1693; and in the Preface he speaks of the difficulty of overcoming "the prejudices in which not only ordinary men, but the learned also, are obstinate." In Hathaway's case, 1702, Chief-Justice Holt, in charging the jury, expresses no disbelief in the possibility of witchcraft, and the indictment implies its existence. Indeed, the natural reaction from the Salem mania of 1692 put an end to belief in devilish compacts and demoniac possessions sooner in New England than elsewhere. The last we hear of it there is in 1720, when Rev. Mr. Turell of Medford detected and exposed an attempted cheat by two girls. Even in 1692, it was the foolish breath of Cotton Mather and others of the clergy that blew the dying embers of this ghastly superstition into a flame; and they were actuated partly by a desire to bring about a religious, revival, which might stay for a while the hastening lapse of their own authority, and still more by that credulous scepticism of feeble-minded piety which dreads the cutting away of an orthodox tumor of misbelief, as if the life-blood of faith would follow, and would keep even a stumbling-block in the way of salvation, if only enough generations had tripped over it to make it venerable. The witches were condemned on precisely the same grounds that in our day led to the condemnation of "Essays and Reviews."

But Puritanism was already in the decline when such things were possible. What had been a wondrous and intimate experience of the soul, a flash into the very crypt and basis of man's nature from the fire of trial, had become ritual and tradition. In prosperous times the faith of one generation becomes the formality of the next. "The necessity of a reformation," set forth by order of the Synod which met at Cambridge in 1679, though no doubt overstating the case, shows how much even at that time the ancient strictness had been loosened. The country had grown rich, its commerce was large, and wealth did its natural work in making life softer and more worldly, commerce in deprovincializing the minds of those engaged in it. But Puritanism had already done its duty. As there are certain creatures whose whole being seems occupied with an egg-laying errand they are sent upon, incarnate ovipositors, their bodies but bags to hold this precious deposit, their legs of use only to carry them where they may safeliest be rid of it, so sometimes a generation seems to have no other end than the conception and ripening of certain germs. Its blind stirrings, its apparently aimless seeking hither and thither, are but the driving of an instinct to be done with its parturient function toward these principles of future life and power. Puritanism, believing itself quick with the seed of religious liberty, laid, without knowing it, the egg of democracy. The English Puritans pulled down church and state to rebuild Zion on the ruins, and all the while it was not Zion, but America, they were building. But if their millennium went by, like the rest, and left men still human; if they, like so many saints and martyrs before them, listened in vain for the sound of that trumpet which was to summon all souls to a resurrection from the body of this death which men call life, — it is not for us, at least, to forget the heavy debt we owe them. It was the drums of Naseby and Dunbar that gathered the minute-men on Lexington Common; it was the red dint of the axe on Charles's block that marked One in our era. The Puritans had their faults. They were narrow, ungenial; they could not understand the text, "I have piped to you and ye have not danced," nor conceive that saving one's soul should be the cheerfullest, and not the dreariest, of businesses. Their preachers had a way, like the painful Mr. Perkins, of pronouncing the word *damn* with such an emphasis as left a doleful echo in their auditors' ears a good while after. And it was natural that men who captained or accompanied the exodus from existing forms and associations into the doubtful wilderness that led to the promised land, should find more to their purpose in the Old Testament than in the New. As respects the New England settlers, however visionary some of their religious tenets may have been, their political ideas savored of the realty, and it was no Nephelococcygia of which they drew the plan, but of a commonwealth whose foundation was to rest on solid and familiar earth. If what they did was done in a corner, the results of it were to be felt to the ends of the earth; and the figure of Winthrop should be as venerable in history as that of Romulus is barbarously grand in legend.

I am inclined to think that many of our national characteristics, which are sometimes attributed to climate and sometimes to institutions, are traceable to the influences of Puritan descent. We are apt to forget how very large a proportion of our population is descended from emigrants who came over before 1660. Those emigrants were in great part representatives of that element of English character which was most susceptible of religious impressions; in other words, the most earnest and imaginative. Our people still differ from their English cousins (as they are fond of calling themselves when they are afraid we may do them a mischief) in a certain capacity for enthusiasm, a devotion to abstract principle, an openness to ideas, a greater aptness for intuitions than for the slow processes of the syllogism, and, as derivative from this, in minds of looser texture, a light-armed, skirmishing habit of thought, and a positive preference of the birds in the bush, — an excellent quality of character *before* you have your bird in the hand.

There have been two great distributing centres of the English race on this continent, Massachusetts and Virginia. Each has impressed the character of its early legislators on the swarms it has sent forth. Their ideas are in some fundamental respects the opposites of each other, and we can only account for it by an antagonism of thought beginning with the early framers of their respective institutions. New England abolished caste; in Virginia they still talk of "quality folks." But it was in making education not only common to all, but in some sense compulsory on all, that the destiny of the free republics of America was practically settled. Every man was to be trained, not only to the use of arms, but of his wits also; and it is these which alone make the others effective weapons for the maintenance of freedom. You may disarm the hands, but not the brains, of a people, and to know what should be defended is the first condition of successful defence. Simple as it seems, it was a great discovery that the key of knowledge could turn both ways, that it could open, as well as lock, the door of power to the many. The only things a New-Englander was ever locked out of were the jails. It is quite true that our Republic is the heir of the English Commonwealth; but as we trace events backward to their causes, we shall find it true also, that what made our Revolution a foregone conclusion was that act of the General Court, passed in May, 1647, which established the system of common schools. "To the end that learning may not be buried in the graves of our forefathers in Church and Commonwealth, the Lord assisting our endeavors, it is therefore ordered by this Court and authority thereof, that every township in this jurisdiction, after the Lord hath increased them to fifty householders, shall then forthwith appoint one within their towns to teach all such children as shall resort to him to write and read."

Passing through some Massachusetts village, perhaps at a distance from any house, it may be in the midst of a piece of woods where four roads meet, one may sometimes even yet see a small square one-story building, whose use would not be long doubtful. It is summer, and the flickering shadows of forest-leaves dapple the roof of the little porch, whose door stands wide, and shows, hanging on either hand, rows of straw hats and bonnets, that look as if they had done good service. As you pass the open windows, you hear whole platoons of high-pitched voices discharging words of two or three syllables with wonderful precision and unanimity. Then there is a pause, and the voice of the officer in command is heard reproving some raw recruit whose vocal musket hung fire. Then the drill of the small infantry begins anew, but pauses again because some urchin — who agrees with Voltaire that the superfluous is a very necessary thing — insists on spelling "subtraction" with an *s* too much.

If you had the good fortune to be born and bred in the Bay State, your mind is thronged with half-sad, half-humorous recollections. The a-b abs of little voices long since hushed in the mould, or ringing now in the pulpit, at the bar, or in the Senate-chamber, come back to the ear of memory. You remember the high stool on which culprits used to be elevated with the tall paper fool's-cap on their heads, blushing to the ears; and you think with wonder how you have seen them since as men climbing the world's penance-stools of ambition without a blush, and gladly giving everything for life's caps and bells. And you have pleasanter memories of going after pond-lilies, of angling for horn-pouts, — that queer bat among the fishes, — of nutting, of walking over the creaking snow-crust in winter, when the warm breath of every household was curling up silently in the keen blue air. You wonder if life has any rewards more solid and permanent than the Spanish dollar that was hung around your neck to be restored again next day, and conclude sadly that it was but too true a prophecy and emblem of all worldly success. But your moralizing is broken short off by a rattle of feet and the pouring forth of the whole swarm, — the boys dancing and shouting, — the mere effervescence of the fixed air of youth and animal spirits uncorked, — the sedater girls in confidential twos and threes decanting secrets out of the mouth of one cape-bonnet into that of another. Times have changed since the jackets and trousers used to draw up on one side of the road, and the petticoats on the other, to salute with bow and courtesy the white neckcloth of the parson or the squire, if it chanced to pass during intermission.

Now this little building, and others like it, were an original kind of fortification invented by the founders of New England. They are the martello-towers that protect our coast. This was the great discovery of our Puritan forefathers. They were the first lawgivers who saw clearly and enforced practically the simple moral and political truth, that knowledge was not an alms to be dependent on the chance charity of private men or the precarious pittance of a trust-fund, but a sacred debt which the Commonwealth owed to every one of her children. The opening of the first grammar-school was the opening of the first trench against monopoly in church and state; the first row of trammels and pothooks which the little Shearjashubs and Elkanahs blotted and blubbered across their copy-books, was the preamble to the Declaration of Independence. The men who gave every man the chance to become a landholder, who made the transfer of land easy, and put knowledge within the reach of all, have been called narrow-minded, because they were intolerant. But intolerant of what? Of what they believed to be dangerous nonsense, which, if left free, would destroy the last hope of civil and religious freedom. They had not come here that every man might do that which seemed good in his own eyes, but in the sight of God. Toleration, moreover, is something which is won, not granted. It is the equilibrium of neutralized forces. The Puritans had no notion of tolerating mischief. They looked upon their little commonwealth as upon their own private estate and homestead, as they had a right to do, and would no more allow the Devil's religion of unreason to be preached therein, than we should permit a prize-fight in our gardens. They were narrow; in other words they had an edge to them, as men that serve in great emergencies must; for a Gordian knot is settled sooner with a sword than a beetle.

The founders of New England are commonly represented in the after-dinner oratory of their descendants as men "before their time," as it is called; in other words, deliberately prescient of events resulting from new relations of circumstances, or even from circumstances new in themselves, and therefore altogether alien from their own experience. Of course, such a class of men is to be reckoned among those non-existent human varieties so gravely catalogued by the ancient naturalists. If a man could shape his action with reference to what should happen a century after his death, surely it might be asked of him to call in the help of that easier foreknowledge which reaches from one day to the next, — a power of prophecy whereof we have no example. I do not object to a wholesome pride of ancestry, though a little mythical, if it be accompanied with the feeling that *noblesse oblige*, and do not result merely in a placid self-satisfaction with our own mediocrity, as if greatness, like righteousness, could be imputed. We can pardon it even in conquered races, like the Welsh and Irish, who make up to themselves for present degradation by imaginary empires in the past whose boundaries they can extend at will, carrying the bloodless conquests of fancy over regions laid down upon no map, and concerning which authentic history is enviously dumb. Those long beadrolls of Keltic kings cannot tyrannize over us, and we can be patient so long as our own crowns are uncracked by the shillalah sceptres of their actual representatives. In our own case, it would not be amiss, perhaps, if we took warning by the example of Teague and Taffy. At least, I think it would be wise in our orators not to put forward so prominently the claim of the Yankee to universal dominion, and his intention to enter upon it forthwith. If we do our duties as honestly and as much in the fear of God as our forefathers did, we need not trouble ourselves much about other titles to empire. The broad foreheads and long heads will win the day at last in spite of all heraldry, and it will be enough if we feel as keenly as our Puritan founders did that those organs of empire may be broadened and lengthened by culture.* That our self-complacency should not increase the complacency of outsiders is not to be wondered at. As *we* sometimes take credit to ourselves (since all commendation of our ancestry is indirect self-flattery) for what the Puritans fathers never were, so there are others who, to gratify a spite against their descendants, blame them for not having been what they could not be; namely, before their time in such matters as slavery, witchcraft, and the like. The view, whether of friend or foe, is equally unhistorical, nay, without the faintest notion of all that makes history worth having as a teacher. That our grandfathers shared in the prejudices of their day is all that makes them human to us; and that nevertheless they could act bravely and wisely on occasion makes them only the more venerable. If certain barbarisms and superstitions disappeared earlier in New England than elsewhere, not by the decision of exceptionally enlightened or humane judges, but by force of public opinion, that is the fact that is interesting and instructive for us. I never thought it an abatement of Hawthorne's genius that he came lineally from one who sat in judgment on the witches in 1692; it was interesting rather to trace some-

* It is curious, that, when Cromwell proposed to transfer a colony from New England to Ireland, one of the conditions insisted on in Massachusetts was that a college should be established.

thing hereditary in the sombre character of his imagination, continually vexing itself to account for the origin of evil, and baffled for want of that simple solution in a personal Devil.

But I have no desire to discuss the merits or demerits of the Puritans, having long ago learned the wisdom of saving my sympathy for more modern objects than Hecuba. My object is to direct the attention of my readers to a collection of documents where they may see those worthies as they were in their daily living and thinking. The collections of our various historical and antiquarian societies can hardly be said to be *published* in the strict sense of the word, and few consequently are aware how much they contain of interest for the general reader no less than the special student. The several volumes of "Winthrop Papers," in especial, are a mine of entertainment. Here we have the Puritans painted by themselves, and, while we arrive at a truer notion of the characters of some among them, and may accordingly sacrifice to that dreadful superstition of being usefully employed which makes so many bores and bored, we can also furtively enjoy the oddities of thought and speech, the humors of the time, which our local historians are too apt to despise as inconsidered trifles. For myself I confess myself heretic to the established theory of the gravity of history, and am not displeased with an opportunity to smile behind my hand at any ludicrous interruption of that sometimes wearisome ceremonial. I am not sure that I would not sooner give up Raleigh spreading his cloak to keep the royal Dian's feet from the mud, than that awful judgment upon the courtier whose Atlantean thighs leaked away in bran through the rent in his trunk-hose. The painful fact that Fisher had his head cut off is somewhat mitigated to me by the circumstance that the Pope should have sent him, of all things in the world, a cardinal's hat after that incapacitation. Theology herself becomes less unamiable to me when I find the Supreme Pontiff writing to the Council of Trent that "they should begin with original sin, *maintaining yet a due respect for the Emperor*." That infallibility should thus courtesy to decorum, shall make me think better of it while I live. I shall accordingly endeavor to give my readers what amusement I can, leaving it to themselves to extract solid improvement from the volumes before us, which include a part of the correspondence of three generations of Winthrops.

Let me premise that there are two men above all others for whom our respect is heightened by these letters, — the elder John Winthrop and Roger Williams. Winthrop appears throughout as a truly magnanimous and noble man in an unobtrusive way, — a kind of greatness that makes less noise in the world, but is on the whole more solidly satisfying than most others, — a man who has been dipped in the river of God (a surer baptism than Styx or dragon's blood) till his character is of perfect proof, and who appears plainly as the very soul and life of the young Colony. Very reverend and godly he truly was, and a respect not merely ceremonious, but personal, a respect that savors of love, shows itself in the letters addressed to him. Charity and tolerance flow so naturally from the pen of Williams that it is plain they were in his heart. He does not show himself a very strong or very wise man, but a thoroughly gentle and good one. His affection for the two Winthrops is evidently of the warmest. We suspect that he lived to see that there was more reason in the drum-head religious discipline which made him, against his will, the founder of a commonwealth, than he may have thought at first. But for the fanaticism (as it is the fashion to call the sagacious straitness) of the abler men who knew how to root the English stock firmly in this new soil on either side of him, his little plantation could never have existed, and he himself would have been remembered only, if at all, as one of the jarring atoms in a chaos of otherwise-mindedness.

Two other men, Emanuel Downing and Hugh Peter, leave a positively unpleasant savor in the nostrils. Each is selfish in his own way, — Downing with the shrewdness of an attorney, Peter with that clerical unction which in a vulgar nature so easily degenerates into greasiness. Neither of them was the man for a forlorn hope, and both returned to England when the civil war opened prospect of preferment there. Both, we suspect, were inclined to value their Puritanism for its rewards in this world rather than the next. Downing's son, Sir George, was basely prosperous, making the good cause pay him so long as it was solvent, and then selling out in season to betray his old commander, Colonel Okey, to the shambles at Charing Cross. Peter became a colonel in the Parliament's army, and under the Protectorate one of Cromwell's chaplains. On his trial, after the Restoration, he made a poor figure, in striking contrast to some of the brave men who suffered with him. At his execution a shocking brutality was shown. "When Mr Cook was cut down and brought to be quartered, one they called Colonel Turner calling to the Sheriff's men to bring Mr Peters near, that he might see it; and by and by the Hangman came to him all besmeared in blood, and rubbing his bloody hands together, he tauntingly asked, *Come, how do you like this, Mr. Peters? How do you like this work?*" * This Colo-

* State Trials, II. 409. One would not reckon too closely with a man on trial for his life, but there is something pitiful in Peter's representing himself as coming back to England "out of the West Indias," in order to evade any complicity with suspected New England.

nel Turner can hardly have been other than the one who four years later came to the hangman's hands for robbery; and whose behavior, both in the dock and at the gallows, makes his trial one of the most entertaining as a display of character. Peter would seem to have been one of those men gifted with what is sometimes called eloquence; that is, the faculty of stating things powerfully from momentary feeling, and not from that conviction of the higher reason which alone can give force and permanence to words. His letters show him subject, like others of like temperament, to fits of "hypocondriacal melancholy," and the only witness he called on his trial was to prove that he was confined to his lodgings by such an attack on the day of the king's beheading. He seems to have been subject to this malady at convenience, as some women to hysterics. Honest John Endicott plainly had small confidence in him, and did not think him the right man to represent the Colony in England. There is a droll resolve in the Massachusetts records by which he is "desired to write to Holland for 500*l.* worth of *peter*, & 40*l.* worth of match." It is with a match that we find him burning his fingers in the present correspondence.

Peter seems to have entangled himself somehow with a Mrs. Deliverance Sheffield, whether maid or widow nowhere appears, but presumably the latter. The following statement of his position is amusing enough: "I have sent Mrs D. Sh. letter, which puts mee to new troubles, for though shee takes liberty upon my Cossen Downing's speeches, yet (Good Sir) let mee not be a foole in Israel. I had many good answers to yesterday's worke [a Fast] and amongst the rest her letter; which (if her owne) doth argue more wisedome than I thought shee had. You have often sayd I could not leave her; what to doe is very considerable. Could I with comfort &

credit desist, this seemes best: could I goe on & content myselfe, that were good. . . . . For though I now seeme free agayne, yet the depth I know not. Had shee come over with me, I thinke I had bin quieter. This shee may know, that I have sought God earnestly, that the nexte weeke I shall bee riper:— I doubt shee gaynes most by such writings: & shee deserves most where shee is further of. If you shall amongst you advise mee to write to hir, I shall forthwith; our towne lookes upon mee contracted & so I have sayd myselfe; what wonder the charge [change?] would make, I know not." Again: "Still pardon my offensive boldnes: I know not well whither Mrs Sh. have set mee at liberty or not: my conclusion is, that if you find I cannot make an honorable retreat, then I shall desire to advance σὺν Θεῷ. Of you I now expect your last advise, viz: whither I must goe on or of, *saluo evangelij honore:* if shee bee in good earnest to leave all agitations this way, then I stand still & wayt God's mind concerning mee. . . . . If I had much mony I would part with it to her free, till wee heare what England doth, supposing I may bee called to some imployment that will not suit a marryed estate": (here another mode of escape presents itself, and he goes on:) "for indeed (Sir) some must looke out & I have very strong thoughts to speake with the Duitch Governor & lay some way there for a supply &c." At the end of the letter, an objection to the lady herself occurs to him: "Once more for Mrs Sh: I had from Mr Hibbins & others, her fellowpassengers, sad discouragements where they saw her in her trim. I would not come of with dishonor, nor come on with griefe, or ominous hesitations." On all this shilly-shally we have a shrewd comment in a letter of Endicott: "I cannot but acquaint you with my thoughts concerning Mr Peter since hee receaued a letter from Mrs Sheffield, which was yesterday in the eveninge after the Fast, shee seeming in her letter to abate of her affeccions towards him & dislikinge to come to Salem vppon such termes as he had written. I finde now that hee begins to play her parte, & if I mistake not, you will see him as greatly in loue with her (if shee will but hold of a little) as euer shee was with him; but he conceales it what he can as yett. The begininge of the next weeke you will heare further from him." The widow was evidently more than a match for poor Peter.

It should appear that a part of his trouble arose from his having coquetted also with a certain Mrs. Ruth, about whom he was "dealt with by Mrs Amee, Mr Phillips & 2 more of the Church, our Elder being one. When Mr Phillips with much violence & sharpnes charged mee home . . . . that I should hinder the mayd of a match at London, which was not so, could not thinke of any kindnes I euer did her, though shee haue had above 300*li.* through my fingers, so as if God uphold me not after an especiall manner, it will sinke me surely . . . . hee told me he would not stop my intended marriage, but assured mee it would not bee good . . . . all which makes mee reflect upon my rash proceedings with Mrs Sh." Panurge's doubts and difficulties about matrimony were not more entertainingly contradictory. Of course, Peter ends by marrying the widow, and presently we have a comment on "her trim." In January, 1639, he writes to Winthrop: "My wife is very thankfull for her apples, & *desires much the new fashioned shooes.*" Eight years later we find him writing from England, where he had been two years: "I am coming over if I must; my wife comes of necessity to New England, having run her selfe out of breath here"; and then in the postscript, "bee sure you never let my wife come away from thence without my leave, & then you love mee." But life is never pure comedy, and the end in this case is tragical. Roger Williams, after his return from England in 1654, writes to John Winthrop, Jr.: "Your brother flourisheth in good esteeme & is eminent for maintaining the Freedome of the Conscience as to matters of Beliefe, Religion, & Worship. Your Father Peters preacheth the same Doctrine though not so zealously as some years since, yet cries out against New English Rigidities & Persecutions, their civil injuries & wrongs to himselfe, & their unchristian dealing with him in excommunicating his distracted wife. All this he tould me in his lodgings at Whitehall, those lodgings which I was tould were Canterburies [the Archbishop], but he himselfe tould me that that Library wherein we were together was Canterburies & given him by the Parliament. His wife lives from him, not wholy but much distracted. He tells me he had but 200 a yeare & he allowed her 4 score per annum of it. Surely, Sir, the most holy Lord is most wise in all the trialls he exerciseth his people with. He tould me that his affliction from his wife stird him up to Action abroad, & when successe tempted him to Pride, the Bitternes in his bozome-comforts was a Cooler & a Bridle to him." Truly the whirligig of time brings about strange revenges. Peter had been driven from England by the persecutions of Laud; a few years later he "stood armed on the scaffold" when that prelate was beheaded, and now we find him installed in the archiepiscopal lodgings. Dr. Palfrey, it appears to me, gives altogether too favorable an opinion both of Peter's character and abilities. I conceive him to have been a vain and selfish man. He may have had the bravery of passionate impulse, but he wanted that steady courage of character which has such a beautiful constancy in Winthrop. He always professed a longing to come back to New England, but it was only a way he had of talking. That he never meant to come is plain from these letters. Nay, when things looked prosperous in England, he writes to the younger Winthrop: "My counsell is you should come hither with your family for certaynly you will bee capable of a comfortable living in this free Commonwealth. I doo seriously advise it. . . . . . G. Downing is worth 500*l.* per annum but 4*l.* per diem — your brother Stephen worth 2000*l.* & a maior. I pray come." But when he is snugly ensconced in Whitehall, and may be presumed to have some influence with the prevailing powers, his zeal cools. "I wish you & all friends to stay there & rather looke to the West Indyes if they remoue, for many are here to seeke when they come ouer." To me Peter's highest promotion seems to have been that he walked with John Milton at the Protector's funeral. He was, I suspect, one of those men, to borrow a charitable phrase of Roger Williams, who "feared God in the main," that is, whenever it was not personally inconvenient. William Coddington saw him in his glory in 1651: "Soe wee toucke the tyme to goe to viset Mr Petters at his chamber. I was mery with him & called him the Arch Bp: of Canterberye, in regard to his adtendance by ministers & gentlemen, & it passed very well." Considering certain charges brought against Peter, (though he is said, when under sentence of death, to have denied the truth of them,) Coddington's statement that he liked to have "gentlewomen waite of him" in his lodgings has not a pleasant look. One last report of him we get (September, 1659) in a letter of John Davenport, — "that Mr Hugh Peters is distracted & under sore horrors of conscience, crying out of himselfe as damned & confessing haynous actings."

Occasionally these letters give us interesting glimpses of persons and things in England. In the letter of Williams just cited, there is a lesson for all parties raised to power by exceptional causes. "Surely, Sir, youre Father & all the people of God in England . . . . are now in the sadle & at the helme, so high that *non datus descensus nisi cadendo :* Some cheere up their spirits with the impossibilitie of another fall or turne, so doth Major G. Harrison . . . . a very gallant most deserving heavenly man, but most highflowne for the Kingdom of the Saints & the 5th Monarchie now risen & their sun never to set againe &c. Others, as, to my knowledge, the Protector . . . . are not so full of that faith of miracles, but still imagine changes & persecutions & the very slaughter of the witnesses before that glorious morning so much desired of a worldly Kingdome, if ever such a Kingdome (as literally it is by so many expounded) be to arise in this present world & dispensation." Poor General Harrison lived to be one of the witnesses so slaughtered. The practical good sense of Cromwell is worth noting, the English understanding struggling against Judaic trammels. Williams gives us another peep through the keyhole of the past : "It pleased the Lord to call me for some time & with some persons to practice the Hebrew, the Greeke, Latine, French & Dutch. The secretarie of the Councell (Mr Milton) for my Dutch I read him, read me many more languages. Grammar rules begin to be esteemed a Tyrannie. I taught 2 young Gentlemen, a Parliament man's sons, as we teach our children English, by words, phrazes, & constant talke, &c." It is plain that Milton had talked over with Williams the theory put forth in his tract on Education, and made a convert of him. We could wish that the good Baptist had gone a little more into particulars. But which of us knows among the men he meets whom time will dignify by curtailing him of the "Mr.," and reducing him to a bare patronymic, as being a kind by himself? We have a glance or two at Oliver, who is always interesting. "The late renowned Oliver confest to me in close discourse about the Protestants affaires &c that he yet feard great persecutions to the protestants from the Romanists before the downfall of the Papacie," writes Williams in 1660. This "close discourse" must have been six years before, when Williams was in England. Within a year after, Oliver interfered to some purpose in behalf of the Protestants of Piedmont, and Mr. Milton wrote his famous sonnet. Of the war with Spain, Williams reports from his letters out of England in 1656: "This diversion against the Spaniard hath turnd the face & thoughts of many English, so that the saying now is, Crowne the Protector with gould,* though the sullen yet cry, Crowne him with thornes."

Again in 1654: "I know the Protector had strong thoughts of Hispaniola & Cuba. Mr Cotton's interpreting of Euphrates to be the West Indies, the supply of gold (to take off taxes), & the provision of a warmer *diverticulum & receptaculum* then N. England is, will make a footing into those parts very precious, & if it shall please God to vouchsafe successe to this fleete, I looke to hear of an invitation at least to these parts for removall from his Highnes who lookes on N. E. only with an eye of pitie, as poore, cold & useless." The mixture of Euphrates and taxes, of the transcendental and practical, prophecy taking precedence of thrift, is characteristic, and recalls Cromwell's famous rule, of fearing God *and* keeping your powder dry. In one of the Protector's speeches,† he insists much on his wish to retire to a private life. There is a curious confirmation of his sincerity in a letter of William Hooke, then belonging to his

* Waller put this into verse:—

"Let the rich ore forthwith be melted down
And the state fixed by making him a crown."

† The *third* in Carlyle, 1654.

household, dated the 13th of April, 1657. The question of the kingly title was then under debate, and Hooke's account of the matter helps to a clearer understanding of the reasons for Cromwell's refusing the title: "The protector is urged *utrinque* & (I am ready to think) willing enough to betake himself to a private life, if it might be. He is a godly man, much in prayer & good discourses, delighting in good men & good ministers, self-denying & ready to promote any good work for Christ."* On the 5th of February, 1654, Captain John Mason, of Pequot memory, writes "a word or twoe of newes as it comes from Mr Eaton, viz: that the Parliament sate in September last; they chose their old Speaker & Clarke. The Protectour told them they were a free Parliament, & soe left them that day. They, considering where the legislative power resided, concluded to vote it on the morrow, & to take charge of the militia. The Protectour hereing of it, sent for some numbers of horse, went to the Parliament House, nayld up the doores, sent for them to the Painted Chamber, told them they should attend the lawes established, & that he would wallow in his blood before he would part with what was conferd upon him, tendering them an oath: 140 engaged." Now it is curious that Mr. Eaton himself, from whom Mason got his news, wrote, only two days before, an account, differing, in some particulars, and especially in tone, from Mason's. Of the speech he says, that it "gave such satisfaction that about 200 have since ingaged to owne the present Government." Yet Carlyle gives the same number of signers (140) as Mason, and there is a sentence in Cromwell's speech, as reported by Carlyle, of precisely the same purport as that quoted by Mason. To me, that "wallow in my blood" has rather more of the Cromwellian ring in it,

* Collections, Third Series, Vol. I. p. 182.

more of the quality of spontaneous speech, than the "rolled into my grave and buried with infamy" of the official reporter. John Haynes (24th July, 1653) reports "newes from England of astonishing nature," concerning the dissolution of the Rump. We quote his story both as a contemporaneous version of the event, and as containing some particulars that explain the causes that led to it. It differs, in some respects, from Carlyle, and is hardly less vivid as a picture: "The Parliament of England & Councell of State are both dissolved, by whom & the manner this: The Lord Cromwell, Generall, went to the house & asked the Speaker & Bradshaw by what power they sate ther. They answered by the same power that he woare his sword. Hee replied they should know they did not, & said they should sitt noe longer, demanding an account of the vast sommes of money they had received of the Commons. They said the matter was of great consequence & they would give him accompt in tenn dayes. He said, Noe, they had sate too long already (& might now take their ease,) for ther inriching themselves & impoverishing the Commons, & then seazed uppon all the Records. Immediatly Lambert, Livetenant Generall, & Hareson Maior Generall (for they two were with him), tooke the Speaker Lenthall by the hands, lift him out of the Chaire, & ledd him out of the house, & commanded the rest to depart, which fortwith was obeied, & the Generall tooke the keyes & locked the doore." He then goes on to give the reasons assigned by different persons for the act. Some said that the General "scented their purpose" to declare themselves perpetual, and to get rid of him by ordering him to Scotland. "Others say this, that the cries of the oppressed preveiled much with him . . . . & hastned the declaracion of that ould principle, *Salus populi suprema lex* &c."

The General, in the heat of his wrath, himself snatching the keys and locking the door, has a look of being drawn from the life. Cromwell, in a letter to General Fortescue (November, 1655), speaks sharply of the disorders and debauchedness, profaneness and wickedness, commonly practised amongst the army sent out to the West Indies. Major Mason gives us a specimen: "It is heere reported that some of the soldiers belonging to the ffleet at Boston, ffell upon the watch: after some bickering they comanded them to goe before the Governour; they retorned that they were Cromwell's boyes." Have we not, in these days, heard of "Sherman's boys"?

Belonging properly to the "Winthrop Papers," but printed in an earlier volume (Third Series, Vol. I. pp. 185–198), is a letter of John Maidstone, which contains the best summary of the Civil War that I ever read. Indeed, it gives a clearer insight into its causes, and a better view of the vicissitudes of the Commonwealth and Protectorate, than any one of the more elaborate histories. There is a singular equity and absence of party passion in it which gives us faith in the author's judgment. He was Oliver's Steward of the Household, and his portrait of him, as that of an eminently fair-minded man who knew him well, is of great value. Carlyle has not copied it, and, as many of my readers may never have seen it, I reproduce it here: "Before I pass further, pardon me in troubling you with the character of his person, which, by reason of my nearness to him, I had opportunity well to observe. His body was well compact and strong; his stature under six feet, (I believe about two inches;) his head so shaped as you might see it a store-house and shop both, of a vast treasury of natural parts. His temper exceeding fiery, as I have known, but the flame of it kept down for the most part or soon allayed with those moral endowments he had. He was naturally compassionate towards objects in distress, even to an effeminate measure; though God had made him a heart wherein was left little room for any fear but what was due to himself, of which there was a large proportion, yet did he exceed in tenderness toward sufferers. A larger soul, I think, hath seldom dwelt in a house of clay than his was. I do believe, if his story were impartially transmitted, and the unprejudiced world well possessed with it, she would add him to her nine worthies and make that number a *decemviri*. He lived and died in comfortable communion with God, as judicious persons near him well observed. He was that Mordecai that sought the welfare of his people and spake peace to his seed. Yet were his temptations such, as it appeared frequently that he that hath grace enough for many men may have too little for himself, the treasure he had being but in an earthen vessel and that equally defiled with original sin as any other man's nature is." There are phrases here that may be matched with the choicest in the life of Agricola; and, indeed, the whole letter, superior to Tacitus in judicial fairness of tone, goes abreast of his best writing in condensation, nay, surpasses it in this, that, while in Tacitus the intensity is of temper, here it is the clear residuum left by the ferment and settling of thought. Just before, speaking of the dissolution of Oliver's last Parliament, Maidstone says: "That was the last which sat during his life, he being compelled to wrestle with the difficulties of his place so well as he could without parliamentary assistance, and in it met with so great a burthen as (I doubt not to say) it drank up his spirits, of which his natural constitution yielded a vast stock, and brought him to his grave, his interment being the seed-time of his glory and England's calamity." Hooke, in a letter of April 16, 1658, has a passage worth quoting: "The dissolucion of the last Parliament puts the supreme powers upon difficulties, though the trueth is the Nacion is so ill spirited that little good is to be expected from these Generall Assemblies. They [the supreme powers, to wit, Cromwell] have been much in Counsell since this disappointment, & God hath been sought by them in the effectuall sense of the need of help from heaven & of the extreme danger impendent on a miscarriage of their advises. But our expences are so vast that I know not how they can avoyde a recurrence to another Session & to make a further tryall. . . . . The land is full of discontents, & the Cavaleerish party doth still expect a day & nourish hopes of a Revolucion. The Quakers do still proceed & are not yet come to their period. The Presbyterians do abound, I thinke, more than ever, & are very bold & confident because some of their masterpieces lye unanswered, particularly theire *Jus Divinum Regiminis Ecclesiastici* which I have sent to Mr. Davenporte. It hath been extant without answer these many years [only four, brother Hooke, if we may trust the title-page]. The Anabaptists abound likewise, & Mr Tombes hath pretended to have answered all the bookes extant against his opinion. I saw him presenting it to the Protectour of late. The Episcopall men ply the Common-Prayer booke with much more boldness then ever since these turnes of things, even in the open face of the City in severall places. I have spoken of it to the Protectour but as yet nothing is done in order to their being suppressed." It should teach us to distrust the apparent size of objects, which is a mere cheat of their nearness to us, that we are so often reminded of how small account things seem to one generation for which another was ready to die. A copy of the *Jus Divinum* held too close to the eyes could shut out the universe with its infinite chances and changes, its splendid indifference to our ephemeral fates. Cromwell, we should gather, had found out the secret of this historical perspective, to distinguish between the blaze of a burning tar-barrel and the final conflagration of all things. He had learned tolerance by the possession of power, — a proof of his capacity for rule. In 1652 Haynes writes: "Ther was a Catechise lately in print ther, that denied the divinity of Christ, yett ther was motions in the house by some, to have it lycenced by authority. Cromwell mainly oposed, & at last it was voted to bee burnt which causes much discontent of somme." Six years had made Cromwell wiser.

One more extract from a letter of Hooke's (30th March, 1659) is worth giving. After speaking of Oliver's death, he goes on to say: "Many prayers were put up solemnly for his life, & some, of great & good note, were too confident that he would not die. . . . . I suppose himselfe had thoughts that he should have outlived this sickness till near his dissolution, perhaps a day or two before; which I collect partly by some words which he was said to speak . . . . & partly from his delaying, almost to the last, to nominate his successor, to the wonderment of many who began sooner to despair of his life. . . . . His eldest son succeedeth him, being chosen by the Council, the day following his father's death, whereof he had no expectation. I have heard him say he had thought to have lived as a country gentleman, & that his father had not employed him in such a way as to prepare him for such employment; which, he thought, he did designedly. I suppose his meaning was lest it should have been apprehended he had prepared & appointed him for such a place, the burthen whereof I have several times heard him complaining under since his coming to the Government, the weighty occasions whereof with continuall oppressing cares had drunk up his father's spirits, in whose body very little blood was found when he was opened: the greatest defect visible was in his heart, which was flaccid & shrunk together. Yet he was one that could bear much without complaining, as one of a strong constitution of brain (as appeared when he was dissected) & likewise of body. His son seemeth to be of another frame, soft & tender, & penetrable with easier cares by much, yet he is of a sweete countenance, vivacious & candid, as is the whole frame of his spirit, only naturally inclined to choler. His reception of multitudes of addresses from towns, cities, & counties doth declare, among several other indiciums, more of ability in him than could, ordinarily, have been expected from him. He spake also with general acceptation & applause when he made his speech before the Parliament, even far beyond the Lord Fynes.* . . . . If this Assembly miss it, we are like to be in an ill condition. The old ways & customs of England, as to worshipe, are in the hearts of the most, who long to see the days again which once they saw. . . . . The hearts of very many are for the house of the Stewarts, & there is a speech as if they would attempt to call the late King's judges into question. . . . . The city, I hear is full of Cavaliers." Poor Richard appears to have inherited little of his father but the inclination to choler. That he could speak far beyond the Lord Fynes seems to have been not much to the purpose. Rhetoric was not precisely the medicine for such a case as he had to deal with. Such were the glimpses which the New England had of the Old. Ishmael must erelong learn to shift for himself.

The temperance question agitated the fathers very much as it still does the children. We have never seen

* This speech may be found in the Annual Register of 1762.

the anti-prohibition argument stated more cogently than in a letter of Thomas Shepard, minister of Cambridge, to Winthrop, in 1639: "This also I doe humbly intreat, that there may be no sin made of *drinking in any case one to another*, for I am confident he that stands here will fall & be beat from his grounds by his own arguments; as also that the consequences will be very sad, and the thing provoking to God & man to make more sins than (as yet is seene) God himself hath made." A principle as wise now as it was then. Our ancestors were also harassed as much as we by the difficulties of domestic service. In a country where land might be had for the asking, it was not easy to keep hold of servants brought over from England. Emanuel Downing, always the hard, practical man, would find a remedy in negro slavery. "A warr with the Narraganset," he writes to Winthrop in 1645, "is verie considerable to this plantation, ffor I doubt whither it be not synne in us, having power in our hands, to suffer them to maynteyne the worship of the devill which their pawwawes often doe; 2lie, If upon a just warre the Lord should deliver them into our hands, wee might easily have men, woemen, & children enough to exchange for Moores, which wilbe more gaynefull pilladge for us than wee conceive, for I doe not see how wee can thrive untill wee gett into a stock of slaves sufficient to doe all our buisenes, for our childrens children will hardly see this great Continent filled with people, soe that our servants will still desire freedome to plant for them selves, & not stay but for verie great wages. And I suppose you know verie well how wee shall maynteyne 20 Moores cheaper than one Englishe servant." The doubt whether it be not sin in us longer to tolerate their devil-worship, considering how much need we have of them as merchandise, is delicious. The way in which Hugh Peter grades the sharp descent from the apostolic to the practical with an *et cetera*, in the following extract, has the same charm: "Sir, Mr Endecot & myself salute you in the Lord Jesus &c. Wee have heard of a dividence of women & children in the bay & would bee glad of a share viz: a young woman or girle & a boy if you thinke good." Peter seems to have got what he asked for, and to have been worse off than before; for we find him writing two years later: "My wife desires my daughter to send to Hanna that was her mayd, now at Charltowne, to know if shee would dwell with us, for truly wee are so destitute (having now but an Indian) that wee know not what to doe." Let any housewife of our day, who does not find the Keltic element in domestic life so refreshing as to Mr. Arnold in literature, imagine a household with one wild Pequot woman, communicated with by signs, for its maid of all work, and take courage. Those were serious times indeed, when your cook might give warning by taking your scalp, or *chignon*, as the case might be, and making off with it into the woods. The fewness and dearness of servants made it necessary to call in temporary assistance for extraordinary occasions, and hence arose the common use of the word *help*. As the great majority kept no servants at all, and yet were liable to need them for work to which the family did not suffice, as, for instance, in harvest, the use of the word was naturally extended to all kinds of service. That it did not have its origin in any false shame at the condition itself, induced by democratic habits, is plain from the fact that it came into use while the word *servant* had a much wider application than now, and certainly implied no social stigma. Downing and Hooke, each at different times, one of them so late as 1667, wished to place a son as "servant" with one of the Winthrops. Roger Williams writes of his daughter, that "she desires to spend some time in service & liked much Mrs Brenton, who wanted." This was, no doubt, in order to be well drilled in housekeeping, an example which might be followed still to advantage. John Tinker, himself the "servant" or steward of the second Winthrop, makes use of *help* in both the senses we have mentioned, and shows the transition of the word from its restricted to its more general application. "We have fallen a pretty deal of timber & drawn some by Goodman Rogers's team, but unless your worship have a good team of your own & a man to go with them, I shall be much distracted for *help* . . . . & when our business is most in haste we shall be most to seek." Again, writing at harvest, as appears both by the date and by an elaborate pun, — "I received the *sithes* you sent but in that there came not also yourself, it maketh me to *sigth*," — he says: "*Help* is scarce and hard to get, difficult to please, uncertain, &c. Means runneth out & wages on & I cannot make choice of my *help*."

It may be some consolation to know that the complaint of a decline in the quality of servants is no modern thing. Shakespeare makes Orlando say to Adam:

> "O, good old man, how well in thee appears
> The constant service of the antique world,
> When service sweat for duty, not for meed!
> Thou art not of the fashion of these times,
> When none will sweat but for promotion."

When the faithful old servant is brought upon the stage, we may be sure he was getting rare. A century later, we have explicit testimony that things were as bad in this respect as they are now. Don Manuel Gonzales, who travelled in England in 1730, says of London servants: "As to common menial servants, they have great wages, are well kept and cloathed, but are notwithstanding the plague of almost every house in town. They form themselves into societies or rather confederacies, contributing to the maintenance of each other when out of place, and if any of them cannot manage the family where they are entertained, as they please, immediately they give notice they will be gone. There is no speaking to them, they are above correction, and if a master should attempt it, he may expect to be handsomely drubbed by the creature he feeds and harbors, or perhaps an action brought against him for it. It is become a common saying, *If my servant ben't a thief, if he be but honest, I can bear with other things.* And indeed it is very rare in London to meet with an honest servant." * Southey writes to his daughter Edith, in 1824, "All the maids eloped because I had turned a man out of the kitchen at eleven o'clock on the preceding night." Nay, Hugh Rhodes, in his *Boke of Nurture* (1577), speaks of servants "ofte fleeting," i. e. leaving one master for another.

One of the most curious things revealed to us in these volumes is the fact that John Winthrop, Jr., was seeking the philosopher's stone, that universal elixir which could transmute all things to its own substance. This is plain from the correspondence of Edward Howes. Howes goes to a certain doctor, professedly to consult him about the method of making a cement for earthen vessels, no doubt crucibles. His account of him is amusing, and reminds one of Ben Jonson's Subtle. This was one of the many quacks who gulled men during that twilight through which alchemy was passing into chemistry. "This Dr, for a Dr he is, brags that if he have but the hint or notice of any useful thing not yet invented, he will undertake to find it out, except some few which he hath vowed not to meddle with as *vitrum maliabile, perpet. motus, via proxima ad Indos & lapis philosi:* all, or

* Collection of Voyages, &c., from the Library of the Earl of Oxford, Vol. I. p. 151.

anything else he will undertake, but for his private gain, to make a monopoly thereof & to sell the use or knowledge thereof at too high rates." This breed of pedlers in science is not yet extinct. The exceptions made by the Doctor show a becoming modesty. Again : "I have been 2 or 3 times with the Dr & can get but small satisfaction about your queries. . . . . Yet I must confess he seemed very free to me, only in the main he was mystical. This he said, that when the will of God is you shall know what you desire, it will come with such a light that it will make a harmony among all your authors, causing them sweetly to agree, & put you forever out of doubt & question." In another letter : "I cannot discover into *terram incognitam*, but I have had a ken of it showed unto me. The way to it is, for the most part, horrible & fearful, the dangers none worse, to them that are *destinati filii*: sometimes I am travelling that way. . . . . I think I have spoken with some that have been there."

Howes writes very cautiously: "Dear friend, I desire with all my heart that I might write plainer to you, but in discovering the mystery, I may diminish its majesty & give occasion to the profane to abuse it, if it should fall into unworthy hands." By and by he begins to think his first doctor a humbug, but he finds a better. Howes was evidently a man of imaginative temper, fit to be captivated by the alchemistic theory of the unity of composition in nature, which was so attractive to Goethe. Perhaps the great poet was himself led to it by his Rosicrucian studies when writing the first part of Faust. Howes tells his friend that "there is all good to be found in unity, & all evil in duality & multiplicity. *Phœnix illa admiranda sola semper existit*, therefore while a man & she is two, he shall never see her," — a truth of very wide application, and too often lost sight of or never seen at all. "The Arabian Philos. I writ to you of, he was styled among us Dr Lyon, the best of all the Rosicrucians * that ever I met withal, far beyond Dr Ewer : they that are of his strain are knowing men ; they pretend [i. e. claim] to live in free light, they honor God & do good to the people among whom they live, & I conceive you are in the right that they had their learning from Arabia."

Howes is a very interesting person, a mystic of the purest kind, and that while learning to be an attorney with Emanuel Downing. How little that perfunctory person dreamed of what was going on under his nose, — as little as of the spiritual wonders that lay beyond the tip of it! Howes was a Swedenborgian before Swedenborg. Take this, for example : "But to our sympathetical business whereby we may communicate our minds one to another though the diameter of the earth interpose. *Diana non est centrum omnium.* I would have you so good a geometrician as to know your own centre. Did you ever yet measure your everlasting self, the length of your life, the breadth of your love, the depth of your wisdom & the height of your light? Let Truth be your centre, & you may do it, otherways not. I could wish you would now begin to leave off being altogether an outward man ; this is but *casa Regentis ;* the Ruler can draw you straight lines from your centre to the confines of an infinite circumference, by which you may pass from any part of the circumference to another without obstacle of earth or secation of lines, if you observe & keep but one & the true & only centre, to pass by it, from it, & to it. Methinks I now see you *intus et extra* & talk to you, but you mind me not because you are from home, you are not within, you look as if you were careless of yourself; your hand & your voice differ ; 't is my friend's hand, I know it well; but

* Howes writes the word symbolically.

the voice is your enemy's. O, my friend, if you love me, get you home, get you in! You have a friend as well as an enemy. Know them by their voices. The one is still driving or enticing you out; the other would have you stay within. Be within and keep within, & all that are within & keep within shall you see know & communicate with to the full, & shall not need to strain your outward senses to see & hear that which is like themselves uncertain & too-too often false, but, abiding forever within, in the centre of Truth, from thence you may behold & understand the innumerable divers emanations within the circumference, & still within; for without are falsities, lies, untruths, dogs &c." Howes was tolerant also, not from want of faith, but from depth of it. "The relation of your fight with the Indians I have read in print, but of the fight among yourselves, *bellum linguarum* the strife of tongues, I have heard much, but little to the purpose. I wonder your people, that pretend to know so much, doe not know that love is the fulfilling of the law, & that against love there is no law." Howes forgot that what might cause only a ripple in London might overwhelm the tiny Colony in Boston. Two years later, he writes more philosophically, and perhaps with a gentle irony, concerning "two monstrous births & a general earthquake." He hints that the people of the Bay might perhaps as well take these signs to themselves as lay them at the door of Mrs. Hutchinson and what not. "Where is there such another people then [as] in New England, that labors might & main to have Christ formed in them, yet would give or appoint him his shape & clothe him too? It cannot be denied that we have conceived many monstrous imaginations of Christ Jesus: the one imagination says, *Lo, here he is;* the other says, *Lo, there he is;* multiplicity of conceptions, but is there any one true shape of Him? And if one of many produce a shape, 't is not the shape of the Son of God, but an ugly horrid metamorphosis. Neither is it a living shape, but a dead one, yet a crow thinks her own bird the fairest, & most prefer their own wisdom before God's, Antichrist before Christ." Howes had certainly arrived at that "centre" of which he speaks and was before his time, as a man of speculation, never a man of action, may sometimes be. He was fitter for Plotinus's colony than Winthrop's. He never came to New England, yet there was always a leaven of his style of thinkers here.

Howes was the true adept, seeking what spiritual ore there might be among the dross of the hermetic philosophy. What he says sincerely and inwardly was the cant of those outward professors of the doctrine who were content to dwell in the material part of it forever. In Jonathan Brewster, we have a specimen of these Wagners. Is it not curious, that there should have been a *balneum Mariæ* at New London two hundred years ago? that *la recherche de l'Absolu* should have been going on there in a log-hut, under constant fear that the Indians would put out, not merely the flame of one little life, but, far worse, the fire of our furnace, and so rob the world of this divine secret, just on the point of revealing itself? Alas! poor Brewster's secret was one that many have striven after before and since, who did not call themselves alchemists, — the secret of getting gold without earning it, — a chase that brings some men to a four-in-hand on Shoddy Avenue, and some to the penitentiary, in both cases advertising its utter vanity. Brewster is a capital specimen of his class, who are better than the average, because they *do* mix a little imagination with their sordidness, and who have also their representatives among us, in those who expect the Jennings and other ideal estates in England. If Hawthorne had but known of him! And yet how perfectly did his genius divine that ideal element in our early New England life, conceiving what must have been without asking proof of what actually was!

An extract or two will sufficiently exhibit Brewster in his lunes. Sending back some alchemistic book to Winthrop, he tells him that if his name be kept secret, "I will write as clear a light, as far as I dare to, in finding the first ingredience. . . . . The first figure in Flamonell doth plainly resemble the first ingredience, what it is, & from whence it comes, & how gotten, as there you may plainly see set forth by 2 resemblances held in a man's hand; for the confections there named is a delusion, for they are but the operations of the work after some time set, as the scum of the Red Sea, which is the Virgin's Milk upon the top of the vessel, white. Red Sea is the sun & moon calcinated & brought & reduced into water mineral which in some time, & most of the whole time, is red. 2ndly, the fat of mercurial wind, that is the fat or quintessence of sun & moon, earth & water, drawn out from them both, & flies aloft & bore up by the operation of our mercury, that is our fire which is our air or wind." This is as satisfactory as Lepidus's account of the generation of the crocodile: "Your serpent of Egypt is bred now of your mud by the operation of your sun: so is your crocodile." After describing the three kinds of fire, that of the lamp, that of ashes, and that against nature, which last "is the fire of fire, that is the secret fire drawn up, being the quintessence of the sun & moon, with the other mercurial water joined with & together, which is fire elemental," he tells us that "these fires are & doth contain the whole mystery of the work." The reader, perhaps, thinks that he has nothing to do but forthwith to turn all the lead he can lay his hands on into gold. But no: "If you had the first ingredience & the proportion of each, yet all were nothing if you had not the certain times & seasons of the planets & signs, when to give more or less of this fire, namely a hot & dry, a cold & moist fire which you must use in the mercurial water before it comes to black & after into white & then red, which is only done by these fires, which when you practise you will easily see & perceive, that you shall stand amazed, & admire at the great & admirable wisdom of God, that can produce such a wonderful, efficacious, powerful thing as this is to convert all metallic bodies to its own nature, which may be well called a first essence. I say by such weak simple means of so little value & so little & easy labor & skill, that I may say with Artephus, 200 page, it is of a worke so easy & short, fitter for women & young children than sage & grave men. . . . . I thank the Lord, I understand the matter perfectly in the said book, yet I could desire to have it again 12 months hence, for about that time I shall have occasion to peruse, whenas I come to the second working which is most difficult, which will be some three or [4] months before the perfect white, & afterwards, as Artephus saith, I may burn my books, for he saith it is one regiment as well for the red as for the white. The Lord in mercy give me life to see the end of it!" — an exclamation I more than once made in the course of some of Brewster's periods.

Again, under pledge of profound secrecy, he sends Winthrop a manuscript, which he may communicate to the owner of the volume formerly lent, because "it gave me such light in the second work as I should not readily have found out by study, also & especially how to work the elixir fit for medicine & healing all maladies which is clean another way of working than we held formerly. Also a light given how to dissolve any hard substance into the elixir, which is also another work.

And many other things which in Ribley [Ripley ?] I could not find out. More works of the same I would gladly see . . . . for, Sir, so it is that any book of this subject, I can understand it, though never so darkly written, having both knowledge & experience of the world,* that now easily I may understand their envious carriages to hide it. . . . . You may marvel why I should give any light to others in this thing before I have perfected my own. This know, that my work being true thus far by all their writings, it cannot fail . . . . for if &c &c you cannot miss if you would, except you break your glass." He confesses he is mistaken as to the time required, which he now, as well as I can make out, reckons at about ten years. "I fear I shall not live to see it finished, in regard partly of the Indians, who, I fear, will raise wars, as also I have a conceit that God sees me not worthy of such a blessing, by reason of my manifold miscarriages." Therefore he "will shortly write all the whole work in few words plainly which may be done in 20 lines from the first to the last & seal it up in a little box & subscribe it to yourself . . . . & will so write it that neither wife nor children shall know thereof." If Winthrop should succeed in bringing the work to perfection, Brewster begs him to remember his wife and children. "I mean if this my work should miscarry by wars of the Indians, for I may not remove it till it be perfected, otherwise I should so unsettle the body by removing sun & moon out of their settled places, that there would then be no other afterworking." Once more he inculcates secrecy, and for a most comical reason: "For it is such a secret as is not fit for every one either for secrecy or for parts to use it, as God's secret for his glory, to do good therewith, or else they may do a great deal of hurt, spend-

* "World" here should clearly be "work."

ing & employing it to satisfy sinful lusts. Therefore, I intreat you, sir, spare to use my name, & let my letters I send either be safely kept or burned that I write about it, for indeed, sir, I am more than before sensible of the evil effects that will arise by the publishing of it. I should never be at quiet, neither at home nor abroad, for one or other that would be enquiring & seeking after knowledge thereof, that I should be tired out & forced to leave the place: nay, it would be blazed abroad into Europe." How much more comic is nature than any comedy! *Mutato nomine de te.* Take heart, ambitious youth, the sun and moon will be no more disconcerted by any effort of yours than by the pots and pans of Jonathan Brewster. It is a curious proof of the duality so common (yet so often overlooked) in human character, that Brewster was all this while manager of the Plymouth trading-post, near what is now New London. The only professors of the transmutation of metals who still impose on mankind are to be found in what is styled the critical department of literature. Their *materia prima*, or universal solvent, serves equally for the lead of Tupper or the brass of Swinburne.

In a letter of Sir Kenelm Digby to J. Winthrop, Jr., we find some odd prescriptions. "For all sorts of agues, I have of late tried the following magnetical experiment with infallible success. Pare the patient's nails when the fit is coming on, & put the parings into a little bag of fine linen or sarsenet, & tie that about a live eel's neck in a tub of water. The eel will die & the patient will recover. And if a dog or hog eat that eel, they will also die."

"The man recovered of the bite,
The dog it was that died!"

"I have known one that cured all deliriums & frenzies whatsoever, & at once taking, with an elixir made of dew, nothing but dew purified & nipped up in a glass & digested 15 months till all of it was become a gray powder, not one drop of humidity remaining. This I know to be true, & that first it was as black as ink, then green, then gray, & at 22 months' end it was as white & lustrous as any oriental pearl. But it cured manias at 15 months' end." Poor Brewster would have been the better for a dose of it, as well as some in our day, who expect to cure men of being men by act of Congress. In the same letter Digby boasts of having made known the properties of *quinquina*, and also of the sympathetic powder, with which latter he wrought a "famous cure" of pleasant James Howell, author of the "Letters." I do not recollect that Howell anywhere alludes to it. In the same letter, Digby speaks of the books he had sent to Harvard College, and promises to send more. In all Paris he cannot find a copy of Blaise Viginere *Des Chiffres*. "I had it in my library in England, but at the plundering of my house I lost it with many other good books. I have *laid out* in all places for it." The words we have underscored would be called a Yankeeism now. The house was Gatehurst, a fine Elizabethan dwelling, still, or lately, standing. Digby made his peace with Cromwell, and professes his readiness to spend his blood for him. He kept well with both sides, and we are not surprised to find Hooke saying that he hears no good of him from any.

The early colonists found it needful to bring over a few trained soldiers, both as drillmasters and engineers. Underhill, Patrick, and Gardner had served in the Low Countries, probably also Mason. As Paris has been said to be not precisely the place for a deacon, so the camp of the Prince of Orange could hardly have been the best training-school for Puritans in practice, however it may have been for masters of casuistic theology. The position of these rough warriors among a people like those of the first emigration must have been a droll one. That of Captain Underhill certainly was. In all our early history, there is no figure so comic. Full of the pedantry of his profession and fond of noble phrases, he is a kind of cross between Dugald Dalgetty and Ancient Pistol, with a slight relish of the *miles gloriosus.* Underhill had taken side with Mr. Wheelwright in his heretical opinions, and there is every reason why he should have maintained, with all the ardor of personal interest, the efficiency of a covenant of grace without reference to the works of the subject of it. Coming back from a visit to England in 1638, he "was questioned for some speeches uttered by him in the ship, viz: that they at Boston were zealous as the scribes and pharisees were and as Paul was before his conversion, which he denying, they were proved to his face by a sober woman whom he had seduced in the ship and drawn to his opinion; but she was afterwards better informed in the truth. Among other passages, he told her how he came by his assurance, saying that, having long lain under a spirit of bondage, and continued in a legal way near five years, he could get no assurance, till at length, as he was taking a pipe of the good creature tobacco, the spirit fell home upon his heart, an absolute promise of free grace, with such assurance and joy, as he never doubted since of his good estate, neither should he, whatsoever sin he should fall into, — a good preparative for such motions as he familiarly used to make to some of that sex. . . . . The next day he was called again and banished. The Lord's day after, he made a speech in the assembly, showing that as the Lord was pleased to convert Paul as he was persecuting &c, so he might manifest himself to him as he was making moderate use of the good creature called tobacco." A week later "he was privately dealt with upon suspicion of incontinency . . . . but his excuse was that the woman was in great trouble of mind, and some temptations, and that he resorted to her to comfort her." He went to the Eastward, and, having run himself out there, thought it best to come back to Boston and reinstate himself by eating his leek. "He came in his worst clothes (being accustomed to take great pride in his bravery and neatness) without a band, in a foul linen cap pulled close to his eyes, and, standing upon a form, he did, with many deep sighs and abundance of tears, lay open his wicked course, his adultery, his hypocrisy &c. He spake well, save that his blubbering &c. interrupted him." We hope he was a sincere penitent, but men of his complexion are apt to be pleased with such a tragi-comedy of self-abasement, if only they can be chief actors and conspicuous enough therein. In the correspondence before us Underhill appears in full turkey-cock proportions. Not having been advanced according to his own opinion of his merits, he writes to Governor Winthrop, with an oblique threat that must have amused him somewhat: "I profess, sir, till I know the cause, I shall not be satisfied, but I hope God will subdue me to his will; yet this I say that such handling of officers in foreign parts hath so far subverted some of them as to cause them turn public rebels against their state & kingdom, which God forbid should ever be found once so much as to appear in my breast." Why, then the world 's mine oyster, which I with sword will open! Next we hear him on a point of military discipline at Salem. "It is this: how they have of their own appointment made them a captain, lieutenant & ensign, & after such a manner as was never heard of in any school of war, nor in no kingdom under heaven. . . . . For my part, if there should not be a reformation in this disordered practise, I would not acknowledge such officers. If officers should be of no better esteem than for constables to place them, & martial discipline to proceed disorderly, I would rather lay down my command than to shame so noble a prince from whom we came." Again: "Whereas it is somewhat questionable whether the three months I was absent, as well in the service of the country as of other particular persons, my request therefore is that this honored Court would be pleased to decide this controversy, myself alleging it to be the custom of Nations that, if a Commander be lent to another State, by that State to whom he is a servant, both his place & means is not detained from him, so long as he doth not refuse the call of his own State to which he is a servant, in case they shall call him home." Then bringing up again his "ancient suit" for a grant of land, he throws in a neat touch of piety: "& if the honored Court shall vouchsafe to make some addition, that which hath not been deserved, by the same power of God, may be in due season." In a postscript, he gives a fine philosophical reason for this desired addition which will go to the hearts of many in these days of high prices and wasteful taxation. "The time was when a little went far; then much was not known nor desired; the reason of the difference lieth only in the error of judgment, for nature requires no more to uphold it now than when it was satisfied with less." The valiant Captain interprets the law of nations, as sovereign powers are wont to do, to suit his advantage in the special case. We find a parallel case in a letter of Bryan Rosseter to John Winthrop, Jr., pleading for a remission of taxes. "The lawes of nations exempt allowed phisitians from personall services, & their estates from rates & assessments." In the Declaration of the town of Southampton on Long Island (1673), the dignity of constable is valued at a juster rate than Underhill was inclined to put upon it. The Dutch, it seems, demanded of them "to deliver up to them the badge of Civil & Military power; namely, the Constable's staffe & the Colonel's." Mayor Munroe of New Orleans did not more effectually magnify his office when he surrendered the city to General Butler.

Underhill's style is always of the finest. His spelling was under the purest covenant of grace. I must give a single specimen of it from a letter whose high moral tone is all the more diverting that it was written while he was under excommunication for the sin which he afterwards confessed. It is addressed to Winthrop and Dudley. "Honnored in the Lord. Youer silenc onc more admirse me. I youse chrischan playnnes. I know you love it. Silenc can not reduce the hart of youer love[g] brother: I would the rightchous would smite me, espeschali youer slfe & the honnored Depoti to whom I also dereckt this letter together with youer honnored slfe. Jesos Christ did wayt; & God his Father did dig and telfe bout the barren figtre before he would cast it of: I would to God you would tender my soule so as to youse playnnes with me." (As if anything could be plainer than excommunication and banishment!) "I wrot to you both, but now [no] answer; & here I am dayli abused by malischous tongse: John Baker I here hath rot to the honnored depoti how as I was dronck & like to be cild, & both falc, upon okachon I delt with Wannerton for intrushon, & findding them resolutli bent to rout out all gud a mong us & advanc there superstischous waye, & by boystrous words indeferd to fritten men to acomplish his end, & he abusing me to my face, dru upon him with intent to corb his insolent and dasterdli sperrite, but now [no] danger of my life, although it might hafe bin just with God to hafe giffen me in the hanse of youer enemise & mine, for they hat the wayse of the Lord & them that profes them, & therfore layes trapes to cachte the pore into there deboyst corses, as ister daye on Pickeren their Chorch Warden caim up to us with intent to mak some of ourse dronc, as is sospeckted, but the Lord soferd him so to misdemen himslfe as he is likli to li by the hielse this too mouth. . . . . My hombel request is that you will be charitabel of me. . . . . Let justies and merci be goyned. . . . . You may plese to soggest youer will to this barrer, you will find him tracktabel." The concluding phrase seems admirably chosen, when we consider the means of making people "tractable" which the magistrates of the Bay had in their hands, and were not slow to exercise, as Underhill himself had experienced.

I cannot deny myself the pleasure of giving one more specimen of the Captain's "grand-delinquent" style, as I once heard such fine writing called by a person who little dreamed what a hit he had made. So far as I have observed, our public defaulters, and others who have nothing to say for themselves, always rise in style as they sink in self-respect. He is speaking of one Scott, who had laid claim to certain lands, and had been called on to show his title. "If he break the comand of the Asembli & bring not in the counterfit portreture of the King imprest in yello waxe, anext to his false perpetuiti of 20 mile square, where by he did chet the Town of Brouckhaven, he is to induer the sentance of the Court of Asisies." Pistol would have been charmed with that splendid amplification of the Great Seal. We have seen nothing like it in our day, except in a speech made to Mr. George Peabody at Danvers, if I recollect, while that gentleman was so elaborately concealing from his left hand what his right had been doing. As examples of Captain Underhill's adroitness in phonetic spelling, I offer *fafarabel* and *poseschonse*, and reluctantly leave him.

Another very entertaining fellow for those who are willing to work through a pretty thick husk of tiresomeness for a genuine kernel of humor underneath is Coddington. The elder Winthrop endured many trials, but I doubt if any were sharper than those which his son had to undergo in the correspondence of this excellently tiresome man. *Tantæ molis Romanam condere gentem!* The dulness of Coddington, always that of no ordinary man, became irritable and aggressive after being stung by the gadfly of Quakerism. Running counter to its proper nature, it made him morbidly uneasy. Already an Anabaptist, his brain does not seem to have been large enough to lodge two maggots at once with any comfort to himself. Fancy John Winthrop, Jr., with all the affairs of the Connecticut Colony on his back, expected to prescribe alike for the spiritual and bodily ailments of all the hypochondriacs in his government, and with Philip's war impending, — fancy him exposed also to perpetual trials like this : "G. F. [George Fox] hath sent thee a book of his by Jere : Bull, & two more now which thou mayest communicate to thy Council & officers. Also I remember before thy last being in England, I sent thee a book written by Francis Howgall against persecution, by Joseph Nicallson which book thou lovingly accepted and communicated to the Commissioners of the United Colonies (as I desired) also J. N. thou entertained with a loving respect which encouraged me" (fatal hospitality!) — "As a token of that ancient love that for this 42 years I have had for thee, I have sent thee three Manuscripts, one of 5 queries, other is of 15, about the love of Jesus &c. The 3d is why we cannot come to the worship which was not set up by Christ Jesus, which I desire thee to communicate to the priests to answer in thy jurisdiction, the Massachusetts, New Plymouth, or elsewhere, & send their answer in writing to me. Also two printed papers to set up in thy house. It 's reported in Barbadoes that thy brother Sammuell shall be sent Governour to Antego." What a mere dust of sugar in the last sentence for such a portentous pill! In his next letter he has other writings of G. F., "not yet copied, which if thou desireth, when I hear from thee, I may convey them unto thee. Also sence G. Ffox departure William Edmondson is arrived at this Island, who having given out a paper to all in authority, which, my wife having copied, I have here inclosed presented thee therewith." Books and manuscripts were not all. Coddington was also glad to bestow on Winthrop any wandering tediousness in the flesh that came to hand. "I now understand of John Stubbs freedom to visit thee (with the said Jo: B.) he is a larned man, as witness the battle door * on 35 languages," — a terrible man this, capable of inflicting himself on three dozen different kindreds of men. It will be observed that Coddington, with his "thou desireths," is not quite so well up in the grammar of his thee-and-thouing as my Lord Coke. Indeed, it is rather pleasant to see that in his alarm about "the enemy," in 1673, he backslides into the second person plural. If Winthrop ever looked over his father's correspondence, he would have read in a letter of Henry Jacie the following dreadful example of retribution: "The last news we heard was that the Bores in Bavaria slew about 300 of the Swedish forces & took about 200 prisoners, of which they put out the eyes of some & cut out the tonges of others & so sent them to the King of Sweden, which caused him to lament bytterly for an hour. Then he sent an army & destroyed those Bores, about 200 or 300 of their towns. Thus we hear." Think of that, Master Coddington!

* The title-page of which our learned Marsh has cited for the etymology of the word.

Could the sinful heart of man always suppress the wish that a Gustavus might arise to do judgment on the Bores of Rhode Island? The unkindest part of it was that, on Coddington's own statement, Winthrop had never persecuted the Quakers, and had even endeavored to save Robinson and Stevenson in 1659.

Speaking of the execution of these two martyrs to the bee in their bonnets, John Davenport gives us a capital example of the way in which Divine "judgments" may be made to work both ways at the pleasure of the interpreter. As the crowd was going home from the hanging, a drawbridge gave way, and some lives were lost. The Quakers, of course, made the most of this lesson to the *pontifices* in the bearing power of timber, claiming it as a proof of God's wrath against the persecutors. This was rather hard, since none of the magistrates perished, and the popular feeling was strongly in favor of the victims of their severity. But Davenport gallantly captures these Quaker guns, and turns them against the enemy himself. "Sir, the hurt that befell so many, by their own rashness, at the Draw Bridge in Boston, being on the day that the Quakers were executed, was not without God's special providence in judgment & wrath, I fear, against the Quakers & their abettors, who will be much hardened thereby." This is admirable, especially as his parenthesis about "their own rashness" assumes that the whole thing was owing to natural causes. The pity for the Quakers, too, implied in the "I fear," is a nice touch. It is always noticeable how much more liberal those who deal in God's command without his power are of his wrath than of his mercy. But we should never understand the Puritans if we did not bear in mind that they were still prisoners in that religion of Fear which casts out Love. The nearness of God was oftener a terror than a comfort to them. Yet perhaps in them was the last apparition of Faith as a wonder-worker in human affairs. Take away from them what you will, you cannot deny them *that,* and its constant presence made them great in a way and measure of which this generation, it is to be feared, can have but a very inadequate conception. If men now-a-days find their tone antipathetic, it would be modest at least to consider whether the fault be wholly theirs, — whether it was they who lacked, or we who have lost. Whether they were right or wrong in their dealing with the Quakers is not a question to be decided glibly after two centuries' struggle toward a conception of toleration very imperfect even yet, perhaps impossible to human nature. If they did not choose what seems to us the wisest way of keeping the Devil out of their household, they certainly had a very honest will to keep him out, which we might emulate with advantage. However it be in other cases, historic toleration must include intolerance among things to be tolerated.

The false notion which the first settlers had of the savages by whom the continent was beflead rather than inhabited, arose in part from what they had heard of Mexico and Peru, in part from the splendid exaggerations of the early travellers, who could give their readers an El Dorado at the cheap cost of a good lie. Hence the kings, dukes, and earls who were so plenty among the red men. Pride of descent takes many odd shapes, none odder than when it hugs itself in an ancestry of filthy barbarians, who daubed themselves for ornament with a mixture of bear's-grease and soot, or colored clay, and were called emperors by Captain John Smith and his compeers. The droll contrast between this imaginary royalty and the squalid reality is nowhere exposed with more ludicrous unconsciousness than in the following passage of a letter from Fitz-John Winthrop to his father, November, 1674 : "The bearer hereof, Mr. Danyell, one of the Royal Indian blood . . . . does desire me to give an account to yourself of the late unhappy accident which has happened to him. A little time since, a careless girl playing with fire at the door, it immediately took hold of the mats, & in an instant consumed it to ashes, with all the common as well as his lady's chamber furniture, & his own wardrobe & armory, Indian plate, & money to the value (as is credibly reported in his estimation) of more than an hundred pounds Indian. . . . . The Indians have handsomely already built him a good house & brought him in several necessaries for his present supply, but that which takes deepest melancholy impression upon him is the loss of an excellent Masathuset cloth cloak & hat, which was only seen upon holy days & their general sessions. His journey at this time is only to intreat your favor & the gentlemen there for a kind relief in his necessity, having no kind of garment but a short jerkin which was charitably given him by one of his Common-Councilmen. He principally aims at a cloak & hat."

"King Stephen was a worthy peer,
His breeches cost him half a crown."

But it will be observed that there is no allusion to any such article of dress in the costume of this prince of Pequot. Some light is perhaps thrown on this deficiency by a line or two in one of Williams's letters, where he says: "I have long had scruples of selling the Natives ought but what may tend or bring to civilizing: I therefore neither brought nor shall sell them loose coats nor breeches." Precisely the opposite course was deemed effectual with the Highland Scotch, between whom and our Indians there was a very close analogy. They were compelled by law to adopt the usages of *Gallia Braccata*, and sansculottism made a penal offence.

What impediment to civilization Williams had discovered in the offending garment it is hard to say. It is a question for Herr Teufelsdröck. Royalty, at any rate, in our day, is dependent for much of its success on the tailor. Williams's opportunities of studying the Indian character were perhaps greater than those of any other man of his time. He was always an advocate for justice toward them. But he seems to have had no better opinion of them than Mr. Parkman,* calling them shortly and sharply, "wolves endowed with men's brains." The same change of feeling has followed the same causes in their case as in that of the Highlanders, — they have become romantic in proportion as they ceased to be dangerous.

As exhibitions of the writer's character, no letters in the collection have interested us more than those of John Tinker, who for many years was a kind of steward for John Winthrop and his son. They show him to have been a thoroughly faithful, grateful, and unselfish servant. He does not seem to have prospered except in winning respect, for when he died his funeral charges were paid by the public. We learn from one of his letters that John Winthrop, Jr., had a negro (presumably a slave) at Paquanet, for he says that a mad cow there "had almost spoiled the neger & made him ferfull to tend the rest of the cattell." That such slaves must have been rare, however, is plain from his constant complaints about the difficulty of procuring "help," some of which we have already quoted. His spelling of the word "ferfull" shows that the New England pronunciation of that word had been brought from the old country. He also uses the word "creatures" for kine, and the like, precisely as our farmers do now. There is one very comical passage in a letter of the 2d of August,

* In his Jesuits in North America.

1660, where he says: "There hath been a motion by some, the chief of the town, (New London) for my keeping an ordinary, or rather under the notion of a tavern, which, *though it suits not with my genius*, yet am almost persuaded to accept for some good grounds." Tinker's modesty is most creditable to him, and we wish it were more common now. No people on the face of the earth suffer so much as we from impostors who keep inconveniences, "under the notion of a tavern," without any call of natural genius thereto; none endure with such unexemplary patience the superb indifference of innkeepers, and the condescending inattention of their gentlemanly deputies. We are the thralls of our railroads and hotels, and we deserve it.

Richard Saltonstall writes to John Winthrop, Jr., in 1636: "The best thing that I have to beg your thoughts for at this present is a motto or two that Mr. Prynne hath writ upon his chamber walls in the Tower." We copy a few phrases, chiefly for the contrast they make with Lovelace's famous verses to Althea. Nothing could mark more sharply the different habits of mind in Puritan and Cavalier. Lovelace is very charming, but he sings

"The sweetness, mercy, majesty,
And glories of *his* King,"

to wit, Charles I. To him "stone walls do not a prison make," so long as he has "freedom in his love, and in his soul is free." Prynne's King was of another and higher kind: "*Carcer excludit mundum, includit Deum. Deus est turris etiam in turre: turris libertatis in turre angustiæ: Turris quietis in turre molestiæ. . . . . Arctari non potest qui in ipsa Dei infinitate incarceratus spatiatur. . . . . Nil crus sentit in nervo si animus sit in cœlo: nil corpus patitur in ergastulo, si anima sit in Christo.*" If Lovelace has the advantage in fancy,

Prynne has it as clearly in depth of sentiment. There could be little doubt which of the parties represented by these men would have the better if it came to a death-grapple.

There is curiously little sentiment in these volumes. Most of the letters, except where some point of doctrine is concerned, are those of shrewd, practical men, busy about the affairs of this world, and earnest to build their New Jerusalem on something more solid than cloud. The truth is, that men anxious about their souls have not been by any means the least skilful in providing for the wants of the body. It was far less the enthusiasm than the common sense of the Puritans which made them what they were in politics and religion. That a great change should be wrought in the settlers by the circumstances of their position was inevitable ; that this change should have had some disillusion in it, that it should have weaned them from the ideal and wonted them to the actual, was equally so. In 1664, not much more than a generation after the settlement, Williams prophesies : "When we that have been the eldest are rotting (to-morrow or next day) a generation will act, I fear, far unlike the first Winthrops and their models of love. I fear that the common trinity of the world (profit, preferment, pleasure) will here be the *tria omnia* as in all the world beside, that Prelacy and Papacy too will in this wilderness predominate, that god Land will be (as now it is) as great a god with us English as god Gold was with the Spaniards. While we are here, noble sir, let us *viriliter hoc agere, rem agere humanam, divinam, Christianam,* which, I believe, is all of a most public genius," or, as we should now say, true patriotism. If Williams means no play on the word *humanam* and *divinam,* the order of precedence in which he marshals them is noticeable. A generation later, what Williams had predicted was in a great measure verified. But what made New England Puritanism narrow was what made Scotch Cameronianism narrow, — its being secluded from the great movement of the nation. Till 1660 the colony was ruled and mostly inhabited by Englishmen closely connected with the party dominant in the mother country, and with their minds broadened by having to deal with questions of state and European policy. After that time they sank rapidly into provincials, narrow in thought, in culture, in creed. Such a pedantic portent as Cotton Mather would have been impossible in the first generation; he was the natural growth of the third, — the manifest judgment of God on a generation who thought Words a saving substitute for Things. Perhaps some injustice has been done to men like the second Governor Dudley, and it should be counted to them rather as a merit than a fault, that they wished to bring New England back within reach of the invigorating influence of national sympathies, and to rescue it from a tradition which had become empty formalism. Puritanism was dead, and its profession had become a wearisome cant before the Revolution of 1688 gave it that vital force in politics which it had lost in religion.

I have gleaned all I could of what is morally picturesque or characteristic from these volumes, but New England history has rather a gregarious than a personal interest. Here, by inherent necessity rather than design, was made the first experiment in practical democracy, and accordingly hence began that reaction of the New World upon the Old whose result can hardly yet be estimated. There is here no temptation to make a hero, who shall sum up in his own individuality and carry forward by his own will that purpose of which we seem to catch such bewitching glances in history, which reveals itself more clearly and constantly, perhaps, in the annals of New

England than elsewhere, and which yet, at best, is but tentative, doubtful of itself, turned this way and that by chance, made up of instinct, and modified by circumstance quite as much as it is directed by deliberate forethought. Such a purpose, or natural craving, or result of temporary influences, may be misguided by a powerful character to his own ends, or, if he be strongly in sympathy with it, may be hastened toward its own fulfilment; but there is no such heroic element in our drama, and what is remarkable is, that, under whatever government, democracy grew with the growth of the New England Colonies, and was at last potent enough to wrench them, and the better part of the continent with them, from the mother country. It is true that Jefferson embodied in the Declaration of Independence the speculative theories he had learned in France, but the impulse to separation came from New England; and those theories had been long since embodied there in the practice of the people, if they had never been formulated in distinct propositions.

I have little sympathy with declaimers about the Pilgrim Fathers, who look upon them all as men of grand conceptions and superhuman foresight. An entire ship's company of Columbuses is what the world never saw. It is not wise to form any theory and fit our facts to it, as a man in a hurry is apt to cram his travelling-bag, with a total disregard of shape or texture. But perhaps it may be found that the facts will only fit comfortably together on a single plan, namely, that the fathers did have a conception (which those will call grand who regard simplicity as a necessary element of grandeur) of founding here a commonwealth on those two eternal bases of Faith and Work; that they had, indeed, no revolutionary ideas of universal liberty, but yet, what answered the purpose quite as well, an abiding faith in the brotherhood of man and the fatherhood of God; and that they did not so much propose to make all things new, as to develop the latent possibilities of English law and English character, by clearing away the fences by which the abuse of the one was gradually discommoning the other from the broad fields of natural right. They were not in advance of their age, as it is called, for no one who is so can ever work profitably in it; but they were alive to the highest and most earnest thinking of their time.

LESSING.*

WHEN Burns's humor gave its last pathetic flicker in his "John, don't let the awkward squad fire over me," was he thinking of actual brother-volunteers, or of possible biographers? Did his words betray only the rhythmic sensitiveness of poetic nerves, or were they a foreboding of that helpless future, when the poet lies at the mercy of the plodder, — of that bi-voluminous shape in which dulness overtakes and revenges itself on genius at last? Certainly Burns has suffered as much as most large-natured creatures from well-meaning efforts to account for him, to explain him away, to bring him into harmony with those well-regulated minds which, during a good part of the last century, found out a way, through rhyme, to snatch a prosiness beyond the reach of prose. Nay, he has been wronged also by that other want of true appreciation, which deals in panegyric, and would put asunder those two things which God has joined, — the poet and the man, — as if it were not the same rash improvidence that was the happiness of the verse and the misfortune of the gauger. But his death-bed was

* G. E. LESSING. *Sein Leben und seine Werke.* Von ADOLF STAHR. Vermehrte und verbesserte Volks-Ausgabe. Dritte Auflage. Berlin. 1864.

The Same. Translated by E. P. EVANS, Ph. D., Professor, &c. in the University of Michigan. Boston: W. V. Spencer. 1866. 2 vols.

G. E. Lessing's Sämmtliche Schriften, herausgegeben von Karl Lachmann. 1853–57. 12 Bände.

at least not haunted by the unappeasable apprehension of a German for his biographer; and that the fame of Lessing should have four times survived this cunningest assault of oblivion is proof enough that its base is broad and deep-set.

There seems to be, in the average German mind, an inability or a disinclination to see a thing as it really is, unless it be a matter of science. It finds its keenest pleasure in divining a profound significance in the most trifling things, and the number of mare's-nests that have been stared into by the German *Gelehrter* through his spectacles passes calculation. They are the one object of contemplation that makes that singular being perfectly happy, and they seem to be as common as those of the stork. In the dark forest of æsthetics, particularly, he finds them at every turn, — "fanno tutto il loco varo." If the greater part of our English criticism is apt only to skim the surface, the German, by way of being profound, too often burrows in delighted darkness quite beneath its subject, till the reader feels the ground hollow beneath him, and is fearful of caving into unknown depths of stagnant metaphysic air at every step. The Commentary on Shakespeare of Gervinus, a really superior man, reminds one of the Roman Campagna, penetrated underground in all directions by strange winding caverns, the work of human borers in search of we know not what. Above are the divine poet's larks and daisies, his incommunicable skies, his broad prospects of life and nature; and meanwhile our Teutonic *teredo* worms his way below, and offers to be our guide into an obscurity of his own contriving. The reaction of language upon style, and even upon thought, by its limitations on the one hand, and its suggestions on the other, is so apparent to any one who has made even a slight study of comparative literature, that we have sometimes thought the German tongue at least an accessory before the fact, if nothing more, in the offences of German literature. The language has such a fatal genius for going stern-foremost, for yawing, and for not minding the helm without some ten minutes' notice in advance, that he must be a great sailor indeed who can safely make it the vehicle for anything but imperishable commodities. Vischer's *Æsthetik*, the best treatise on the subject, ancient or modern, is such a book as none but a German could write, and it is written as none but a German could have written it. The abstracts of its sections are sometimes nearly as long as the sections themselves, and it is as hard to make out which head belongs to which tail, as in a knot of snakes thawing themselves into sluggish individuality under a spring sun. The average German professor spends his life in making lanterns fit to guide us through the obscurest passages of all the *ologies* and *ysics*, and there are none in the world of such honest workmanship. They are durable, they have intensifying glasses, reflectors of the most scientific make, capital sockets in which to set a light, and a handsome lump of potentially illuminating tallow is thrown in. But, in order to *see* by them, the explorer must make his own candle, supply his own cohesive wick of common-sense, and light it himself. And yet the admirable thoroughness of the German intellect! We should be ungrateful indeed if we did not acknowledge that it has supplied the raw material in almost every branch of science for the defter wits of other nations to work on; yet we have a suspicion that there are certain lighter departments of literature in which it may be misapplied, and turn into something very like clumsiness. Delightful as Jean Paul's humor is, how much more so would it be if he only knew when to stop! Ethereally deep as is his sentiment, should we not feel it more if he sometimes gave us a little less of it, — if he would only not always deal out his wine by beer-measure? *So* thorough is the German mind, that might it not seem now and then to work quite through its subject, and expatiate in cheerful unconsciousness on the other side thereof?

With all its merits of a higher and deeper kind, it yet seems to us that German literature has not quite satisfactorily answered that so long-standing question of the French Abbé about *esprit.* Hard as it is for a German to be clear, still harder to be light, he is more than ever awkward in his attempts to produce that quality of style, so peculiarly French, which is neither wit nor liveliness taken singly, but a mixture of the two that must be drunk while the effervescence lasts, and will not bear exportation into any other language. German criticism, excellent in other respects, and immeasurably superior to that of any other nation in its constructive faculty, in its instinct for getting at whatever principle of life lies at the heart of a work of genius, is seldom lucid, almost never entertaining. It may turn its light, if we have patience, into every obscurest cranny of its subject, one after another, but it never flashes light *out* of the subject itself, as Sainte-Beuve, for example, so often does, and with such unexpected charm. We should be inclined to put Julian Schmidt at the head of living critics in all the more essential elements of his outfit; but with him is not one conscious at too frequent intervals of the professorial grind, — of that German tendency to bear on too heavily, where a French critic would touch and go with such exquisite measure? The Great Nation, as it cheerfully calls itself, is in nothing greater than its talent for saying little things agreeably, which is perhaps the very top of mere culture, and in literature is the next best thing to the power of saying great things as easily as if they were little.

German learning, like the elephants of Pyrrhus, is always in danger of turning upon what it was intended to adorn and reinforce, and trampling it ponderously to death. And yet what do we not owe it? Mastering all languages, all records of intellectual man, it has been able, or has enabled others, to strip away the husks of nationality and conventionalism from the literatures of many races, and to disengage that kernel of human truth which is the germinating principle of them all. Nay, it has taught us to recognize also a certain value in those very husks, whether as shelter for the unripe or food for the fallen seed.

That the general want of style in German authors is not wholly the fault of the language is shown by Heine (a man of mixed blood), who can be daintily light in German; that it is not altogether a matter of race, is clear from the graceful airiness of Erasmus and Reuchlin in Latin, and of Grimm in French. The sense of heaviness which creeps over the reader from so many German books is mainly due, we suspect to the language, which seems wellnigh incapable of that aerial perspective so delightful in first-rate French, and even English, writing. But there must also be in the national character an insensibility to proportion, a want of that instinctive discretion which we call tact. Nothing short of this will account for the perpetual groping of German imaginative literature after some foreign mould in which to cast its thought or feeling, now trying a Louis Quatorze pattern, then something supposed to be Shakespearian, and at last going back to ancient Greece, or even Persia. Goethe himself, limpidly perfect as are many of his shorter poems, often fails in giving artistic coherence to his longer works. Leaving deeper qualities wholly out of the question, Wilhelm Meister seems a mere aggregation of episodes if compared with such a masterpiece as Paul and Virginia, or even with a happy improvisation like the Vicar of Wakefield. The second part of Faust, too, is rather a reflection of Geothe's own changed view of life and man's relation to it, than an harmonious completion of the original conception. Full of placid wisdom and exquisite poetry it certainly is; but if we look at it as a poem, it seems more as if the author had striven to get in all he could, than to leave out all he might. We cannot help asking what business have paper money and political economy and geognosy here? We confess that Thales and the Homunculus weary us not a little, unless, indeed, a poem be nothing, after all, but a prolonged conundrum. Many of Schiller's lyrical poems — though the best of them find no match in modern verse for rapid energy, the very axles of language kindling with swiftness — seem disproportionately long in parts, and the thought too often has the life wellnigh squeezed out of it in the sevenfold coils of diction, dappled though it be with splendid imagery.

In German sentiment, which runs over so easily into sentimentalism, a foreigner cannot help being struck with a certain incongruousness. What can be odder, for example, than the mixture of sensibility and sausages in some of Goethe's earlier notes to Frau von Stein, unless, to be sure, the publishing them? It would appear that Germans were less sensible to the ludicrous — and we are far from saying that this may not have its compensatory advantages — than either the English or the French. And what is the source of this sensibility, if it be not an instinctive perception of the incongruous and disproportionate? Among all races, the English has ever shown itself most keenly alive to the fear of making itself ridiculous; and among all, none has produced so many humorists, only one of them, indeed, so profound as Cervantes, yet all masters in their several ways. What English-speaking man, except Boswell, could have arrived at Weimar, as Goethe did, in that absurd *Werther-montirung?* And where, out of Germany, could he have found a reigning Grand Duke to put his whole court into the same sentimental livery of blue and yellow, leather breeches, boots, and all, excepting only Herder, and that not on account of his clerical profession, but of his age? To be sure, it might be asked also where else in Europe was a prince to be met with capable of manly friendship with a man whose only decoration was his genius? But the comicality of the other fact no less remains. Certainly the German character is in no way so little remarkable as for its humor. If we were to trust the evidence of Herr Hub's dreary *Deutsche komische und humoristische Dichtung*, we should believe that no German had even so much as a suspicion of what humor meant, unless the book itself, as we are half inclined to suspect, be a joke in three volumes, the *want* of fun being the real point thereof. If German patriotism can be induced to find a grave delight in it, we congratulate Herr Hub's publishers, and for ourselves advise any sober-minded man who may hereafter "be merry," not to "sing psalms," but to read Hub as the more serious amusement of the two. There are epigrams there that make life more solemn, and, if taken in sufficient doses, would make it more precarious. Even Jean Paul, the greatest of German humorous authors, and never surpassed in comic conception or in the pathetic quality of humor, is not to be named with his master, Sterne, as a creative humorist. What are Siebenkäs, Fixlein, Schmelzle, and Fibel, (a single lay-figure to be draped at will with whimsical sentiment and reflection, and put in various attitudes,) compared with the living reality of Walter Shandy and his brother Toby, characters which we do not see merely as puppets in the author's mind, but poetically projected from it in an independent being of their own? Heine himself, the most graceful, sometimes the most touching, of modern poets, and clearly the most easy of German humorists, seems to me wanting in a refined perception of that inward propriety which is only another name for poetic proportion, and shocks us sometimes with an *Unfläthigkeit*, as at the end of his *Deutschland*, which, if it make Germans laugh, as we should be sorry to believe, makes other people hold their noses. Such things have not been possible in English since Swift, and the *persifleur* Heine cannot offer the same excuse of savage cynicism that might be pleaded for the Irishman.

I have hinted that Herr Stahr's Life of Lessing is not precisely the kind of biography that would have been most pleasing to the man who could not conceive that an author should be satisfied with anything more than truth in praise, or anything less in criticism. My respect for what Lessing was, and for what he did, is profound. In the history of literature it would be hard to find a man so stalwart, so kindly, so sincere,* so capable of great ideas, whether in their influence on the intellect or the life, so unswervingly true to the truth, so free from the common weaknesses of his class. Since Luther, Germany has given birth to no such intellectual athlete, — to no son so German to the core. Greater poets she has had, but no greater writer; no nature more finely tempered. Nay, may we not say that great character is as rare a thing as great genius, if it be not even a nobler form of it? For surely it is easier to embody fine thinking, or delicate sentiment, or lofty aspiration, in a book than in a life. The written leaf, if it be, as some few are, a safe-keeper and conductor of celestial fire, is se-

* "If I write at all, it is not possible for me to write otherwise than just as I think and feel." — Lessing to his father, 21st December, 1767.

cure. Poverty cannot pinch, passion swerve, or trial shake it. But the man Lessing, harassed and striving life-long, always poor and always hopeful, with no patron but his own right-hand, the very shuttlecock of fortune, who saw ruin's ploughshare drive through the hearth on which his first home-fire was hardly kindled, and who, through all, was faithful to himself, to his friend, to his duty, and to his ideal, is something more inspiring for us than the most glorious utterance of merely intellectual power. The figure of Goethe is grand, it is rightfully pre-eminent, it has something of the calm, and something of the coldness, of the immortals; but the Valhalla of German letters can show one form, in its simple manhood, statelier even than his.

Manliness and simplicity, if they are not necessary coefficients in producing character of the purest tone, were certainly leading elements in the Lessing who is still so noteworthy and lovable to us when eighty-six years have passed since his bodily presence vanished from among men. He loved clearness, he hated exaggeration in all its forms. He was the first German who had any conception of style, and who could be full without spilling over on all sides. Herr Stahr, we think, is not just the biographer he would have chosen for himself. His book is rather a panegyric than a biography. There is sometimes an almost comic disproportion between the matter and the manner, especially in the epic details of Lessing's onslaughts on the nameless herd of German authors. It is as if Sophocles should have given a strophe to every bullock slain by Ajax in his mad foray upon the Grecian commissary stores. He is too fond of striking an attitude, and his tone rises unpleasantly near a scream, as he calls the personal attention of heaven and earth to something which Lessing himself would have thought a very matter-of-course affair. He who lays it down as an axiom, that "genius loves simplicity," would hardly have been pleased to hear the "Letters on Literature" called the "burning thunderbolts of his annihilating criticism," or the Anti-Götze pamphlets, "the hurtling arrows that sped from the bow of the immortal hero." Nor would he with whom accuracy was a matter of conscience have heard patiently that the Letters "appeared in a period distinguished for its lofty tone of mind, and in their own towering boldness they are a true picture of the intrepid character of the age."* If the age was what Herr Stahr represents it to have been, where is the great merit of Lessing? He would have smiled, we suspect, a little contemptuously, at Herr Stahr's repeatedly quoting a certificate from the "historian of the proud Britons," that he was "the first critic in Europe." Whether we admit or not Lord Macaulay's competence in the matter, we are sure that Lessing would not have thanked his biographer for this soup-ticket to a ladleful of fame. If ever a man stood firmly on his own feet, and asked help of none, that man was Gotthold Ephraim Lessing.

Herr Stahr's desire to *make* a hero of his subject, and his love for sonorous sentences like those we have quoted above, are apt to stand somewhat in the way of our chance at taking a fair measure of the man, and seeing in what his heroism really lay. He furnishes little material for a comparative estimate of Lessing, or for judging of the foreign influences which helped from time to time in making him what he was. Nothing is harder than to worry out a date from Herr Stahr's haystacks of praise and quotation. Yet dates are of special value

* "I am sure that Kleist would rather have taken another wound with him into his grave than have such stuff jabbered over him (*sich solch Zeug nachschwatzen lassen*)." Lessing to Gleim, 6th September, 1759.

in tracing the progress of an intellect like Lessing's, which, little actuated by an inward creative energy, was commonly stirred to motion by the impulse of other minds, and struck out its brightest flashes by collision with them. He himself tells us that a critic should "first seek out some one with whom he can contend," and quotes in justification from one of Aristotle's commentators, *Solet Aristoteles quærere pugnam in suis libris.* This Lessing was always wont to do. He could only feel his own strength, and make others feel it, — could only call it into full play in an intellectual wrestling-bout. He was always anointed and ready for the ring, but with this distinction, that he was no mere prize-fighter, or bully for the side that would pay him best, nor even a contender for mere sentiment, but a self-forgetful champion for the truth as he saw it. Nor is this true of him only as a critic. His more purely imaginative works — his Minna, his Emilia, his Nathan — were all written, not to satisfy the craving of a poetic instinct, nor to rid head and heart of troublous guests by building them a lodging outside himself, as Goethe used to do, but to prove some thesis of criticism or morals by which Truth could be served. His zeal for her was perfectly unselfish. "Does one write, then, for the sake of being always in the right? I think I have been as serviceable to Truth," he says, "when I miss her, and my failure is the occasion of another's discovering her, as if I had discovered her myself." * One would almost be inclined to think, from Herr Stahr's account of the matter, that Lessing had been an autochthonous birth of the German soil, without intellectual ancestry or helpful kindred. That this is the sufficient natural history of no original mind we need hardly say, since originality consists quite as much in the power of using to purpose what it finds

* Letter to Klotz, 9th June, 1766.

ready to its hand, as in that of producing what is absolutely new. Perhaps we might say that it was nothing more than the faculty of combining the separate, and therefore ineffectual, conceptions of others, and making them into living thought by the breath of its own organizing spirit. A great man without a past, if he be not an impossibility, will certainly have no future. He would be like those conjectural Miltons and Cromwells of Gray's imaginary Hamlet. The only privilege of the original man is, that, like other sovereign princes, he has the right to call in the current coin and reissue it stamped with his own image, as was the practice of Lessing.

Herr Stahr's over-intensity of phrase is less offensive than amusing when applied to Lessing's early efforts in criticism. Speaking of poor old Gottsched, he says: "Lessing assailed him sometimes with cutting criticism, and again with exquisite humor. In the notice of Gottsched's poems, he says, among other things, 'The exterior of the volume is so handsome that it will do great credit to the bookstores, and it is to be hoped that it will continue to do so for a long time. But to give a satisfactory idea of the interior surpasses our powers.' And in conclusion he adds, 'These poems cost two thalers and four groschen. The two thalers pay for the ridiculous, and the four groschen pretty much for the useful.'" Again, he tells us that Lessing concludes his notice of Klopstock's Ode to God "with these inimitably roguish words: 'What presumption to beg thus earnestly for a woman!' Does not a whole book of criticism lie in these nine words?" For a young man of twenty-two, Lessing's criticisms show a great deal of independence and maturity of thought; but humor he never had, and his wit was always of the bluntest, — crushing rather than cutting. The mace, and not the scymitar, was his weapon. Let Herr Stahr put all Lessing's "inimitably roguish words" together, and compare them with these few intranslatable lines from Voltaire's letter to Rousseau, thanking him for his *Discours sur l'Inégalité:* "On n'a jamais employé tant d'esprit à vouloir nous rendre bêtes; il prend envie de marcher à quatre pattes quand on lit votre ouvrage." Lessing from the first was something far better than a wit. Force was always much more characteristic of him than cleverness. Sometimes Herr Stahr's hero-worship leads him into positive misstatement. For example, speaking of Lessing's Preface to the "Contributions to the History and Reform of the Theatre," he tells us that "his eye was directed chiefly to the English theatre and Shakespeare." Lessing at that time (1749) was only twenty, and knew little more than the names of any foreign dramatists except the French. In this very Preface his English list skips from Shakespeare to Dryden, and in the Spanish he omits Calderon, Tirso de Molina, and Alarcon. Accordingly, we suspect that the date is wrongly assigned to Lessing's translation of *Toda la Vida es Sueño.* His mind was hardly yet ready to feel the strange charm of this most imaginative of Calderon's dramas.

Even where Herr Stahr undertakes to give us light on the *sources* of Lessing, it is something of the dimmest. He attributes "Miss Sara Sampson" to the influence of the "Merchant of London," as Mr. Evans translates it literally from the German, meaning our old friend, "George Barnwell." But we are strongly inclined to suspect from internal evidence that Moore's more recent "Gamester" gave the prevailing impulse. And if Herr Stahr must needs tell us anything of the Tragedy of Middle-Class Life, he ought to have known that on the English stage it preceded Lillo by more than a century, — witness the "Yorkshire Tragedy," — and that something very like it was even much older in France. We are inclined to complain, also, that he does not bring out more clearly how much Lessing owed to Diderot both as dramatist and critic, nor give us so much as a hint of what already existing English criticism did for him in the way of suggestion and guidance. But though we feel it to be our duty to say so much of Herr Stahr's positive faults and negative short-comings, yet we leave him in very good humor. While he is altogether too full upon certain points of merely transitory importance, — such as the quarrel with Klotz, — yet we are bound to thank him both for the abundance of his extracts from Lessing, and for the judgment he has shown in the choice of them. Any one not familiar with his writings will be able to get a very good notion of the quality of his mind, and the amount of his literary performance, from these volumes; and that, after all, is the chief matter. As to the absolute merit of his works other than critical, Herr Stahr's judgment is too much at the mercy of his partiality to be of great value.

Of Mr. Evans's translation we can speak for the most part with high commendation. There are great difficulties in translating German prose; and whatever other good things Herr Stahr may have learned from Lessing, terseness and clearness are not among them. We have seldom seen a translation which read more easily, or was generally more faithful. That Mr. Evans should nod now and then we do not wonder, nor that he should sometimes choose the wrong word. We have only compared him with the original where we saw reason for suspecting a slip; but, though we have not found much to complain of, we have found enough to satisfy us that his book will gain by a careful revision. We select a few oversights, mainly from the first volume, as examples. On page 34, comparing Lessing with Goethe on arriving at the University, Mr. Evans, we think, obscures, if he does not wholly lose the meaning, when he translates *Leben* by "social relations," and is altogether wrong in rendering *Patrizier* by "aristocrat." At the top of the next page, too, "suspicious" is not the word for *bedenklich.* Had he been writing English, he would surely have said "questionable." On page 47, "overtrodden shoes" is hardly so good as the idiomatic "down at the heel." On page 104, "A very humorous representation" is oddly made to "confirm the documentary evidence." The reverse is meant. On page 115, the sentence beginning "the tendency in both" needs revising. On page 138, Mr. Evans speaks of the "Poetical Village-younker of Destouches." This, we think, is hardly the English of *Le Poète Campagnard,* and almost recalls Lieberkühn's theory of translation, toward which Lessing was so unrelenting, — "When I do not understand a passage, why, I translate it word for word." On page 149, "Miss Sara Sampson" is called "the first social tragedy of the German Drama." All tragedies surely are *social,* except the "Prometheus." *Bürgerliche Tragödie* means a tragedy in which the protagonist is taken from common life, and perhaps cannot be translated clearly into English except by "tragedy of middle-class life." So on page 170 we find Emilia Galotti called a "Virginia *bourgeoise,*" and on page 172 a hospital becomes a *lazaretto.* On page 190 we have a sentence ending in this strange fashion: "in an episode of the English original, which Wieland omitted entirely, one of its characters nevertheless appeared in the German tragedy." On page 205 we have the Seven Years' War called "a bloody *process.*" This is mere carelessness, for Mr. Evans, in the second volume, translates it rightly "*lawsuit.*" What English reader would know what "You are intriguing me" means, on page 228? On page 264,

Vol. II., we find a passage inaccurately rendered, which we consider of more consequence, because it is a quotation from Lessing. "O, out upon the man who claims, Almighty God, to be a preacher of Thy word, and yet so impudently asserts that, in order to attain Thy purposes, there was only one way in which it pleased *Thee* to make Thyself known to him!" This is very far from *nur den einzigen Weg gehabt den Du Dir gefallen lassen ihm kund zu machen!* The *ihm* is scornfully emphatic. We hope Professor Evans will go over his version for a second edition much more carefully than we have had any occasion to do. He has done an excellent service to our literature, for which we heartily thank him, in choosing a book of this kind to translate, and translating it so well. We would not look such a gift horse too narrowly in the mouth.

Let us now endeavor to sum up the result of Lessing's life and labor with what success we may.

Gotthold Ephraim Lessing was born (January 22, 1729) at Camenz, in Upper Lusatia, the second child and eldest son of John Gottfried Lessing, a Lutheran clergyman. Those who believe in the persistent qualities of race, or the cumulative property of culture, will find something to their purpose in his Saxon blood and his clerical and juristic ancestry. It is worth mentioning, that his grandfather, in the thesis for his doctor's degree, defended the right to entire freedom of religious belief. The name first comes to the surface in Parson Clement Lessigk, nearly three centuries ago, and survives to the present day in a painter of some distinction. It has almost passed into a proverb, that the mothers of remarkable children have been something beyond the common. If there be any truth in the theory, the case of Lessing was an exception, as might have been inferred, perhaps, from the peculiarly masculine type of his character and intellect. His mother was in no wise superior, but his father seems to have been a man somewhat above the pedantic average of the provincial clergymen of his day, and to have been a scholar in the ampler meaning of the word. Besides the classics, he had possessed himself of French and English, and was somewhat versed in the Oriental languages. The temper of his theology may be guessed from his having been, as his son tells us with some pride, one of "the earliest translators of Tillotson." We can only conjecture him from the letters which Lessing wrote to him, from which we should fancy him as on the whole a decided and even choleric old gentleman, in whom the wig, though not a predominant, was yet a notable feature, and who was, like many other fathers, permanently astonished at the fruit of his loins. He would have preferred one of the so-called learned professions for his son, — theology above all, — and would seem to have never quite reconciled himself to his son's distinction, as being in none of the three careers which alone were legitimate. Lessing's bearing towards him, always independent, is really beautiful in its union of respectful tenderness with unswerving self-assertion. When he wished to evade the maternal eye, Gotthold used in his letters to set up a screen of Latin between himself and her; and we conjecture the worthy Pastor Primarius playing over again in his study at Camenz, with some scruples of conscience, the old trick of Chaucer's fox: —

> "Mulier est hominis confusio;
> Madam, the sentence of this Latin is,
> Woman is mannës joy and mannës bliss."

He appears to have snatched a fearful and but ill-concealed joy from the sight of the first collected edition of his son's works, unlike Tillotson as they certainly were. Ah, had they only been *Opera!* Yet were they not volumes, after all, and able to stand on their own edges beside the immortals, if nothing more?

After grinding with private-tutor Mylius the requisite time, Lessing entered the school of Camenz, and in his thirteenth year was sent to the higher institution at Meissen. We learn little of his career there, except that Theophrastus, Plautus, and Terence were already his favorite authors, that he once characteristically distinguished himself by a courageous truthfulness, and that he wrote a Latin poem on the valor of the Saxon soldiers, which his father very sensibly advised him to shorten. In 1750, four years after leaving the school, he writes to his father: "I believed even when I was at Meissen that one must learn much there which he cannot make the least use of in real life (*der Welt*), and I now [after trying Leipzig and Wittenberg] see it all the more clearly," — a melancholy observation which many other young men have made under similar circumstances. Sent to Leipzig in his seventeenth year, he finds himself an awkward, ungainly lad, and sets diligently to perfecting himself in the somewhat unscholastic accomplishments of riding, dancing, and fencing. He also sedulously frequents the theatre, and wrote a play, "The Young Scholar," which attained the honor of representation. Meanwhile his most intimate companion was a younger brother of his old tutor Mylius, a young man of more than questionable morals, and who had even written a satire on the elders of Camenz, for which — over-confidently trusting himself in the outraged city — he had been fined and imprisoned; so little could the German Muse, celebrated by Klopstock for her swiftness of foot, protect her son. With this scandalous person and with play-actors, more than probably of both sexes, did the young Lessing share a Christmas cake sent him by his mother. Such news was not long in reaching Camenz, and we can easily fancy how tragic it seemed in the little parsonage there, to what cabinet councils it gave rise in the paternal study, to what ominous shaking of the clerical wig in that domestic Olympus. A pious fraud is practised on the boy, who hurries home thinly clad through the winter weather, his ill-eaten Christmas cake wringing him with remorseful indigestion, to receive the last blessing, if such a prodigal might hope for it, of a broken-hearted mother. He finds the good dame in excellent health, and softened toward him by a cold he has taken on his pious journey. He remains at home several months, now writing Anacreontics of such warmth that his sister (as volunteer representative of the common hangman) burns them in the family stove; now composing sermons to convince his mother that "he could be a preacher any day," — a theory of that sacred office unhappily not yet extinct. At Easter, 1747, he gets back to Leipzig again, with some scant supply of money in his pocket, but is obliged to make his escape thence between two days somewhere toward the middle of the next year, leaving behind him some histrionic debts (chiefly, we fear, of a certain Mademoiselle Lorenz) for which he had confidingly made himself security. Stranded, by want of floating or other capital, at Wittenberg, he enters himself, with help from home, as a student there, but soon migrates again to Berlin, which had been his goal when making his hegira from Leipzig. In Berlin he remained three years, applying himself to his chosen calling of author at all work, by doing whatever honest job offered itself, — verse, criticism, or translation, — and profitably studious in a very wide range of languages and their literature. Above all, he learned the great secret, which his stalwart English contemporary, Johnson, also acquired, of being able to "dine heartily" for threepence.

Meanwhile he continues in a kind of colonial dependence on the parsonage at Camenz, the bonds gradually slackening, sometimes shaken a little rudely, and always giving alarming hints of approaching and inevitable autonomy. From the few home letters of Lessing which remain, (covering the period before 1753, there are only eight in all,) we are able to surmise that a pretty constant maternal cluck and shrill paternal warning were kept up from the home coop. We find Lessing defending the morality of the stage and his own private morals against charges and suspicions of his parents, and even making the awful confession that he does not consider the Christian religion itself as a thing "to be taken on trust," nor a Christian by mere tradition so valuable a member of society as "one who has *prudently* doubted, and by the way of examination has arrived at conviction, or at least striven to arrive." Boyish scepticism of the superficial sort is a common phenomenon enough, but the Lessing variety of it seems to us sufficiently rare in a youth of twenty. What strikes us mainly in the letters of these years is not merely the maturity they show, though that is remarkable, but the tone. We see already in them the cheerful and never overweening self-confidence which always so pleasantly distinguished Lessing, and that strength of tackle, so seldom found in literary men, which brings the mind well home to its anchor, enabling it to find holding-ground and secure riding in any sea. "What care I to live in plenty," he asks gayly, "if I only live?" Indeed, Lessing learned early, and never forgot, that whoever would be life's master, and not its drudge, must make it a means, and never allow it to become an end. He could say more truly than Goethe, *Mein Acker ist die Zeit*, since he not only sowed in it the seed of thought for other men and other times, but cropped it for his daily bread. Above all, we find

Lessing even thus early endowed with the power of keeping his eyes wide open to what he was after, to what would help or hinder him, — a much more singular gift than is commonly supposed. Among other jobs of this first Berlin period, he had undertaken to arrange the library of a certain Herr Rüdiger, getting therefor his meals and "other receipts," whatever they may have been. His father seems to have heard with anxiety that this arrangement had ceased, and Lessing writes to him: "I never wished to have anything to do with this old man longer than *until I had made myself thoroughly acquainted with his great library*. This is now accomplished, and we have accordingly parted." This was in his twenty-first year, and we have no doubt, from the *range* of scholarship which Lessing had at command so young, that it was perfectly true. All through his life he was thoroughly German in this respect also, that he never *quite* smelted his knowledge clear from some slag of learning.

In the early part of the first Berlin residence, Pastor Primarius Lessing, hearing that his son meditated a movement on Vienna, was much exercised with fears of the temptation to Popery he would be exposed to in that capital. We suspect that the attraction thitherward had its source in a perhaps equally catholic, but less theological magnet, — the Mademoiselle Lorenz above mentioned. Let us remember the perfectly innocent passion of Mozart for an actress, and be comforted. There is not the slightest evidence that Lessing's life at this time, or any other, though careless, was in any way debauched. No scandal was ever coupled with his name, nor is any biographic chemistry needed to bleach spots out of his reputation. What cannot be said of Wieland, of Goethe, of Schiller, of Jean Paul, may be safely affirmed of this busy and single-minded man. The parental fear of Popery brought him a seasonable supply of money from home, which enabled him to clothe himself decently enough to push his literary fortunes, and put on a bold front with publishers. Poor enough he often was, but never in so shabby a pass that he was forced to write behind a screen, like Johnson.

It was during this first stay in Berlin that Lessing was brought into personal relations with Voltaire. Through an acquaintance with the great man's secretary, Richier, he was employed as translator in the scandalous Hirschel lawsuit, so dramatically set forth by Carlyle in his Life of Frederick, though Lessing's share in it seems to have been unknown to him. The service could hardly have been other than distasteful to him; but it must have been with some thrill of the *anche io!* kind that the poor youth, just fleshing his maiden pen in criticism, stood face to face with the famous author, with whose name all Europe rang from side to side. This was in February, 1751. Young as he was, we fancy those cool eyes of his making some strange discoveries as to the real nature of that lean nightmare of Jesuits and dunces. Afterwards the same secretary lent him the manuscript of the *Siècle de Louis XIV.*, and Lessing thoughtlessly taking it into the country with him, it was not forthcoming when called for by the author. Voltaire naturally enough danced with rage, screamed all manner of unpleasant things about robbery and the like, cashiered the secretary, and was, we see no reason to doubt, really afraid of a pirated edition. *This* time his cry of wolf must have had a quaver of sincerity in it. Herr Stahr, who can never keep separate the Lessing as he then was and the Lessing as he afterwards became, takes fire at what he chooses to consider an unworthy suspicion of the Frenchman, and treats himself to some rather cheap indignation on the subject. For ourselves, we think Voltaire altogether in the right, and we respect Lessing's honesty too much to suppose, with his biographer, that it was this which led him, years afterwards, to do such severe justice to *Merope*, and other tragedies of the same author. The affair happened in December, 1751, and a year later Lessing calls Voltaire a "great man," and says of his *Amalie*, that "it has not only beautiful passages, it is beautiful throughout, and the tears of a reader of feeling will justify our judgment." Surely there is no resentment here. Our only wonder would be at its being written after the Hirschel business. At any rate, we cannot allow Herr Stahr to shake our faith in the sincerity of Lessing's motives in criticism,— he could not in the soundness of the criticism itself,— by tracing it up to a spring at once so petty and so personal.

During a part of 1752,* Lessing was at Wittenberg again as student of medicine, the parental notion of a strictly professional career of some kind not having yet been abandoned. We must give his father the credit of having done his best, in a well-meaning paternal fashion, to make his son over again in his own image, and to thwart the design of nature by coaxing or driving him into the pinfold of a prosperous obscurity. But Gotthold, with all his gifts, had no talent whatever for contented routine. His was a mind always in solution, which the divine order of things, as it is called, could not precipitate into any of the traditional forms of crys-

* Herr Stahr heads the fifth chapter of his Second Book, "Lessing at Wittenberg. December, 1751, to November, 1752." But we never feel quite sure of his dates. The Richier affair puts Lessing in Berlin in December, 1751, and he took his Master's degree at Wittenberg, 29th April, 1752. We are told that he finally left Wittenberg "toward the end" of that year. He himself, writing from Berlin in 1754, says that he has been absent from that city *nur ein halbes Jahr* since 1748. There is only one letter for 1752, dated at Wittenberg, 9th June.

14

tallization, and in which the time to come was already fermenting. The principle of growth was in the young literary hack, and he must obey it or die. His was to the last a *natura naturans*, never a *naturata*. Lessing seems to have done what he could to be a dutiful failure. But there was something in him stronger and more sacred than even filial piety; and the good old pastor is remembered now only as the father of a son who would have shared the benign oblivion of his own theological works, if he could only have had his wise way with him. Even after never so many biographies and review articles, genius continues to be a marvellous and inspiring thing. At the same time, considering the then condition of what was pleasantly called literature in Germany, there was not a little to be said on the paternal side of the question, though it may not seem now a very heavy mulct to give up one son out of ten to immortality, — at least the Fates seldom decimate in *this* way. Lessing had now, if we accept the common standard in such matters, "completed his education," and the result may be summed up in his own words to Michaelis, 16th October, 1754: "I have studied at the Fürstenschule at Meissen, and after that at Leipzig and Wittenberg. But I should be greatly embarrassed if I were asked to tell *what*." As early as his twentieth year he had arrived at some singular notions as to the uses of learning. On the 20th of January, 1749, he writes to his mother: "I found out that books, indeed, would make me learned, *but never make me a man*." Like most men of great knowledge, as distinguished from mere scholars, he seems to have been always a rather indiscriminate reader, and to have been fond, as Johnson was, of "browsing" in libraries. Johnson neither in amplitude of literature nor exactness of scholarship could be deemed a match for Lessing; but they were alike in the power of readily applying whatever they had learned, whether for purposes of illustration or argument. They resemble each other, also, in a kind of absolute common-sense, and in the force with which they could plant a direct blow with the whole weight both of their training and their temperament behind it. As a critic, Johnson ends where Lessing begins. The one is happy in the lower region of the understanding: the other can breathe freely in the ampler air of reason alone. Johnson acquired learning, and stopped short from indolence at a certain point. Lessing assimilated it, and accordingly his education ceased only with his life. Both had something of the intellectual sluggishness that is apt to go with great strength; and both had to be baited by the antagonism of circumstances or opinions, not only into the exhibition, but into the possession of their entire force. Both may be more properly called original men than, in the highest sense, original writers.

From 1752 to 1760, with an interval of something over two years spent in Leipzig to be near a good theatre, Lessing was settled in Berlin, and gave himself wholly and earnestly to the life of a man of letters. A thoroughly healthy, cheerful nature he most surely had, with something at first of the careless light-heartedness of youth. Healthy he was not always to be, not always cheerful, often very far from light-hearted, but manly from first to last he eminently was. Downcast he could never be, for his strongest instinct, invaluable to him also as a critic, was to see things as they really are. And this not in the sense of a cynic, but of one who measures himself as well as his circumstances, — who loves truth as the most beautiful of all things and the only permanent possession, as being of one substance with the soul. In a man like Lessing, whose character is even more interesting than his works, the tone and turn of thought are what we like to get glimpses of. And for this his letters are more helpful than those of most authors, as might be expected of one who said of himself, that, in his more serious work, " he must profit by his first heat to accomplish anything." He began, we say, light-heartedly. He did not believe that "one should thank God only for good things." "He who is only in good health, and is willing to work, has nothing to fear in the world." "What another man would call want, I call comfort." "Must not one often act thoughtlessly, if one would provoke Fortune to do something for him?" In his first inexperience, the life of "the sparrow on the house-top" (which we find oddly translated "roof") was the one he would choose for himself. Later in life, when he wished to marry, he was of another mind, and perhaps discovered that there was something in the old father's notion of a fixed position. "The life of the sparrow on the house-top is only right good if one need not expect any end to it. If it cannot always last, every day it lasts too long," — he writes to Ebert in 1770. Yet even then he takes the manly view. "Everything in the world has its time, everything may be overlived and overlooked, if one only have health." Nor let any one suppose that Lessing, full of courage as he was, found professional authorship a garden of Alcinoüs. From creative literature he continually sought refuge, and even repose, in the driest drudgery of mere scholarship. On the 26th of April, 1768, he writes to his brother with something of his old gayety: "Thank God, the time will soon come when I cannot call a penny in the world my own but I must first earn it. I am unhappy if it must be by writing." And again in May, 1771: "Among all the wretched, I think him the most wretched who must work with his head, even if he is not conscious of having one. But what is the good of complaining?" Lessing's life, if it is a noble example, so far as it concerned himself alone, is also a warning when another is to be asked to share it. He too would have profited had he earlier learned and more constantly borne in mind the profound wisdom of that old saying, *Si sit prudentia.* Let the young poet, however he may believe of his art that "all other pleasures are not worth its pains," consider well what it is to call down fire from heaven to keep the pot boiling, before he commit himself to a life of authorship as something fine and easy. That fire will not condescend to such office, though it come without asking on ceremonial days to the free service of the altar.

Lessing, however, never would, even if he could, have so desecrated his better powers. For a bare livelihood, he always went sturdily to the market of hack-work, where his learning would fetch him a price. But it was only in extremest need that he would claim that benefit of clergy. "I am worried," he writes to his brother Karl, 8th April, 1773, "and work because working is the only means to cease being so. But you and Voss are very much mistaken if you think that it could ever be indifferent to me, under such circumstances, on what I work. Nothing less true, whether as respects the work itself or the principal object wherefor I work. I have been in my life before now in very wretched circumstances, yet never in such that I would have written for bread in the true meaning of the word. I have begun my 'Contributions' because this work helps me . . . . to live from one day to another." It is plain that he does not call this kind of thing in any high sense writing. Of that he had far other notions; for though he honestly disclaimed the title, yet his dream was always to be a poet. But he *was* willing to work, as he claimed to be, because he had one ideal higher than that of being a poet, namely, to be thoroughly a man. To Nicolai he writes in 1758: "All ways of earning his bread are alike becoming to an honest man, whether to split wood or to sit at the helm of state. It does not concern his conscience how useful he is, but how useful he would be." Goethe's poetic sense was the Minotaur to which he sacrificed everything. To make a study, he would soil the maiden petals of a woman's soul; to get the delicious sensation of a reflex sorrow, he would wring a heart. All that saves his egoism from being hateful is, that, with its immense reaches, it cheats the sense into a feeling of something like sublimity. A patch of sand is unpleasing; a desert has all the awe of ocean. Lessing also felt the duty of self-culture; but it was not so much for the sake of feeding fat this or that faculty as of strengthening character, — the only soil in which real mental power can root itself and find sustenance. His advice to his brother Karl, who was beginning to write for the stage, is two parts moral to one literary. "Study ethics diligently, learn to express yourself well and correctly, and cultivate your own character. Without that I cannot conceive a good dramatic author." Marvellous counsel this will seem to those who think that wisdom is only to be found in the fool's paradise of Bohemia!

We said that Lessing's dream was to be a poet. In comparison with success as a dramatist, he looked on all other achievement as inferior in kind. In 1767 he writes to Gleim (speaking of his call to Hamburg): "Such circumstances were needed to rekindle in me an almost extinguished love for the theatre. I was just beginning to lose myself in other studies which would have made me unfit for any work of genius. My *Laocoön* is now a secondary labor." And yet he never fell into the mistake of overvaluing what he valued so highly. His unflinching common-sense would have saved him from that, as it afterwards enabled him to see that something was wanting in him which must enter into the making of true poetry, whose distinction from prose is an inward one of nature, and not an outward one of form. While yet under thirty, he assures Mendelssohn that he was quite right in neglecting poetry for philosophy, because "only a part of our youth should be given up to the arts of the beautiful. We must practise ourselves in weightier things before we die. An old man, who lifelong has done nothing but rhyme, and an old man who lifelong has done nothing but pass his breath through a stick with holes in it, — I doubt much whether such an old man has arrived at what he was meant for."

This period of Lessing's life was a productive one, though none of its printed results can be counted of permanent value, except his share in the "Letters on German Literature." And even these must be reckoned as belonging to the years of his apprenticeship and training for the master-workman he afterwards became. The small fry of authors and translators were hardly fitted to call out his full strength, but his vivisection of them taught him the value of certain structural principles. "To one dissection of the fore quarter of an ass," says Haydon in his diary, "I owe my information." Yet even in his earliest criticisms we are struck with the same penetration and steadiness of judgment, the same firm grasp of the essential and permanent, that were afterwards to make his opinions law in the courts of taste. For example, he says of Thomson, that, "as a dramatic poet, he had the fault of never knowing when to leave off; he lets every character talk so long as anything can be said; accordingly, during these prolonged conversations, the action stands still, and the story becomes tedious." Of "Roderick Random," he says that "its author is neither a Richardson nor a Fielding; he is one of those writers of whom there are plenty among the Germans and French." We cite these merely because their firmness of tone seems to us uncommon in a youth of twenty-four. In the "Letters," the range is much wider, and the application of principles more consequent. He had already secured for himself a position among the literary men of that day, and was beginning to be feared for the inexorable justice of his criticisms. His "Fables" and his "Miss Sara Sampson" had been translated into French, and had attracted the attention of Grimm, who says of them (December, 1754): "These Fables commonly contain in a few lines a new and profound moral meaning. M. Lessing has much wit, genius, and invention; the dissertations which follow the Fables prove moreover that he is an excellent critic." In Berlin, Lessing made friendships, especially with Mendelssohn, Von Kleist, Nicolai, Gleim, and Ramler. For Mendelssohn and Von Kleist he seems to have felt a real love; for the others at most a liking, as the best material that could be had. It certainly was not of the juiciest. He seems to have worked hard and played hard, equally at home in his study and Baumann's wine-cellar. He was busy, poor, and happy.

But he was restless. We suspect that the necessity of forever picking up crumbs, and their occasional scarcity, made the life of the sparrow on the house-top less agreeable than he had expected. The imagined freedom was not quite so free after all, for necessity is as short a tether as dependence, or official duty, or what not, and the regular occupation of grub-hunting is as tame and wearisome as another. Moreover, Lessing had probably by this time sucked his friends dry of any intellectual stimulus they could yield him; and when friendship reaches that pass, it is apt to be anything but inspiring. Except Mendelssohn and Von Kleist, they were not men capable of rating him at his true value; and Lessing was one of those who always burn up the fuel of life at a fearful rate. Admirably dry as the supplies of Ramler and the rest no doubt were, they had not substance enough to keep his mind at the high temperature it needed, and he would soon be driven to the cutting of green stuff from his own wood-lot, more rich in smoke than fire. Besides this, he could hardly have been at ease among intimates most of whom could not even conceive of that intellectual honesty, that total disregard of all personal interests where truth was concerned, which was an innate quality of Lessing's mind. Their theory of criticism was, Truth, or even worse if possible, for all who do not belong to our set; for us, that delicious falsehood which is no doubt a slow poison, but then so *very* slow. Their nerves were unbraced by that fierce democracy of thought, trampling on all prescription, all tradition, in which Lessing loved to shoulder his way and advance his insupportable foot. "What is called a heretic," he says in his Preface to *Berengarius*, "has a very good side. It is a man who at least *wishes* to see with his own eyes." And again, "I know not if it be a duty to offer up fortune and life to the truth; . . . . but I know it *is* a duty, if one undertake to teach the truth, to teach the whole of it, or none at all." Such men as Gleim and Ramler were mere *dilettanti*, and could have no notion how sacred his convictions are to a militant thinker like Lessing. His creed as to the rights of friendship in criticism might be put in the words of Selden, the firm tread of whose mind was like his own: "Opinion and affection extremely differ. Opinion is something wherein I go about to give reason why all the world should think as I think. Affection is a thing wherein I look after the pleasing of myself." How little his friends were capable of appreciating this view of the matter is plain from a letter of Ramler to Gleim, cited by Herr Stahr. Lessing had shown up the weaknesses of a certain work by the Abbé Batteux (long ago gathered to his literary fathers as conclusively as poor old Ramler himself), without regard to the important fact that the Abbé's book had been translated by a friend. Horrible to think of at best, thrice horrible when the friend's name was Ramler! The impression thereby made on the friendly heart may be conceived. A ray of light penetrated the rather opaque substance of Herr Ramler's mind, and revealed to him the dangerous character of Lessing. "I know well," he says, "that Herr Lessing means to speak his own opinion, and" — what is the dreadful inference? — "and, by suppressing others, to gain air, and make room for himself. This disposition is not to be overcome." * Fortunately not, for Lessing's opinion always meant something, and was worth having. Gleim no doubt sympathized deeply with the sufferer by this treason, for he too had been shocked at some disrespect for La Fontaine, as a disciple of whom he had announced himself.

Berlin was hardly the place for Lessing, if he could not take a step in any direction without risk of treading on somebody's gouty foot. This was not the last time that he was to have experience of the fact that the critic's pen, the more it has of truth's celestial temper, the more it is apt to reverse the miracle of the archangel's spear, and to bring out whatever is toadlike in the nature of him it touches. We can well understand the sadness with which he said,

"Der Blick des Forscher's fand
Nicht selten mehr als er zu finden wünschte."

* "Ramler," writes Georg Forster, "ist die Ziererei, die Eigenliebe, die Eitelkeit in eigener Person."

Here, better than anywhere, we may cite something which he wrote of himself to a friend of Klotz. Lessing, it will be remembered, had literally "suppressed" Klotz. "What do you apprehend, then, from me? The more faults and errors you point out to me, so much the more I shall learn of you; the more I learn of you, the more thankful shall I be. . . . . I wish you knew me more thoroughly. If the opinion you have of my learning and genius (*Geist*) should perhaps suffer thereby, yet I am sure the idea I would like you to form of my character would gain. I am not the insufferable, unmannerly, proud, slanderous man Herr Klotz proclaims me. It cost me a great deal of trouble and compulsion to be a little bitter against him."* Ramler and the rest had contrived a nice little society for mutual admiration, much like that described by Goldsmith, if, indeed, he did not convey it from the French, as was not uncommon with him. "'What, have you never heard of the admirable Brandellius or the ingenious Mogusius, one the eye and the other the heart of our University, known all over the world?' 'Never,' cried the traveller; 'but pray inform me what Brandellius is particularly remarkable for.' 'You must be little acquainted with the republic of letters,' said the other, 'to ask such a question. Brandellius has written a most sublime panegyric on Mogusius.' 'And, prithee, what has Mogusius done to deserve so great a favor?' 'He has written an excellent poem in praise of Brandellius.'" Lessing was not the man who could narrow himself to the proportions of a clique; lifelong he was the terror of the Brandellii and Mogusii, and, at the signal given by him,

* Lessing to Von Murr, 25th November, 1768. The whole letter is well worth reading.

"They, but now who seemed
In bigness to surpass Earth's giant sons,
Now less than smallest dwarfs in narrow room
Throng numberless."

Besides whatever other reasons Lessing may have had for leaving Berlin, we fancy that his having exhausted whatever means it had of helping his spiritual growth was the chief. Nine years later, he gave as a reason for not wishing to stay long in Brunswick, "Not that I do not like Brunswick, but because nothing comes of being long in a place which one likes." * Whatever the reason, Lessing, in 1760, left Berlin for Breslau, where the post of secretary had been offered him under Frederick's tough old General Tauentzien. "I will spin myself in for a while like an ugly worm, that I may be able to come to light again as a brilliant winged creature," says his diary. Shortly after his leaving Berlin, he was chosen a member of the Academy of Sciences there. Herr Stahr, who has no little fondness for the foot-light style of phrase, says, "It may easily be imagined that he himself regarded his appointment as an insult rather than as an honor." Lessing himself merely says that it was a matter of indifference to him, which is much more in keeping with his character and with the value of the intended honor.

The Seven Years' War began four years before Lessing took up his abode in Breslau, and it may be asked how he, as a Saxon, was affected by it. We might answer, hardly at all. His position was that of armed neutrality. Long ago at Leipzig he had been accused of Prussian leanings; now in Berlin he was thought too Saxon. Though he disclaimed any such sentiment as

* A favorite phrase of his, which Egbert has preserved for us with its Saxon accent, was, *Es kommt doch nischt dabey heraus*, implying that one might do something better for a constancy than shearing swine.

patriotism, and called himself a cosmopolite, it is plain enough that his position was simply that of a German. Love of country, except in a very narrow parochial way, was as impossible in Germany then as in America during the Colonial period. Lessing himself, in the latter years of his life, was librarian of one of those petty princelets who sold their subjects to be shot at in America, — creatures strong enough to oppress, too weak to protect their people. Whoever would have found a Germany to love must have pieced it together as painfully as Isis did the scattered bits of Osiris. Yet he says that "the true patriot is by no means extinguished" in him. It was the noisy ones that he could not abide; and, writing to Gleim about his "Grenadier" verses, he advises him to soften the tone of them a little, he himself being a "declared enemy of imprecations," which he would leave altogether to the clergy. We think Herr Stahr makes too much of these anti-patriot flings of Lessing, which, with a single exception, occur in his letters to Gleim, and with reference to a kind of verse that could not but be distasteful to him, as needing no more brains than a drum, nor other inspiration than serves a trumpet. Lessing undoubtedly had better uses for his breath than to spend it in shouting for either side in this "bloody lawsuit," as he called it, in which he was not concerned. He showed himself German enough, and in the right way, in his persistent warfare against the tyranny of French taste.

He remained in Breslau the better part of five years, studying life in new phases, gathering a library, which, as commonly happens, he afterwards sold at great loss, and writing his *Minna* and his *Laocoön*. He accompanied Tauentzien to the siege of Schweidnitz, where Frederick was present in person. He seems to have lived a rather free-and-easy life during his term of office, kept shockingly late hours, and learned, among other things, to gamble,—a fact for which Herr Stahr thinks it needful to account in a high philosophical fashion. We prefer to think that there are *some* motives to which remarkable men are liable in common with the rest of mankind, and that they may occasionally do a thing merely because it is pleasant, without forethought of medicinal benefit to the mind. Lessing's friends (whose names were *not*, as the reader might be tempted to suppose, Eliphaz, Bildad, and Zophar) expected him to make something handsome out of his office; but the pitiful result of those five years of opportunity was nothing more than an immortal book. Unthrifty Lessing, to have been so nice about your fingers, (and so near the mint, too,) when your general was wise enough to make his fortune! As if ink-stains were the only ones that would wash out, and no others had ever been covered with white kid from the sight of all reasonable men! In July, 1764, he had a violent fever, which he turned to account in his usual cheerful way: "The serious epoch of my life is drawing nigh. I am beginning to become a man, and flatter myself that in this burning fever I have raved away the last remains of my youthful follies. Fortunate illness!" He had never intended to bind himself to an official career. To his father he writes: "I have more than once declared that my present engagement could not continue long, that I have not given up my old plan of living, and that I am more than ever resolved to withdraw from any service that is not wholly to my mind. I have passed the middle of my life, and can think of nothing that could compel me to make myself a slave for the poor remainder of it. I write you this, dearest father, and must write you this, in order that you may not be astonished if, before long, you should see me once more very far removed from all hopes of, or claims to, a settled prosperity, as it is called." Before the middle of the next year he was back in Berlin again.

There he remained for nearly two years, trying the house-top way of life again, but with indifferent success, as we have reason to think. Indeed, when the metaphor resolves itself into the plain fact of living just on the other side of the roof, — in the garret, namely, — and that from hand to mouth, as was Lessing's case, we need not be surprised to find him gradually beginning to see something more agreeable in a *fixirtes Glück* than he had once been willing to allow. At any rate, he was willing, and even heartily desirous, that his friends should succeed in getting for him the place of royal librarian. But Frederick, for some unexplained reason, would not appoint him. Herr Stahr thinks it had something to do with the old *Siècle* manuscript business. But this seems improbable, for Voltaire's wrath was not directed against Lessing; and even if it had been, the great king could hardly have carried the name of an obscure German author in his memory through all those anxious and warlike years. Whatever the cause, Lessing early in 1767 accepts the position of Theatrical Manager at Hamburg, as usual not too much vexed with disappointment, but quoting gayly

"Quod non dant proceres, dabit histrio."

Like Burns, he was always "contented wi' little and canty wi' mair." In connection with his place as Manager he was to write a series of dramatic essays and criticisms. It is to this we owe the *Dramaturgie*, — next to the *Laocoön* the most valuable of his works. But Lessing — though it is plain that he made his hand as light as he could, and wrapped his lash in velvet — soon found that actors had no more taste for truth than authors. He was obliged to drop his remarks on the special merits or demerits of players, and to confine himself to those of the pieces represented. By this his work gained in value; and the latter part of it, written without reference to a particular stage, and devoted to the discussion of those general principles of dramatic art on which he had meditated long and deeply, is far weightier than the rest. There are few men who can put forth all their muscle in a losing race, and it is characteristic of Lessing that what he wrote under the dispiritment of failure should be the most lively and vigorous. Circumstances might be against him, but he was incapable of believing that a cause could be lost which had once enlisted his conviction.

The theatrical enterprise did not prosper long; but Lessing had meanwhile involved himself as partner in a publishing business which harassed him while it lasted, and when it failed, as was inevitable, left him hampered with debt. Help came in his appointment (1770) to take charge of the Duke of Brunswick's library at Wolfenbüttel, with a salary of six hundred thalers a year. This was the more welcome, as he soon after was betrothed with Eva König, widow of a rich manufacturer.* Her husband's affairs, however, had been left in confusion, and this, with Lessing's own embarrassments, prevented their being married till October, 1776. Eva König was

* I find surprisingly little about Lessing in such of the contemporary correspondence of German literary men as I have read. A letter of Boie to Merck (10 April, 1775) gives us a glimpse of him. "Do you know that Lessing will probably marry Reiske's widow and come to Dresden in place of Hagedorn? The restless spirit! How he will get along with the artists, half of them, too, Italians, is to be seen. . . . . Liffert and he have met and parted good friends. He has worn ever since on his finger the ring with the skeleton and butterfly which Liffert gave him. He is reported to be much dissatisfied with the theatrical filibustering of Goethe and Lenz, especially with the remarks on the drama in which so little respect is shown for his Aristotle, and the Leipzig folks are said to be greatly rejoiced at getting such an ally."

every way worthy of him. Clever, womanly, discreet, with just enough coyness of the will to be charming when it is joined with sweetness and good sense, she was the true helpmate of such a man, — the serious companion of his mind and the playfellow of his affections. There is something infinitely refreshing to me in the love-letters of these two persons. Without wanting sentiment, there is such a bracing air about them as breathes from the higher levels and strong-holds of the soul. They show that self-possession which can alone reserve to love the power of new self-surrender, — of never cloying, because never wholly possessed. Here is no invasion and conquest of the weaker nature by the stronger, but an equal league of souls, each in its own realm still sovereign. Turn from such letters as these to those of St. Preux and Julie, and you are stifled with the heavy perfume of a demirep's boudoir, — to those of Herder to his Caroline, and you sniff no doubtful odor of professional unction from the sermon-case. Manly old Dr. Johnson, who could be tender and true to a plain woman, knew very well what he meant when he wrote that single poetic sentence of his, — "The shepherd in Virgil grew at last acquainted with Love, and found him to be a native of the rocks."

In January, 1778, Lessing's wife died from the effects of a difficult childbirth. The child, a boy, hardly survived its birth. The few words wrung out of Lessing by this double sorrow are to me as deeply moving as anything in tragedy. "I wished for once to be as happy (*es so gut haben*) as other men. But it has gone ill with me!" "And I was so loath to lose him, this son!" "My wife is dead; and I have had this experience also. I rejoice that I have not many more such experiences left to make, and am quite cheerful." "If you had known her! But they say that to praise one's wife is self-praise. Well, then, I say no more of her! But if you had known her!" *Quite cheerful!* On the 10th of August he writes to Elise Reimarus, — he is writing to a woman now, an old friend of his and his wife, and will be less restrained: "I am left here all alone. I have not a single friend to whom I can wholly confide myself. . . . . How often must I curse my ever wishing to be for once as happy as other men! How often have I wished myself back again in my old, isolated condition, — to be nothing, to wish nothing, to do nothing, but what the present moment brings with it! . . . . Yet I am too proud to think myself unhappy. I just grind my teeth, and let the boat go as pleases wind and waves. Enough that I will not overset it myself." It is plain from this letter that suicide had been in his mind, and, with his antique way of thinking on many subjects, he would hardly have looked on it as a crime. But he was too brave a man to throw up the sponge to fate, and had work to do yet. Within a few days of his wife's death he wrote to Eschenburg: "I am right heartily ashamed if my letter betrayed the least despair. Despair is not nearly so much my failing as levity, which often expresses itself with a little bitterness and misanthropy." A stoic, not from insensibility or cowardice, as so many are, but from stoutness of heart, he blushes at a moment's abdication of self-command. And he will not roil the clear memory of his love with any tinge of the sentimentality so much the fashion, and to be had so cheap, in that generation. There is a moderation of sincerity peculiar to Lessing in the epithet of the following sentence: "How dearly must I pay for the single year I have lived with a *sensible* wife!" Werther had then been published four years. Lessing's grief has that pathos which he praised in sculpture, — he may writhe, but he must not scream. Nor is this a new thing with him. On the death of a younger brother, he wrote to his father, fourteen years before: "Why should those who grieve communicate their grief to each other purposely to increase it? .... Many mourn in death what they loved not living. I will love in life what nature bids me love, and after death strive to bewail it as little as I can."

We think Herr Stahr is on his stilts again when he speaks of Lessing's position at Wolfenbüttel. He calls it an "assuming the chains of feudal service, being buried in a corner, a martyrdom that consumed the best powers of his mind and crushed him in body and spirit forever." To crush *forever* is rather a strong phrase, Herr Stahr, to apply to the spirit, if one must ever give heed to the sense as well as the sound of what one is writing. But eloquence has no bowels for its victims. We have no doubt the Duke of Brunswick meant well by Lessing, and the salary he paid him was as large as he would have got from the frugal Frederick. But one whose trade it was to be a Duke could hardly have had much sympathy with his librarian after he had once found out what he really was. For even if he was not, as Herr Stahr affirms, a republican, and we doubt very much if he was, yet he was not a man who could play with ideas in the light French fashion. At the ardent touch of his sincerity, they took fire, and grew dangerous to what is called the social fabric. The logic of wit, with its momentary flash, is a very different thing from that consequent logic of thought, pushing forward its deliberate sap day and night with a fixed object, which belonged to Lessing. The men who attack abuses are not so much to be dreaded by the reigning house of Superstition as those who, as Dante says, syllogize hateful truths. As for "the chains of feudal service," they might serve a Fenian Head-Centre on a pinch, but are wholly out of place here. The slavery that Lessing had really taken on him was that of a great library, an Alcina that could always too easily witch him away from the more serious duty of his genius. That a mind like his could be buried in a corner is mere twaddle, and of a kind that has done great wrong to the dignity of letters. Where-ever Lessing sat, was the head of the table. That he suffered at Wolfenbüttel is true; but was it nothing to be in love and in debt at the same time, and to feel that his fruition of the one must be postponed for uncertain years by his own folly in incurring the other? If the sparrow-life must end, surely a wee bush is better than nae beild. One cause of Lessing's occasional restlessness and discontent Herr Stahr has failed to notice. It is evident from many passages in his letters that he had his share of the hypochondria which goes with an imaginative temperament. But in him it only serves to bring out in stronger relief his deep-rooted manliness. He spent no breath in that melodious whining which, beginning with Rousseau, has hardly yet gone out of fashion. Work of some kind was his medicine for the blues, — if not always of the kind he would have chosen, then the best that was to be had; for the useful, too, had for him a sweetness of its own. Sometimes he found a congenial labor in rescuing, as he called it, the memory of some dead scholar or thinker from the wrongs of ignorance or prejudice or falsehood; sometimes in fishing a manuscript out of the ooze of oblivion, and giving it, after a critical cleansing, to the world. Now and then he warmed himself and kept his muscle in trim with buffeting soundly the champions of that shallow artificiality and unctuous wordiness, one of which passed for orthodox in literature, and the other in theology. True religion and creative genius were both so beautiful to him that he could never abide the mediocre counterfeit of either, and he who put so much of his own life into all he wrote could not but hold all scripture sacred in which a divine soul had recorded itself. It would be doing Lessing great wrong to confound his controversial writing with the paltry quarrels of authors. His own personal relations enter into them surprisingly little, for his quarrel was never with men, but with falsehood, cant, and misleading tradition, in whomsoever incarnated. Save for this, they were no longer readable, and might be relegated to that herbarium of Billingsgate gathered by the elder Disraeli.

So far from being "crushed in spirit" at Wolfenbüttel, the years he spent there were among the most productive of his life. "Emilia Galotti," begun in 1758, was finished there and published in 1771. The controversy with Götze, by far the most important he was engaged in, and the one in which he put forth his maturest powers, was carried on thence. His "Nathan the Wise" (1779), by which almost alone he is known as a poet outside of Germany, was conceived and composed there. The last few years of his life were darkened by ill-health and the depression which it brings. His Nathan had not the success he hoped. It is sad to see the strong, self-sufficing man casting about for a little sympathy, even for a little praise. "It is really needful to me that you should have some small good opinion of it [Nathan], in order to make me once more contented with myself," he writes to Elise Reimarus in May, 1779. That he was weary of polemics, and dissatisfied with himself for letting them distract him from better things, appears from his last pathetic letter to the old friend he loved and valued most, — Mendelssohn. "And in truth, dear friend, I sorely need a letter like yours from time to time, if I am not to become wholly out of humor. I think you do not know me as a man that has a very hot hunger for praise. But the coldness with which the world is wont to convince certain people that they do not suit it, if not deadly, yet stiffens one with chill. I am not astonished that *all* I have written lately does not please *you*. . . . . At best, a passage here and there may have cheated you by recalling our better days. I, too, was then a sound, slim sapling, and am now such a rotten, gnarled trunk!" This was written on the 19th of December, 1780; and on the 15th of February, 1781, Lessing died, not quite fifty-two years old. Goethe was then in his thirty-second year, and Schiller ten years younger.

Of Lessing's relation to metaphysics the reader will find ample discussion in Herr Stahr's volumes. We are not particularly concerned with them, because his interest in such questions was purely speculative, and because he was more concerned to exercise the powers of his mind than to analyze them. His chief business, his master impulse always, was to be a man of letters in the narrower sense of the term. Even into theology he only made occasional raids across the border, as it were, and that not so much with a purpose of reform as in defence of principles which applied equally to the whole domain of thought. He had even less sympathy with heterodoxy than with orthodoxy, and, so far from joining a party or wishing to form one, would have left belief a matter of choice to the individual conscience. "From the bottom of my heart I hate all those people who wish to found sects. For it is not error, but sectarian error, yes, even sectarian truth, that makes men unhappy, or would do so if truth would found a sect." * Again he says, that in his theological controversies he is "much less concerned about theology than about sound

* To his brother Karl, 20th April, 1774.

common-sense, and only therefore prefer the old orthodox (at bottom *tolerant*) theology to the new (at bottom *intolerant*), because the former openly conflicts with sound common-sense, while the latter would fain corrupt it. I reconcile myself with my open enemies in order the better to be on my guard against my secret ones." * At another time he tells his brother that he has a wholly false notion of his (Lessing's) relation to orthodoxy. "Do you suppose I grudge the world that anybody should seek to enlighten it?—that I do not heartily wish that every one should think rationally about religion? I should loathe myself if even in my scribblings I had any other end than to help forward those great views. But let me choose my own way, which I think best for this purpose. And what is simpler than this way? I would not have the impure water, which has long been unfit to use, preserved; but I would not have it thrown away before we know whence to get purer. . . . . Orthodoxy, thank God, we were pretty well done with; a partition-wall had been built between it and Philosophy, behind which each could go her own way without troubling the other. But what are they doing now? They are tearing down this wall, and, under the pretext of making us rational Christians, are making us very irrational philosophers. . . . . We are agreed that our old religious system is false; but I cannot say with you that it is a patchwork of bunglers and half-philosophers. I know nothing in the world in which human acuteness has been more displayed or exercised than in that."† Lessing was always for freedom, never for looseness, of thought, still less for laxity of principle. But it must be a real freedom, and not that vain struggle to become a majority, which, if it succeed, escapes from heresy

* To the same, 20th March, 1777.

† To the same, 2d February, 1774.

only to make heretics of the other side. *Abire ad plures* would with him have meant, not bodily but spiritual death. He did not love the fanaticism of innovation a whit better than that of conservatism. To his sane understanding, both were equally hateful, as different masks of the same selfish bully. Coleridge said that toleration was impossible till indifference made it worthless. Lessing did not wish for toleration, because that implies authority, nor could his earnest temper have conceived of indifference. But he thought it as absurd to regulate opinion as the color of the hair. Here, too, he would have agreed with Selden, that "it is a vain thing to talk of an heretic, for a man for his heart cannot think any otherwise than he does think." Herr Stahr's chapters on this point, bating a little exaltation of tone, are very satisfactory; though, in his desire to make a leader of Lessing, he almost represents him as being what he shunned, — the founder of a sect. The fact is, that Lessing only formulated in his own way a general movement of thought, and what mainly interests us is that in him we see a layman, alike indifferent to clerisy and heresy, giving energetic and pointed utterance to those opinions of his class which the clergy are content to ignore so long as they remain esoteric. At present the world has advanced to where Lessing stood, while the Church has done its best to stand stock-still; and it would be a curious were it not a melancholy spectacle, to see the indifference with which the laity look on while theologians thrash their wheatless straw, utterly unconscious that there is no longer any common term possible that could bring their creeds again to any point of bearing on the practical life of men. Fielding never made a profounder stroke of satire than in Squire Western's indignant "Art not in the pulpit now! When art got up there, I never mind what dost say."

As an author, Lessing began his career at a period when we cannot say that German literature was at its lowest ebb, only because there had not yet been any flood-tide. That may be said to have begun with him. When we say German literature, we mean so much of it as has any interest outside of Germany. That part of the literary histories which treats of the dead waste and middle of the eighteenth century reads like a collection of obituaries, and were better reduced to the conciseness of epitaph, though the authors of them seem to find a melancholy pleasure, much like that of undertakers, in the task by which they live. Gottsched reigned supreme on the legitimate throne of dulness. In Switzerland, Bodmer essayed a more republican form of the same authority. At that time a traveller reports eight hundred authors in Zürich alone! Young aspirant for lettered fame, in imagination clear away the lichens from their forgotten headstones, and read humbly the "As I am, so thou must be," on all! Everybody remembers how Goethe, in the seventh book of his autobiography, tells the story of his visit to Gottsched. He enters by mistake an inner room at the moment when a frightened servant brings the discrowned potentate a periwig large enough to reach to the elbows. That awful emblem of pretentious sham seems to be the best type of the literature then predominant. We always fancy it set upon a pole, like Gessler's hat, with nothing in it that was not wooden, for all men to bow down before. The periwig style had its natural place in the age of Louis XIV., and there were certainly brains under it. But it had run out in France, as the tie-wig style of Pope had in England. In Germany it was the mere imitation of an imitation. Will it be believed that Gottsched recommends his Art of Poetry to beginners, in preference to Breitinger's, because it "*will enable them to produce every* *species of poem in a correct style,* while out of that no one can learn to make an ode or a cantata"? "Whoever," he says, "buys Breitinger's book *in order to learn how to make poems,* will too late regret his money." * Gottsched, perhaps, did some service even by his advocacy of French models, by calling attention to the fact that there *was* such a thing as style, and that it was of some consequence. But not one of the authors of that time can be said to survive, nor to be known even by name except to Germans, unless it be Klopstock, Herder, Wieland, and Gellert. And the latter's immortality, such as it is, reminds us somewhat of that Lady Gosling's, whose obituary stated that she was "mentioned by Mrs. Barbauld in her Life of Richardson 'under the name of Miss M., afterwards Lady G.'" Klopstock himself is rather remembered for what he was than what he is, — an immortality of unreadableness; and we much doubt if many Germans put the "Oberon" in their trunks when they start on a journey. Herder alone survives, if not as a contributor to literature, strictly so called, yet as a thinker and as part of the intellectual impulse of the day. But at the time, though there were two parties, yet within the lines of each there was a loyal reciprocity of what is called on such occasions appreciation. Wig ducked to wig, each blockhead had a brother, and there was a universal apotheosis of the mediocrity of our set. If the greatest happiness of the greatest number be the true theory, this was all that could be desired. Even Lessing at one time looked up to Hagedorn as the German Horace. If Hagedorn were pleased, what mattered it to Horace? Worse almost than this was the universal pedantry. The solemn bray of one pedagogue was taken up and prolonged in a thousand echoes. There was not only no originality, but no

* Gervinus, IV. 62.

desire for it, — perhaps even a dread of it, as something that would break the *entente cordiale* of placid mutual assurance. No great writer had given that tone of good-breeding to the language which would gain it entrance to the society of European literature. No man of genius had made it a necessity of polite culture. It was still as rudely provincial as the Scotch of Allan Ramsay. Frederick the Great was to be forgiven if, with his practical turn, he gave himself wholly to French, which had replaced Latin as a cosmopolitan tongue. It had lightness, ease, fluency, elegance, — in short, all the good qualities that German lacked. The study of French models was perhaps the best thing for German literature before it got out of long-clothes. It was bad only when it became a tradition and a tyranny. Lessing did more than any other man to overthrow this foreign usurpation when it had done its work.

The same battle had to be fought on English soil also, and indeed is hardly over yet. For the renewed outbreak of the old quarrel between Classical and Romantic grew out of nothing more than an attempt of the modern spirit to free itself from laws of taste laid down by the *Grand Siècle.* But we must not forget the debt which all modern prose literature owes to France. It is true that Machiavelli was the first to write with classic pith and point in a living language; but he is, for all that, properly an ancient. Montaigne is really the first modern writer, — the first who assimilated his Greek and Latin, and showed that an author might be original and charming, even classical, if he did not try too hard. He is also the first modern critic, and his judgments of the writers of antiquity are those of an equal. He made the ancients his servants, to help him think in Gascon French; and, in spite of his endless quotations, began the crusade against pedantry. It was not, however, till a century later, t[illegible] reform became complete in France, and then crossed the Channel. Milton is still a pedant in his prose, and not seldom even in his great poem. Dryden was the first Englishman who wrote perfectly easy prose, and he owed his style and turn of thought to his French reading. His learning sits easily on him, and has a modern cut. So far, the French influence was one of unmixed good, for it rescued us from pedantry. It must have done something for Germany in the same direction. For its effect on poetry we cannot say as much; and its traditions had themselves become pedantry in another shape when Lessing made an end of it. He himself certainly learned to write prose of Diderot; and whatever Herr Stahr may think of it, his share in the "Letters on German Literature" got its chief inspiration from France.

It is in the *Dramaturgie* that Lessing first properly enters as an influence into European literature. He may be said to have begun the revolt from pseudo-classicism in poetry, and to have been thus unconsciously the founder of romanticism. Wieland's translation of Shakespeare had, it is true, appeared in 1762; but Lessing was the first critic whose profound knowledge of the Greek drama and apprehension of its principles gave weight to his judgment, who recognized in what the true greatness of the poet consisted, and found him to be really nearer the Greeks than any other modern. This was because Lessing looked always more to the life than the form, — because he knew the classics, and did not merely cant about them. But if the authority of Lessing, by making people feel easy in their admiration for Shakespeare, perhaps increased the influence of his works, and if his discussions of Aristotle have given a new starting-point to modern criticism, it may be doubted whether the immediate effect on literature of his own critical essays was so great as Herr Stahr supposes. Surely "Götz" and "The Robbers" are nothing like what he would have called Shakespearian, and the whole *Sturm und Drang* tendency would have roused in him nothing but antipathy. Fixed principles in criticism are useful in helping us to form a judgment of works already produced, but it is questionable whether they are not rather a hindrance than a help to living production. Ben Jonson was a fine critic, intimate with the classics as few men have either the leisure or the strength of mind to be in this age of many books, and built regular plays long before they were heard of in France. But he continually trips and falls flat over his metewand of classical propriety, his personages are abstractions, and fortunately neither his precepts nor his practice influenced any one of his greater coevals.* In breadth of understanding, and the gravity of purpose that comes of it, he was far above Fletcher or Webster, but how far below either in the subtler, the incalculable, qualities of a dramatic poet! Yet Ben, with his principles off, could soar and sing with the best of them; and there are strains in his lyrics which Herrick, the most Catullian of poets since Catullus, could imitate, but never match. A constant reference to the statutes which taste has codified would only bewilder the creative instinct. Criticism can at best teach writers without genius what is to be avoided or imitated. It cannot communicate life;

* It should be considered, by those sagacious persons who think that the most marvellous intellect of which we have any record could not master so much Latin and Greek as would serve a sophomore, that Shakespeare must through conversation have possessed himself of whatever principles of art Ben Jonson and the other university men had been able to deduce from their study of the classics. That they should not have discussed these matters over their sack at the Mermaid is incredible; that Shakespeare, who left not a drop in any orange he squeezed, could not also have got all the juice out of this one, is even more so.

and its effect, when reduced to rules, has commonly been to produce that correctness which is so praiseworthy and so intolerable. It cannot give taste, it can only demonstrate who has had it. Lessing's essays in this kind were of service to German literature by their manliness of style, whose example was worth a hundred treatises, and by the stimulus there is in all original thinking. Could he have written such a poem as he was capable of conceiving, his influence would have been far greater. It is the living soul, and not the metaphysical abstraction of it, that is genetic in literature. If to do were as easy as to know what were good to be done! It was out of his own failures to reach the ideal he saw so clearly, that Lessing drew the wisdom which made him so admirable a critic. Even here, too, genius can profit by no experience but its own.

For, in spite of Herr Stahr's protest, we must acknowledge the truth of Lessing's own characteristic confession, that he was no poet. A man of genius he unquestionably was, if genius may be claimed no less for force than fineness of mind, — for the intensity of conviction that inspires the understanding as much as for that apprehension of beauty which gives energy of will to imagination, — but a poetic genius he was not. His mind kindled by friction in the process of thinking, not in the flash of conception, and its delight is in demonstration, not in bodying forth. His prose can leap and run, his verse is always thinking of its feet. Yet in his "Minna" and his "Emilia"* he shows one faculty of

* In "Minna" and "Emilia" Lessing followed the lead of Diderot. In the Preface to the second edition of Diderot's *Théâtre*, he says: "I am very conscious that my taste, without Diderot's example and teaching, would have taken quite another direction. Perhaps one more my own, yet hardly one with which my understanding would in the long run have been so well content." Diderot's choice of prose was dictated and justified by the accentual poverty of his mother-

the dramatist, that of construction, in a higher degree than any other German.* Here his critical deductions served him to some purpose. The action moves rapidly, there is no speechifying, and the parts are coherent. Both plays act better than anything of Goethe or Schiller. But it is the story that interests us, and not the characters. These are not, it is true, the incorporation of certain ideas, or, still worse, of certain dogmas, but they certainly seem something like machines by which the motive of the play is carried on; and there is nothing of that interplay of plot and character which makes Shakespeare more real in the closet than other dramatists with all the helps of the theatre. It is a striking illustration at once of the futility of mere critical insight and of Lessing's want of imagination, that in the Emilia he should have thought a Roman motive consistent with modern habits of thought, and that in Nathan he should have been guilty of anachronisms which violate not only the accidental truth of fact, but the essential truth of

tongue. Lessing certainly revised his judgment on this point (for it was not equally applicable to German), and wrote his maturer "Nathan" in what he took for blank verse. There was much kindred between the minds of the two men. Diderot always seems to us a kind of deboshed Lessing. Lessing was also indebted to Burke, Hume, the two Wartons, and Hurd, among other English writers. Not that he borrowed anything of them but the quickening of his own thought. It should be remembered that Rousseau was seventeen, Diderot and Sterne sixteen, and Winckelmann twelve years older than Lessing. Wieland was four years younger.

* Goethe's appreciation of Lessing grew with his years. He writes to Lavater, 18th March, 1781: "Lessing's death has greatly depressed me. I had much pleasure in him and much hope of him." This is a little patronizing in tone. But in the last year of his life, talking with Eckermann, he naturally antedates his admiration, as reminiscence is wont to do: "You can conceive what an effect this piece (*Minna*) had upon us young people. It was, in fact, a shining meteor. It made us aware that something higher existed than anything whereof that feeble literary epoch had a notion. The first two acts are truly a masterpiece of exposition, from which one learned much and can always learn."

character. Even if we allowed him imagination, it must be only on the lower plane of prose; for of verse as anything more than so many metrical feet he had not the faintest notion. Of that exquisite sympathy with the movement of the mind, with every swifter or slower pulse of passion, which proves it another species from prose, the very ἀφροδίτη καὶ λύρα of speech, and not merely a higher one, he wanted the fineness of sense to conceive. If we compare the prose of Dante or Milton, though both were eloquent, with their verse, we see at once which was the most congenial to them. Lessing has passages of freer and more harmonious utterance in some of his most careless prose essays, than can be found in his Nathan from the first line to the last. In the *numeris lege solutis* he is often snatched beyond himself, and becomes truly dithyrambic; in his pentameters the march of the thought is comparatively hampered and irresolute. His best things are not poetically delicate, but have the tougher fibre of proverbs. Is it not enough, then, to be a great prose-writer? They are as rare as great poets, and if Lessing have the gift to stir and to dilate that something deeper than the mind which genius only can reach, what matter if it be not done to music? Of his minor poems we need say little. Verse was always more or less mechanical with him, and his epigrams are almost all stiff, as if they were bad translations from the Latin. Many of them are shockingly coarse, and in liveliness are on a level with those of our Elizabethan period. Herr Stahr, of course, cannot bear to give them up, even though Gervinus be willing. The prettiest of his shorter poems (*Die Namen*) has been appropriated by Coleridge, who has given it a grace which it wants in the original. His Nathan, by a poor translation of which he is chiefly known to English readers, is an Essay on Toleration in the form of a dialogue. As a play, it has not the interest of Minna or Emilia, though the Germans, who have a praiseworthy national stoicism where one of their great writers is concerned, find in seeing it represented a grave satisfaction, like that of subscribing to a monument. There is a sober lustre of reflection in it that makes it very good reading; but it wants the molten interfusion of thought and phrase which only imagination can achieve.

As Lessing's mind was continually advancing, — always open to new impressions, and capable, as very few are, of apprehending the many-sidedness of truth, — as he had the rare quality of being honest with himself, — his works seem fragmentary, and give at first an impression of incompleteness. But one learns at length to recognize and value this very incompleteness as characteristic of the man who was growing lifelong, and to whom the selfish thought that any share of truth could be exclusively *his* was an impossibility. At the end of the ninety-fifth number of the *Dramaturgie* he says: "I remind my readers here, that these pages are by no means intended to contain a dramatic system. I am accordingly not bound to solve all the difficulties which I raise. I am quite willing that my thoughts should seem to want connection, — nay, even to contradict each other, — if only there are thoughts in which they [my readers] find material for thinking themselves. I wish to do nothing more than scatter the *fermenta cognitionis*." That is Lessing's great praise, and gives its chief value to his works, — a value, indeed, imperishable, and of the noblest kind. No writer can leave a more precious legacy to posterity than this; and beside this shining merit, all mere literary splendors look pale and cold. There is that life in Lessing's thought which engenders life, and not only thinks for us, but makes us think. Not sceptical, but forever testing and inquiring, it is out of the cloud of his own doubt that the flash comes at last with sudden and vivid illumination. Flashes they indeed are, his finest intuitions, and of very different quality from the equable north-light of the artist. He felt it, and said it of himself, "Ever so many flashes of lightning do not make daylight." We speak now of those more rememberable passages where his highest individuality reveals itself in what may truly be called a passion of thought. In the "Laocoön" there is daylight of the serenest temper, and never was there a better example of the discourse of reason, though even that is also a fragment.

But it is as a nobly original man, even more than as an original thinker, that Lessing is precious to us, and that he is so considerable in German literature. In a higher sense, but in the same kind, he is to Germans what Dr. Johnson is to us, — admirable for what he was. Like Johnson's, too, but still from a loftier plane, a great deal of his thought has a direct bearing on the immediate life and interests of men. His genius was not a St. Elmo's fire, as it so often is with mere poets, — as it was in Shelley, for example, playing in ineffectual flame about the points of his thought, — but was interfused with his whole nature and made a part of his very being. To the Germans, with their weak nerve of sentimentalism, his brave common-sense is a far wholesomer tonic than the cynicism of Heine, which is, after all, only sentimentalism soured. His jealousy for maintaining the just boundaries whether of art or speculation may warn them to check with timely dikes the tendency of their thought to diffuse inundation. Their fondness in æsthetic discussion for a nomenclature subtile enough to split a hair at which even a Thomist would have despaired, is rebuked by the clear simplicity of his style.*

* Nothing can be droller than the occasional translation by Vischer of a sentence of Lessing into his own jargon.

But he is no exclusive property of Germany. As a complete man, constant, generous, full of honest courage, as a hardy follower of Thought wherever she might lead him, above all, as a confessor of that Truth which is forever revealing itself to the seeker, and is the more loved because never wholly revealable, he is an ennobling possession of mankind. Let his own striking words characterize him: —

"Not the truth of which any one is, or supposes himself to be, possessed, but the upright endeavor he has made to arrive at truth, makes the worth of the man. For not by the possession, but by the investigation, of truth are his powers expanded, wherein alone his ever-growing perfection consists. Possession makes us easy, indolent, proud.

"If God held all truth shut in his right hand, and in his left nothing but the ever-restless instinct for truth, though with the condition of for ever and ever erring, and should say to me, Choose! I should bow humbly to his left hand, and say, Father, give! pure truth is for Thee alone!"

It is not without reason that fame is awarded only after death. The dust-cloud of notoriety which follows and envelopes the men who drive with the wind bewilders contemporary judgment. Lessing, while he lived, had little reward for his labor but the satisfaction inherent in all work faithfully done; the highest, no doubt, of which human nature is capable, and yet perhaps not so sweet as that sympathy of which the world's praise is but an index. But if to perpetuate herself beyond the grave in healthy and ennobling influences be the noblest aspiration of the mind, and its fruition the only reward she would have deemed worthy of herself, then is Lessing to be counted thrice fortunate. Every year since he was laid prematurely in the earth has seen his power for good increase, and made him more precious to the hearts and intellects of men. "Lessing," said Goethe, "would have declined the lofty title of a Genius; but his enduring influence testifies against himself. On the other hand, we have in literature other and indeed important names of men who, while they lived, were esteemed great geniuses, but whose influence ended with their lives, and who, accordingly, were less than they and others thought. For, as I have said, there is no genius without a productive power that continues forever operative." *

* Eckermann, Gespräche mit Goethe, III. 229.

ROUSSEAU AND THE SENTIMENTALISTS.*

"WE have had the great professor and founder of the philosophy of Vanity in England. As I had good opportunities of knowing his proceedings almost from day to day, he left no doubt in my mind that he entertained no principle either to influence his heart or to guide his understanding but vanity; with this vice he was possessed to a degree little short of madness. Benevolence to the whole species, and want of feeling for every individual with whom the professors come in contact, form the character of the new philosophy. Setting up for an unsocial independence, this their hero of vanity refuses the just price of common labor, as well as the tribute which opulence owes to genius, and which, when paid, honors the giver and the receiver, and then pleads his beggary as an excuse for his crimes. He melts with tenderness for those only who touch him by the remotest relation, and then, without one natural pang, casts away, as a sort of offal and excrement, the spawn of his disgustful amours, and sends his children to the hospital of foundlings. The bear loves, licks, and forms her young; but bears are not philosophers."

This was Burke's opinion of the only contemporary

* *Histoire des Idées Morales et Politiques en France au XVIII*me *Siècle.* Par M. JULES BARNI, Professeur à l'Académie de Genève. Tome II. Paris. 1867.

who can be said to rival him in fervid and sustained eloquence, to surpass him in grace and persuasiveness of style. Perhaps we should have been more thankful to him if he had left us instead a record of those "proceedings almost from day to day" which he had such "good opportunities of knowing," but it probably never entered his head that posterity might care as much about the doings of the citizen of Geneva as about the sayings of even a British Right Honorable. Vanity eludes recognition by its victims in more shapes, and more pleasing, than any other passion, and perhaps had Mr. Burke been able imaginatively to translate Swiss Jean Jacques into Irish Edmund, he would have found no juster equivalent for the obnoxious trisyllable than "righteous self-esteem." For Burke was himself also, in the subtler sense of the word, a sentimentalist, that is, a man who took what would now be called an æsthetic view of morals and politics. No man who ever wrote English, except perhaps Mr. Ruskin, more habitually mistook his own personal likes and dislikes, tastes and distastes, for general principles, and this, it may be suspected, is the secret of all merely eloquent writing. He hints at madness as an explanation of Rousseau, and it is curious enough that Mr. Buckle was fain to explain *him* in the same way. It is not, we confess, a solution that we find very satisfactory in this latter case. Burke's fury against the French Revolution was nothing more than was natural to a desperate man in self-defence. It was his own life, or, at least, all that made life dear to him, that was in danger. He had all that abstract political wisdom which may be naturally secreted by a magnanimous nature and a sensitive temperament, absolutely none of that rough-and-tumble kind which is so needful for the conduct of affairs. Fastidiousness is only another form of egotism; and all men who know not where to look for truth save in the narrow well of self will find their own image at the bottom, and mistake it for what they are seeking. Burke's hatred of Rousseau was genuine and instinctive. It was so genuine and so instinctive as no hatred can be but that of self, of our own weaknesses as we see them in another man. But there was also something deeper in it than this. There was mixed with it the natural dread in the political diviner of the political logician, — in the empirical, of the theoretic statesman. Burke, confounding the idea of society with the form of it then existing, would have preserved that as the only specific against anarchy. Rousseau, assuming that society as it then existed was but another name for anarchy, would have reconstituted it on an ideal basis. The one has left behind him some of the profoundest aphorisms of political wisdom; the other, some of the clearest principles of political science. The one, clinging to Divine right, found in the fact that things were, a reason that they ought to be; the other, aiming to solve the problem of the Divine order, would deduce from that abstraction alone the claim of anything to be at all. There seems a mere oppugnancy of nature between the two, and yet both were, in different ways, the dupes of their own imaginations.

Now let us hear the opinion of a philosopher who *was* a bear, whether bears be philosophers or not. Boswell had a genuine relish for what was superior in any way, from genius to claret, and of course he did not let Rousseau escape him. "One evening at the Mitre, Johnson said sarcastically to me, 'It seems, sir, you have kept very good company abroad, — Rousseau and Wilkes!' I answered with a smile, 'My dear sir, you don't call Rousseau bad company; do you really think *him* a bad man?' JOHNSON. 'Sir, if you are talking jestingly of this, I don't talk with you. If you mean to be serious,

I think him one of the worst of men, a rascal who ought to be hunted out of society, as he has been. Three or four nations have expelled him, and it is a shame that he is protected in this country. Rousseau, sir, is a very bad man. I would sooner sign a sentence for his transportation, than that of any felon who has gone from the Old Bailey these many years. Yes, I should like to have him work in the plantations.'" *We* were the plantations then, and Rousseau was destined to work there in another and much more wonderful fashion than the gruff old Ursa Major imagined. However, there is always a refreshing heartiness in his growl, a masculine bass with no snarl in it. The Doctor's logic is of that fine old crusted Port sort, the native manufacture of the British conservative mind. Three or four nations *have*, therefore England ought. A few years later, had the Doctor been living, if three or four nations had treated their kings as France did hers, would he have thought the *ergo* a very stringent one for England?

Mr. Burke, who could speak with studied respect of the Prince of Wales, and of his vices with that charity which thinketh no evil and can afford to think no evil of so important a living member of the British Constitution, surely could have had no unmixed moral repugnance for Rousseau's "disgustful amours." It was because they were *his* that they were so loathsome. Mr. Burke was a snob, though an inspired one. Dr. Johnson, the friend of that wretchedest of lewd fellows, Richard Savage, and of that gay man about town, Topham Beauclerk, — himself sprung from an amour that would have been disgustful had it not been royal, — must also have felt something more in respect of Rousseau than the mere repugnance of virtue for vice. We must sometimes allow to personal temperament its right of peremptory challenge. Johnson had not that fine sensitiveness to the political atmosphere which made Burke presageful of coming tempest, but both of them felt that there was something dangerous in this man. Their dislike has in it somewhat of the energy of fear. Neither of them had the same feeling toward Voltaire, the man of supreme talent, but both felt that what Rousseau was possessed by was genius, with its terrible force either to attract or repel.

"By the pricking of my thumbs,
Something wicked this way comes."

Burke and Johnson were both of them sincere men, both of them men of character as well as of intellectual force; and we cite their opinions of Rousseau with the respect which is due to an honest conviction which has apparent grounds for its adoption, whether we agree with it or no. But it strikes us as a little singular that one whose life was so full of moral inconsistency, whose character is so contemptible in many ways, in some we might almost say so revolting, should yet have exercised so deep and lasting an influence, and on minds so various, should still be an object of minute and earnest discussion, — that he should have had such vigor in his intellectual loins as to have been the father of Châteaubriand, Byron, Lamartine, George Sand, and many more in literature, in politics of Jefferson and Thomas Paine, — that the spots he had haunted should draw pilgrims so unlike as Gibbon and Napoleon, nay, should draw them still, after the lapse of near a century. Surely there must have been a basis of sincerity in this man seldom matched, if it can prevail against so many reasons for repugnance, aversion, and even disgust. He could not have been the mere sentimentalist and rhetorician for which the rough-and-ready understanding would at first glance be inclined to condemn him. In a certain sense he was both of these, but he was something more. It will bring us a little nearer the point we are aiming at if we quote one other and more recent English opinion of him.

Mr. Thomas Moore, returning pleasantly in a travelling-carriage from a trip to Italy, in which he had never forgotten the poetical shop at home, but had carefully noted down all the pretty images that occurred to him for future use, — Mr. Thomas Moore, on his way back from a visit to his noble friend Byron, at Venice, who had there been leading a life so gross as to be talked about, even amid the crash of Napoleon's fall, and who was just writing "Don Juan" for the improvement of the world, — Mr. Thomas Moore, fresh from the reading of Byron's Memoirs, which were so scandalous that, by some hocus-pocus, three thousand guineas afterward found their way into his own pocket for consenting to suppress them, — Mr. Thomas Moore, the *ci-devant* friend of the Prince Regent, and the author of Little's Poems, among other objects of pilgrimage visits *Les Charmettes*, where Rousseau had lived with Madame de Warens. So good an opportunity for occasional verses was not to be lost, so good a text for a little virtuous moralizing not to be thrown away; and accordingly Mr. Moore pours out several pages of octosyllabic disgust at the sensuality of the dead man of genius. There was no horror for Byron. Toward him all was suavity and decorous *bienséance*. That lively sense of benefits to be received made the Irish Anacreon wink with both his little eyes. In the judgment of a liberal like Mr. Moore, were not the errors of a lord excusable? But with poor Rousseau the case was very different. The son of a watchmaker, an outcast from boyhood up, always on the perilous edge of poverty, — what right had he to indulge himself in any immoralities? So it is always with the sentimentalists. It is never the thing in itself that is bad or good, but the thing in its relation to some conventional and mostly selfish standard. Moore could be a moralist, in this case, without any trouble, and with the advantage of winning Lord Lansdowne's approval; he could write some graceful verses which everybody would buy, and for the rest it is not hard to be a stoic in eight-syllable measure and a travelling-carriage. The next dinner at Bowood will taste none the worse. Accordingly he speaks of

"The mire, the strife
And vanities of this man's life,
Who more than all that e'er have glowed
With fancy's flame (and it was his
In fullest warmth and radiance) showed
What an impostor Genius is;
How, with that strong mimetic art
Which forms its life and soul, it takes
All shapes of thought, all hues of heart,
Nor feels itself one throb it wakes;
How, like a gem, its light may shine,
O'er the dark path by mortals trod,
Itself as mean a worm the while
As crawls at midnight o'er the sod;
. . . .
How, with the pencil hardly dry
From coloring up such scenes of love
And beauty as make young hearts sigh,
And dream and think through heaven they rove," &c., &c.

Very spirited, is it not? One has only to overlook a little threadbareness in the similes, and it is very good oratorical verse. But would we believe in it, we must never read Mr. Moore's own journal, and find out how thin a piece of veneering his own life was, — how he lived in sham till his very nature had become subdued to it, till he could persuade himself that a sham could be written into a reality, and actually made experiment thereof in his Diary.

One verse in this diatribe deserves a special comment, —

"What an impostor Genius is!"

In two respects there is nothing to be objected to in it. It is of eight syllables, and "is" rhymes unexceptionably with "his." But is there the least filament of truth in it? We venture to assert, not the least. It was not Rousseau's genius that was an impostor. It was the one thing in him that was always true. We grant that, in allowing that a man has genius. Talent is that which is in a man's power; genius is that in whose power a man is. That is the very difference between them. We might turn the tables on Moore, the man of talent, and say truly enough, What an impostor talent is! Moore talks of the mimetic power with a total misapprehension of what it really is. The mimetic power had nothing whatever to do with the affair. Rousseau had none of it; Shakespeare had it in excess; but what difference would it make in our judgment of Hamlet or Othello if a manuscript of Shakespeare's memoirs should turn up, and we should find out that he had been a pitiful fellow? None in the world; for he is not a professed moralist, and his life does not give the warrant to his words. But if Demosthenes, after all his Philippics, throws away his shield and runs, we feel the contemptibleness of the contradiction. With genius itself we never find any fault. It would be an over-nicety that would do that. We do not get invited to nectar and ambrosia so often that we think of grumbling and saying we have better at home. No; the same genius that mastered him who wrote the poem masters us in reading it, and we care for nothing outside the poem itself. How the author lived, what he wore, how he looked, — all that is mere gossip, about which we need not trouble ourselves. Whatever he was or did, somehow or other God let him be worthy to write *this*, and that is enough for us. We forgive everything to the genius; we are inexorable to the man. Shakespeare, Goethe, Burns, —

what have their biographies to do with us? Genius is not a question of character. It may be sordid, like the lamp of Aladdin, in its externals; what care we, while the touch of it builds palaces for us, makes us rich as only men in dream-land are rich, and lords to the utmost bound of imagination? So, when people talk of the ungrateful way in which the world treats its geniuses, they speak unwisely. There is no work of genius which has not been the delight of mankind, no word of genius to which the human heart and soul have not, sooner or later, responded. But the man whom the genius takes possession of for its pen, for its trowel, for its pencil, for its chisel, *him* the world treats according to his deserts. Does Burns drink? It sets him to gauging casks of gin. For, remember, it is not to the practical world that the genius appeals; it *is* the practical world which judges of the man's fitness for its uses, and has a right so to judge. No amount of patronage could have made distilled liquors less toothsome to Robbie Burns, as no amount of them could make a Burns of the Ettrick Shepherd.

There is an old story in the *Gesta Romanorum* of a priest who was found fault with by one of his parishioners because his life was in painful discordance with his teaching. So one day he takes his critic out to a stream, and, giving him to drink of it, asks him if he does not find it sweet and pure water. The parishioner, having answered that it was, is taken to the source, and finds that what had so refreshed him flowed from between the jaws of a dead dog. "Let this teach thee," said the priest, "that the very best doctrine may take its rise in a very impure and disgustful spring, and that excellent morals may be taught by a man who has no morals at all." It is easy enough to see the fallacy here. Had the man known beforehand from what a carrion fountain-head the stream issued, he could not have drunk of it without loathing. Had the priest merely bidden him to *look* at the stream and see how beautiful it was, instead of tasting it, it would have been quite another matter. And this is precisely the difference between what appeals to our æsthetic and to our moral sense, between what is judged of by the taste and the conscience.

It is when the sentimentalist turns preacher of morals that we investigate his character, and are justified in so doing. He may express as many and as delicate shades of feeling as he likes, — for this the sensibility of his organization perfectly fits him, no other person could do it so well, — but the moment he undertakes to establish his feeling as a rule of conduct, we ask at once how far are his own life and deed in accordance with what he preaches? For every man feels instinctively that all the beautiful sentiments in the world weigh less than a single lovely action; and that while tenderness of feeling and susceptibility to generous emotions are accidents of temperament, goodness is an achievement of the will and a quality of the life. Fine words, says our homely old proverb, butter no parsnips; and if the question be how to render those vegetables palatable, an ounce of butter would be worth more than all the orations of Cicero. The only conclusive evidence of a man's sincerity is that he give *himself* for a principle. Words, money, all things else, are comparatively easy to give away; but when a man makes a gift of his daily life and practice, it is plain that the truth, whatever it may be, has taken possession of him. From that sincerity his words gain the force and pertinency of deeds, and his money is no longer the pale drudge 'twixt man and man, but, by a beautiful magic, what erewhile bore the image and superscription of Cæsar seems now to bear the image and superscription of God. It is thus that there is a genius for goodness, for magnanimity, for self-sacrifice, as well as for creative art; and it is thus that by a more refined sort of Platonism the Infinite Beauty dwells in and shapes to its own likeness the soul which gives it body and individuality. But when Moore charges genius with being an impostor, the confusion of his ideas is pitiable. There is nothing so true, so sincere, so downright and forthright, as genius. It is always truer than the man himself is, greater than he. If Shakespeare the man had been as marvellous a creature as the genius that wrote his plays, that genius so comprehensive in its intelligence, so wise even in its play, that its clowns are moralists and philosophers, so penetrative that a single one of its phrases reveals to us the secret of our own character, would his contemporaries have left us so wholly without record of him as they have done, distinguishing him in no wise from his fellow-players?

Rousseau, no doubt, was weak, nay, more than that, was sometimes despicable, but yet is not fairly to be reckoned among the herd of sentimentalists. It is shocking that a man whose preaching made it fashionable for women of rank to nurse their own children should have sent his own, as soon as born, to the foundling hospital, still more shocking that, in a note to his *Discours sur l'Inégalité*, he should speak of this crime as one of the consequences of our social system. But for all that there was a faith and an ardor of conviction in him that distinguish him from most of the writers of his time. Nor were his practice and his preaching always inconsistent. He contrived to pay regularly, whatever his own circumstances were, a pension of one hundred *livres* a year to a maternal aunt who had been kind to him in childhood. Nor was his asceticism a sham. He might have turned his gift into laced coats and *châteaux* as easily as Voltaire, had he not held it too sacred to be bartered away in any such losing exchange.

But what is worthy of especial remark is this, — that in nearly all that he wrote his leading object was the good of his kind, and that through all the vicissitudes of a life which illness, sensibility of temperament, and the approaches of insanity rendered wretched, — the associate of infidels, the foundling child, as it were, of an age without belief, least of all in itself, — he professed and evidently felt deeply a faith in the goodness both of man and of God. There is no such thing as scoffing in his writings. On the other hand, there is no stereotyped morality. He does not ignore the existence of scepticism; he recognizes its existence in his own nature, meets it frankly face to face, and makes it confess that there are things in the teaching of Christ that are deeper than its doubt. The influence of his early education at Geneva is apparent here. An intellect so acute as his, trained in the school of Calvin in a republic where theological discussion was as much the amusement of the people as the opera was at Paris, could not fail to be a good logician. He had the fortitude to follow his logic wherever it led him. If the very impressibility of character which quickened his perception of the beauties of nature, and made him alive to the charm of music and musical expression, prevented him from being in the highest sense an original writer, and if his ideas were mostly suggested to him by books, yet the clearness, consecutiveness, and eloquence with which he stated and enforced them made them his own. There was at least that original fire in him which could fuse them and run them in a novel mould. His power lay in this very ability of manipulating the thoughts of others. Fond of paradox he doubtless was, but he had a way of putting things that arrested attention and excited thought.

It was, perhaps, this very sensibility of the surrounding atmosphere of feeling and speculation, which made Rousseau more directly influential on contemporary thought (or perhaps we should say sentiment) than any writer of his time. And this is rarely consistent with enduring greatness in literature. It forces us to remember, against our will, the oratorical character of his works. They were all pleas, and he a great advocate, with Europe in the jury-box. Enthusiasm begets enthusiasm, eloquence produces conviction for the moment, but it is only by truth to nature and the everlasting intuitions of mankind that those abiding influences are won that enlarge from generation to generation. Rousseau was in many respects — as great pleaders always are — a man of the day, who must needs become a mere name to posterity, yet he could not but have had in him some not inconsiderable share of that principle by which man eternizes himself. For it is only to such that the night cometh not in which no man shall work, and he is still operative both in politics and literature by the principles he formulated or the emotions to which he gave a voice so piercing and so sympathetic.

In judging Rousseau, it would be unfair not to take note of the malarious atmosphere in which he grew up. The constitution of his mind was thus early infected with a feverish taint that made him shiveringly sensitive to a temperature which hardier natures found bracing. To him this rough world was but too literally a rack. Good-humored Mother Nature commonly imbeds the nerves of her children in a padding of self-conceit that serves as a buffer against the ordinary shocks to which even a life of routine is liable, and it would seem at first sight as if Rousseau had been better cared for than usual in this regard. But as his self-conceit was enormous, so was the reaction from it proportionate, and the fretting suspiciousness of temper, sure mark of an unsound mind, which rendered him incapable of intimate friendship, while passionately longing for it, became inevitably, when turned inward, a tormenting self-distrust. To dwell in unrealities is the doom of the sentimentalist; but it should not be forgotten that the same fitful intensity of emotion which makes them real as the means of elation, gives them substance also for torture. Too irritably jealous to endure the rude society of men, he steeped his senses in the enervating incense that women are only too ready to burn. If their friendship be a safeguard to the other sex, their homage is fatal to all but the strongest, and Rousseau was weak both by inheritance and early training. His father was one of those feeble creatures for whom a fine phrase could always satisfactorily fill the void that non-performance leaves behind it. If he neglected duty, he made up for it by that cultivation of the finer sentiments of our common nature which waters flowers of speech with the brineless tears of a flabby remorse, without one fibre of resolve in it, and which impoverishes the character in proportion as it enriches the vocabulary. He was a very Apicius in that digestible kind of woe which makes no man leaner, and had a favorite receipt for cooking you up a sorrow *à la douleur inassouvie* that had just enough delicious sharpness in it to bring tears into the eyes by tickling the palate. "When he said to me, 'Jean Jacques, let us speak of thy mother,' I said to him, 'Well, father, we are going to weep, then,' and this word alone drew tears from him. 'Ah!' said he, groaning, 'give her back to me, console me for her, fill the void she has left in my soul!'" Alas! in such cases, the void she leaves is only that she found. The grief that seeks any other than its own society will erelong want an object. This admirable parent allowed his son to become an outcast at sixteen, without any attempt to reclaim him, in order to enjoy unmolested a petty inheritance to which the boy was entitled in right of his mother. "This conduct," Rousseau tells us, "of a father whose tenderness and virtue were so well known to me, caused me to make reflections on myself which have not a little contributed to make my heart sound. I drew from it this great maxim of morals, the only one perhaps serviceable in practice, to avoid situations which put our duties in opposition to our interest, and which show us our own advantage in the wrong of another, sure that in such situations, *however sincere may be one's love of virtue*, it sooner or later grows weak without our perceiving it, *and that we become unjust and wicked in action without having ceased to be just and good in soul.*"

This maxim may do for that "fugitive and cloistered virtue, unexercised and unbreathed, that never sallies out and seeks its adversary," which Milton could not praise, — that is, for a manhood whose distinction it is not to be manly, — but it is chiefly worth notice as being the characteristic doctrine of sentimentalism. This disjoining of deed from will, of practice from theory, is to put asunder what God has joined by an indissoluble sacrament. The soul must be tainted before the action become corrupt; and there is no self-delusion more fatal than that which makes the conscience dreamy with the anodyne of lofty sentiments, while the life is grovelling and sensual, — witness Coleridge. In his case we feel something like disgust. But where, as in his son Hartley, there is hereditary infirmity, where the man sees the principle that might rescue him slip from the clutch of a nerveless will, like a rope through the fingers of a drowning man, and the confession of faith is the moan of despair, there is room for no harsher feeling than pity. Rousseau showed through life a singular proneness for being convinced by his own eloquence; he was always his own first convert; and this reconciles his power as a writer with his weakness as a man. He and all like him mistake emotion for conviction, velleity for resolve, the brief eddy of sentiment for the midcurrent of ever-gathering faith in duty that draws to itself all the affluents of conscience and will, and gives continuity of purpose to life. They are like men who love the stimulus of being under conviction, as it is called, who, forever getting religion, never get capital enough to retire upon and spend for their own need and the common service.

The sentimentalist is the spiritual hypochondriac, with whom fancies become facts, while facts are a discomfort because they will not be evaporated into fancy. In his eyes, Theory is too fine a dame to confess even a country-cousinship with coarse-handed Practice, whose homely ways would disconcert her artificial world. The very susceptibility that makes him quick to feel, makes him also incapable of deep and durable feeling. He loves to think he suffers, and keeps a pet sorrow, a blue-devil familiar, that goes with him everywhere, like Paracelsus's black dog. He takes good care, however, that it shall not be the true sulphurous article that sometimes takes a fancy to fly away with his conjurer. René says: "In my madness I had gone so far as even to wish I might experience a misfortune, so that my suffering might at least have a real object." But no; selfishness is only active egotism, and there is nothing and nobody, with a single exception, which this sort of creature will not sacrifice, rather than give any other than an imaginary pang to his idol. Vicarious pain he is not unwilling to endure, nay, will even commit suicide by proxy, like the German poet who let his wife kill herself to give him a sensation. Had young Jerusalem been anything like Goethe's portrait of him in Werther, he would have taken very good care not to blow out the brains which he would have thought only too precious. Real sorrows are uncomfortable things, but purely æsthetic ones are by no means unpleasant, and I have always fancied the handsome young Wolfgang writing those distracted letters to Auguste Stolberg with a looking-glass in front of him to give back an image of his desolation, and finding it rather pleasant than otherwise to shed the tear of sympathy with self that would seem so bitter to his fair correspondent. The tears that have real salt in them will keep; they are the difficult, manly tears that are shed in secret; but the pathos soon evaporates from that fresh-water with which a man can bedew a dead donkey in public, while his wife is having a good cry over his neglect of her at home. We do not think the worse of Goethe for hypothetically desolating himself in the fashion aforesaid, for with many constitutions it is as purely natural a crisis as dentition, which the stronger worry through, and turn out very sensible, agreeable fellows. But where there is an arrest of development, and the heartbreak of the patient is audibly prolonged through life, we have a spectacle which the toughest heart would wish to get as far away from as possible.

We would not be supposed to overlook the distinction, too often lost sight of, between sentimentalism and sentiment, the latter being a very excellent thing in its way, as genuine things are apt to be. Sentiment is intellectualized emotion, emotion precipitated, as it were, in pretty crystals by the fancy. This is the delightful staple of the poets of social life like Horace and Béranger, or Thackeray, when he too rarely played with verse. It puts into words for us that decorous average of feeling to the expression of which society can consent without danger of being indiscreetly moved. It is excellent for people who are willing to save their souls alive to any extent that shall not be discomposing. It is even satisfying till some deeper experience has given us a hunger which what we so glibly call "the world" cannot sate, just as a water-ice is nourishment enough to a man who has had his dinner. It is the sufficing lyrical interpreter of those lighter hours that should make part of every healthy man's day, and is noxious only when it palls men's appetite for the truly profound poetry which is very passion of very soul sobered by afterthought and embodied in eternal types by imagination. True sentiment is emotion ripened by a slow ferment of the mind and qualified to an agreeable temperance by that taste which is the conscience of polite society. But the sentimentalist always insists on taking his emotion neat, and, as his sense gradually deadens to the stimulus, increases his dose till he ends in a kind of moral deliquium. At first the debaucher, he becomes at last the victim of his sensations.

Among the ancients we find no trace of sentimentalism. Their masculine mood both of body and mind left no room for it, and hence the bracing quality of their literature compared with that of recent times, its tonic property, that seems almost too astringent to palates relaxed by a daintier diet. The first great example of the degenerate modern tendency was Petrarch, who may be said to have given it impulse and direction. A more perfect specimen of the type has not since appeared. An intellectual voluptuary, a moral *dilettante*, the first instance of that character, since too common, the gentleman in search of a sensation, seeking a solitude at Vaucluse because it made him more likely to be in demand at Avignon, praising philosophic poverty with a sharp eye to the next rich benefice in the gift of his patron, commending a good life but careful first of a good living, happy only in seclusion but making a dangerous journey to enjoy the theatrical show of a coronation in the Capitol, cherishing a fruitless passion which broke his heart three or four times a year and yet could not make an end of him till he had reached the ripe age of seventy and survived his mistress a quarter of a century, — surely a more exquisite perfection of inconsistency would be hard to find.

When Petrarch returned from his journey into the North of Europe in 1332, he balanced the books of his unrequited passion, and, finding that he had now been in love seven years, thought the time had at last come to call deliberately on Death. Had Death taken him at his word, he would have protested that he was only in fun. For we find him always taking good care of an excellent constitution, avoiding the plague with commendable assiduity, and in the very year when he declares it absolutely essential to his peace of mind to die for good and all, taking refuge in the fortress of Capranica, from a wholesome dread of having his throat cut by robbers. There is such a difference between dying in a sonnet with a cambric handkerchief at one's eyes, and the prosaic reality of demise certified in the parish register! Practically it is inconvenient to be dead. Among other things, it puts an end to the manufacture of sonnets. But there seems to have been an excellent understanding between Petrarch and Death, for he was brought to that grisly monarch's door so often, that, otherwise, nothing short of a miracle or the nine lives of that animal whom love also makes lyrical could have saved him. "I consent," he cries, "to live and die in Africa among its serpents, upon Caucasus, or Atlas, if, while I live, to breathe a pure air, and after my death a little corner of earth where to bestow my body, may be allowed me.

This is all I ask, but this I cannot obtain. Doomed always to wander, and to be a stranger everywhere, O Fortune, Fortune, fix me at last to some one spot! I do not covet thy favors. Let me enjoy a tranquil poverty, let me pass in this retreat the few days that remain to me!" The pathetic stop of Petrarch's poetical organ was one he could pull out at pleasure, — and indeed we soon learn to distrust literary tears, as the cheap subterfuge for want of real feeling with natures of this quality. Solitude with him was but the pseudonyme of notoriety. Poverty was the archdeaconry of Parma, with other ecclesiastical pickings. During his retreat at Vaucluse, in the very height of that divine sonneteering love of Laura, of that sensitive purity which called Avignon Babylon, and rebuked the sinfulness of Clement, he was himself begetting that kind of children which we spell with a *b*. We believe that, if Messer Francesco had been present when the woman was taken in adultery, he would have flung the first stone without the slightest feeling of inconsistency, nay, with a sublime sense of virtue. The truth is, that it made very little difference to him what sort of proper sentiment he expressed, provided he could do it elegantly and with unction.

Would any one feel the difference between his faint abstractions and the Platonism of a powerful nature fitted alike for the withdrawal of ideal contemplation and for breasting the storms of life, — would any one know how wide a depth divides a noble friendship based on sympathy of pursuit and aspiration, on that mutual help which souls capable of self-sustainment are the readiest to give or to take, and a simulated passion, true neither to the spiritual nor the sensual part of man, — let him compare the sonnets of Petrarch with those which Michel Angelo addressed to Vittoria Colonna. In them the airiest pinnacles of sentiment and speculation are buttressed with solid mason-work of thought, and of an actual, not fancied experience, and the depth of feeling is measured by the sobriety and reserve of expression, while in Petrarch's all ingenuousness is frittered away into ingenuity. Both are cold, but the coldness of the one is self-restraint, while the other chills with pretence of warmth. In Michel Angelo's, you feel the great architect; in Petrarch's the artist who can best realize his conception in the limits of a cherry-stone. And yet this man influenced literature longer and more widely than almost any other in modern times. So great is the charm of elegance, so unreal is the larger part of what is written!

Certainly I do not mean to say that a work of art should be looked at by the light of the artist's biography, or measured by our standard of his character. Nor do I reckon what was genuine in Petrarch — his love of letters, his refinement, his skill in the superficial graces of language, that rhetorical art by which the music of words supplants their meaning, and the verse moulds the thought instead of being plastic to it — after any such fashion. I have no ambition for that character of *valet de chambre* which is said to disenchant the most heroic figures into mere every-day personages, for it implies a mean soul no less than a servile condition. But we have a right to demand a certain amount of reality, however small, in the emotion of a man who makes it his business to endeavor at exciting our own. We have a privilege of nature to shiver before a painted flame, how cunningly soever the colors be laid on. Yet our love of minute biographical detail, our desire to make ourselves spies upon the men of the past, seems so much of an instinct in us, that we must look for the spring of it in human nature, and that somewhat deeper than mere curiosity or love of gossip. It should seem to arise from what must be considered on the whole a creditable feeling, namely, that we value character more than any amount of talent, — the skill to *be* something, above that of doing anything but the best of its kind. The highest creative genius, and that only, is privileged from arrest by this personality, for there the thing produced is altogether disengaged from the producer. But in natures incapable of this escape from themselves, the author is inevitably mixed with his work, and we have a feeling that the amount of his sterling character is the security for the notes he issues. Especially we feel so when truth to self, which is always self-forgetful, and not truth to nature, makes an essential part of the value of what is offered us; as where a man undertakes to narrate personal experience or to enforce a dogma. This is particularly true as respects sentimentalists, because of their intrusive self-consciousness; for there is no more universal characteristic of human nature than the instinct of men to apologize to themselves for themselves, and to justify personal failings by generalizing them into universal laws. A man would be the keenest devil's advocate against himself, were it not that he has always taken a retaining fee for the defence; for we think that the indirect and mostly unconscious pleas in abatement which we read between the lines in the works of many authors are oftener written to set themselves right in their own eyes than in those of the world. And in the real life of the sentimentalist it is the same. He is under the wretched necessity of keeping up, at least in public, the character he has assumed, till he at last reaches that last shift of bankrupt self-respect, to play the hypocrite with himself. Lamartine, after passing round the hat in Europe and America, takes to his bed from wounded pride when the French Senate votes him a subsidy, and sheds tears of humiliation. Ideally, he resents it; in practical coin, he will accept the shame without a wry face.

George Sand, speaking of Rousseau's "Confessions," says that an autobiographer always makes himself the hero of his own novel, and cannot help idealizing, even if he would. But the weak point of all sentimentalists is that they always have been, and always continue under every conceivable circumstance to be, their own ideals, whether they are writing their own lives or no. Rousseau opens his book with the statement: "I am not made like any of those I have seen; I venture to believe myself unlike any that exists. If I am not worth more, at least I am different." O exquisite cunning of self-flattery! It is this very imagined difference that makes us worth more in our own foolish sight. For while all men are apt to think, or to persuade themselves that they think, all other men their accomplices in vice or weakness, they are not difficult of belief that they are singular in any quality or talent on which they hug themselves. More than this; people who are truly original are the last to find it out, for the moment we become conscious of a virtue it has left us or is getting ready to go. Originality does not consist in a fidgety assertion of selfhood, but in the faculty of getting rid of it altogether, that the truer genius of the man, which commerces with universal nature and with other souls through a common sympathy with that, may take all his powers wholly to itself, — and the truly original man could no more be jealous of his peculiar gift, than the grass could take credit to itself for being green. What is the reason that all children are geniuses, (though they contrive so soon to outgrow that dangerous quality,) except that they never cross-examine themselves on the subject? The moment that process begins, their speech loses its gift of unexpectedness, and they become as tediously impertinent as the rest of us.

If there never was any one like him, if he constituted a genus in himself, to what end write confessions in which no other human being could ever be in a condition to take the least possible interest? All men are interested in Montaigne in proportion as all men find more of themselves in him, and all men see but one image in the glass which the greatest of poets holds up to nature, an image which at once startles and charms them with its familiarity. Fabulists always endow their animals with the passions and desires of men. But if an ox could dictate his confessions, what glimmer of understanding should we find in those bovine confidences, unless on some theory of pre-existence, some blank misgiving of a creature moving about in worlds not realized? The truth is, that we recognize the common humanity of Rousseau in the very weakness that betrayed him into this conceit of himself; we find he is just like the rest of us in this very assumption of essential difference, for among all animals man is the only one who tries to pass for more than he is, and so involves himself in the condemnation of seeming less.

But it would be sheer waste of time to hunt Rousseau through all his doublings of inconsistency, and run him to earth in every new paradox. His first two books attacked, one of them literature, and the other society. But this did not prevent him from being diligent with his pen, nor from availing himself of his credit with persons who enjoyed all the advantages of that inequality whose evils he had so pointedly exposed. Indeed, it is curious how little practical communism there has been, how few professors it has had who would not have gained by a general dividend. It is perhaps no frantic effort of generosity in a philosopher with ten crowns in his pocket when he offers to make common stock with a neighbor who has ten thousand of yearly income, nor is it an uncommon thing to see such theories knocked clean out of a man's head by the descent of a thumping legacy. But, consistent or not, Rousseau remains permanently interesting as the highest and most perfect type of the sentimentalist of genius. His was perhaps the acutest mind that was ever mated with an organization so diseased, the brain most far-reaching in speculation that ever kept itself steady and worked out its problems amid such disordered tumult of the nerves.* His letter to the Archbishop of Paris, admirable for its lucid power and soberness of tone, and his *Rousseau juge de Jean Jacques*, which no man can read and believe him to have been sane, show him to us in his strength and weakness, and give us a more charitable, let us hope therefore a truer, notion of him than his own apology for himself. That he was a man of genius appears unmistakably in his impressibility by the deeper meaning of the epoch in which he lived. Before an eruption, clouds steeped through and through with electric life gather over the crater, as if in sympathy and expectation. As the mountain heaves and cracks, these vapory masses are seamed with fire, as if they felt and answered the dumb agony that is struggling for utterance below. Just such flashes of eager sympathetic fire break continually from the cloudy volumes of Rousseau, the result at once and the warning of that convulsion of which Paris was to be the crater and all Europe to feel the spasm. There are symptoms enough elsewhere of that want of faith in the existing order which made the Revolution inevitable, — even so shallow an observer as Horace Walpole could forebode it so early as 1765, — but Rousseau more than all others is the unconscious expression of the groping

* Perhaps we should except Newton.

after something radically new, the instinct for a change that should be organic and pervade every fibre of the social and political body. Freedom of thought owes far more to the jester Voltaire, who also had his solid kernel of earnest, than to the sombre Genevese, whose earnestness is of the deadly kind. Yet, for good or evil, the latter was the father of modern democracy, and without him our Declaration of Independence would have wanted some of those sentences in which the immemorial longings of the poor and the dreams of solitary enthusiasts were at last affirmed as axioms in the manifesto of a nation, so that all the world might hear.

Though Rousseau, like many other fanatics, had a remarkable vein of common sense in him, (witness his remarks on duelling, on landscape-gardening, on French poetry, and much of his thought on education,) we cannot trace many practical results to his teaching, least of all in politics. For the great difficulty with his system, if system it may be called, is, that, while it professes to follow nature, it not only assumes as a starting-point that the individual man may be made over again, but proceeds to the conclusion that man himself, that human nature, must be made over again, and governments remodelled on a purely theoretic basis. But when something like an experiment in this direction was made in 1789, not only did it fail as regarded man in general, but even as regards the particular variety of man that inhabited France. The Revolution accomplished many changes, and beneficent ones, yet it left France peopled, not by a new race without traditions, but by Frenchmen. Still, there could not but be a wonderful force in the words of a man who, above all others, had the secret of making abstractions glow with his own fervor; and his ideas — dispersed now in the atmosphere of thought

— have influenced, perhaps still continue to influence, speculative minds, which prefer swift and sure generalization to hesitating and doubtful experience.

Rousseau has, in one respect, been utterly misrepresented and misunderstood. Even Châteaubriand most unfilially classes him and Voltaire together. It appears to me that the inmost core of his being was religious. Had he remained in the Catholic Church he might have been a saint. Had he come earlier, he might have founded an order. His was precisely the nature on which religious enthusiasm takes the strongest hold, — a temperament which finds a sensuous delight in spiritual things, and satisfies its craving for excitement with celestial debauch. He had not the iron temper of a great reformer and organizer like Knox, who, true Scotchman that he was, found a way to weld this world and the other together in a cast-iron creed; but he had as much as any man ever had that gift of a great preacher to make the oratorical fervor which persuades himself while it lasts into the abiding conviction of his hearers. That very persuasion of his that the soul could remain pure while the life was corrupt, is not unexampled among men who have left holier names than he. His "Confessions," also, would assign him to that class with whom the religious sentiment is strong, and the moral nature weak. They are apt to believe that they may, as special pleaders say, confess and avoid. Hawthorne has admirably illustrated this in the penance of Mr. Dimmesdale. With all the soil that is upon Rousseau, I cannot help looking on him as one capable beyond any in his generation of being divinely possessed; and if it happened otherwise, when we remember the much that hindered and the little that helped in a life and time like his, we shall be much readier to pity than to condemn. It was his very fitness for being something better that makes him able to shock us so with what in too many respects he unhappily was. Less gifted, he had been less hardly judged. More than any other of the sentimentalists, except possibly Sterne, he had in him a staple of sincerity. Compared with Châteaubriand, he is honesty, compared with Lamartine, he is manliness itself. His nearest congener in our own tongue is Cowper.

In the whole school there is a sickly taint. The strongest mark which Rousseau has left upon literature is a sensibility to the picturesque in Nature, not with Nature as a strengthener and consoler, a wholesome tonic for a mind ill at ease with itself, but with Nature as a kind of feminine echo to the mood, flattering it with sympathy rather than correcting it with rebuke or lifting it away from its unmanly depression, as in the wholesomer fellow-feeling of Wordsworth. They seek in her an accessary, and not a reproof. It is less a sympathy with Nature than a sympathy with ourselves as we compel her to reflect us. It is solitude, Nature for her estrangement from man, not for her companionship with him, — it is desolation and ruin, Nature as she has triumphed over man, — with which this order of mind seeks communion and in which it finds solace. It is with the hostile and destructive power of matter, and not with the spirit of life and renewal that dwells in it, that they ally themselves. And in human character it is the same. St. Preux, René, Werther, Manfred, Quasimodo, they are all anomalies, distortions, ruins, — so much easier is it to caricature life from our own sickly conception of it, than to paint it in its noble simplicity; so much cheaper is unreality than truth.

Every man is conscious that he leads two lives, — the one trivial and ordinary, the other sacred and recluse; one which he carries to society and the dinner-table, the other in which his youth and aspiration survive for him, and which is a confidence between himself and God. Both may be equally sincere, and there need be no contradiction between them, any more than in a healthy man between soul and body. If the higher life be real and earnest, its result, whether in literature or affairs, will be real and earnest too. But no man can produce great things who is not thoroughly sincere in dealing with himself, who would not exchange the finest show for the poorest reality, who does not so love his work that he is not only glad to give himself for it, but finds rather a gain than a sacrifice in the surrender. The sentimentalist does not think of what he does so much as of what the world will think of what he does. He translates should into would, looks upon the spheres of duty and beauty as alien to each other, and can never learn how life rounds itself to a noble completeness between these two opposite but mutually sustaining poles of what we long for and what we must.

Did Rousseau, then, lead a life of this quality? Perhaps, when we consider the contrast which every man who looks backward must feel between the life he planned and the life which circumstance within him and without him has made for him, we should rather ask, Was this the life he meant to lead? Perhaps, when we take into account his faculty of self-deception, — it may be no greater than our own, — we should ask, Was this the life he believed he led? Have we any right to judge this man after our blunt English fashion, and condemn him, as we are wont to do, on the finding of a jury of average householders? Is French reality precisely our reality? Could we tolerate tragedy in rhymed alexandrines, instead of blank verse? The whole life of Rousseau is pitched on this heroic key, and for the most trivial occasion he must be ready with the sublime sentiments that are supposed to suit him rather than it. It is one of the most curious features of the sentimental ailment, that, while it shuns the contact of men, it courts publicity. In proportion as solitude and communion with self lead the sentimentalist to exaggerate the importance of his own personality, he comes to think that the least event connected with it is of consequence to his fellow-men. If he change his shirt, he would have mankind aware of it. Victor Hugo, the greatest living representative of the class, considers it necessary to let the world know by letter from time to time his opinions on every conceivable subject about which it is not asked nor is of the least value unless we concede to him an immediate inspiration. We men of colder blood, in whom self-consciousness takes the form of pride, and who have deified *mauvaise honte* as if our defect were our virtue, find it especially hard to understand that artistic impulse of more southern races to *pose* themselves properly on every occasion, and not even to die without some tribute of deference to the taste of the world they are leaving. Was not even mighty Cæsar's last thought of his drapery? Let us not condemn Rousseau for what seems to us the indecent exposure of himself in his "Confessions."

Those who allow an oratorical and purely conventional side disconnected with our private understanding of the facts, and with life, in which everything has a wholly parliamentary sense where truth is made subservient to the momentary exigencies of eloquence, should be charitable to Rousseau. While we encourage a distinction which establishes two kinds of truth, one for the world, and another for the conscience, while we take pleasure in a kind of speech that has no relation to the real thought of speaker or hearer, but to the rostrum only, we must not be hasty to condemn a sentimentalism which we do our best to foster. We listen in public with the gravity oı augurs to what we smile at when we meet a brother adept. France is the native land of eulogy, of truth padded out to the size and shape demanded by *comme-il-faut.* The French Academy has, perhaps, done more harm by the vogue it has given to this style, than it has done good by its literary purism; for the best purity of a language depends on the limpidity of its source in veracity of thought. Rousseau was in many respects a typical Frenchman, and it is not to be wondered at if he too often fell in with the fashion of saying what was expected of him, and what he thought due to the situation, rather than what would have been true to his inmost consciousness. Perhaps we should allow something also to the influence of a Calvinistic training, which certainly helps men who have the least natural tendency towards it to set faith above works, and to persuade themselves of the efficacy of an inward grace to offset an outward and visible defection from it.

As the sentimentalist always takes a fanciful, sometimes an unreal, life for an ideal one, it would be too much to say that Rousseau was a man of earnest convictions. But he was a man of fitfully intense ones, as suited so mobile a temperament, and his writings, more than those of any other of his tribe, carry with them that persuasion that was in him while he wrote. In them at least he is as consistent as a man who admits new ideas can ever be. The children of his brain he never abandoned, but clung to them with paternal fidelity. Intellectually he was true and fearless; constitutionally, timid, contradictory, and weak; but never, if we understand him rightly, false. He was a little too credulous of sonorous sentiment, but he was never, like Châteaubriand or Lamartine, the lackey of fine phrases. If, as some fanciful physiologists have assumed, there be a masculine and feminine lobe of the brain, it would seem that in men of sentimental turn the masculine half fell in love with and made an idol of the other, obeying and admiring all the pretty whims of this *folle du logis.* In Rousseau the mistress had some noble elements of character, and less taint of the *demi-monde* than is visible in more recent cases of the same illicit relation.

THE END

Cambridge: Printed by Welch, Bigelow, and Company.

www.ingramcontent.com/pod-product-compliance
Lightning Source LLC
LaVergne TN
LVHW020119110826
845151LV00001B/215

* 9 7 8 1 4 2 5 5 4 1 7 7 4 *